THE

Brooklyn
Reader

THE
Brooklyn
Reader

30 Writers
Celebrate America's
Favorite Borough

EDITED BY

ANDREA WYATT SEXTON

AND ALICE LECCESE POWERS

INTRODUCTION BY PETE HAMILL

HARMONY BOOKS / NEW YORK

Published by Harmony Books, a division of Crown Publishers, Inc., 201
East 50th Street, New York, New York 10022. Member of the Crown
Publishing Group.

Random House, Inc. New York, Toronto, London, Sydney, Auckland

HARMONY and colophon are trademarks of Crown Publishers, Inc.

Manufactured in the United States of America

Ornaments by Jennifer Harper

Library of Congress Cataloging-in-Publication Data

The Brooklyn reader : 30 writers celebrate America's favorite borough / edited by Andrea
    Wyatt Sexton and Alice Leccese Powers—1st ed.
    1. Brooklyn (New York, N.Y.)—Literary collections.   2. American
literature—New York (N.Y.)   I. Powers, Alice.   II. Wyatt, Andrea.
PS509.N5B76   1994
810.8'03274723—dc20
93-14527
CIP

ISBN 0-517-59134-0
10   9   8   7   6   5   4   3   2

$\mathcal{C}$ontents

Acknowledgments

With grateful acknowledgment to Abby Sexton for finding the perfect John Tunis excerpt; to Lansing Sexton for his advice and support; to Muriel Manning for her warm hospitality, and to William Korff for unearthing a copy of *The Brooklyn Cantata* at the Lincoln Center Library for the Performing Arts; to Isaac Asimov for his good counsel; to Catherine Shapleigh, Doug Lang, and JoAnn Bradeen for their valuable suggestions, and to Beverly Silberstein, Connie and Henry Becker, and Alvin Silver for giving me a lifetime of Brooklyn memories.

A.W.S

Many thanks to Peter Guzzardi and Valerie Kuscenko, my editors at Harmony, and to Jane Dystel, my agent; to my fellow writers for their wise advice—Beth Joselow, Michael Leccese, Kem Sawyer, and Erich Parker; to my Brooklyn family with deep gratitude, especially Lil and Dan DiSanto and Arcangela and Michael Leccese; and to my parents, Gaetana and Vito Leccese. And for their unfailing support and patience—Brian, Alison, Christina, and Brenna Powers.

A.L.P.

Introduction

You begin with the light. If you want to make Brooklyn in words or film or paint, you must see the way the sun defines the silent streets on an early Sunday morning, sculpting trees, buildings, fire hydrants, stray dogs, and wandering people with an almost perfect clarity. You can see the Brooklyn light on summer afternoons, on any morning after a snowfall, in the glittering chilly days of October. You can see it in elegant photographs and artless snapshots, in paintings by Edward Hopper and William Merrit Chase. But the Brooklyn light is not unique: the same luminous quality suffuses the work of the Dutch masters. I gaze at Vermeer and feel the presence of Brooklyn; those first seventeenth-century Dutch settlers must have looked at this empty western end of Long Island and seen the lowlands of Holland.

If you have ever lived in Brooklyn, or if you grew up on its streets, you carry that light with you forever. The distinctiveness of the light does not explain why so many writers came from this largest of New York's five boroughs; no single element ever explains a writer. But that Vermeer light always seems to find its way into the work. That, and other things.

The most powerful of all factors is also the most American: the pull of the past. Writers are rememberers, or they are nothing. Millions of older Brooklynites, those who stayed and those who departed, live with a sense of a lost Eden in their imaginations, a collective memory of a time and place in which they were young and innocent and happy. Some of this is delusion, of course; but the delusions are as vivid and concrete as any great fiction. The details of such powerful nostalgias are different for every generation, often for every neighborhood, but the impulse is persistent. A voice seems always to whisper: *There was another place here once and it was better than this.* When I was a boy in the 1940s and 1950s, I sometimes met old-timers who traced the ruin of Brooklyn to the opening of the Brooklyn Bridge in 1888 or to the forced welding of Brooklyn to Greater New York ten years later or to the driving of the subways out past Prospect Park around the time of World War I. They talked with regret about the farms that had vanished, the families ruined, the strangers who had come among them. To them, as to so many other Americans, the past truly was another country. Listening to them, I envied their knowledge of that lost Brooklyn and was certain that my own Brooklyn of cement and street gangs was the vast borough's final form.

My certainty had its reasons. Until the mid-1950s, my Brooklyn never changed in any major way. The Second World War had combined with the Great Depression to freeze all of us in place. Men went away to the war; most of them returned; but nobody ever moved more than three blocks. We played stickball on the same streets where the war veterans played when they were boys. We went through eight grades of school with the same kids, year after year, getting to know each other better than we ever knew anybody else. Every day, the *Brooklyn Eagle* arrived at the door, and every spring, the Dodgers returned to Ebbets Field. In the summer we took the trolley south to Coney Island, with its honkytonk midway, hotdogs and orange drinks, sand and sea. We thought that world would last for the rest of our lives.

It didn't. Highways opened up eastern Long Island; the GI Bill provided low-cost mortgages; the great flight to the suburbs was soon under way. The *Brooklyn Eagle* folded in 1955. The Dodgers fled to California two years later. Heroin arrived in the neighborhoods, followed by the plague of guns, and nobody played stickball anymore. Factories began closing, as New York's economy shifted from manufacturing to services, and the humiliation of unemployment started to destroy families. The European immigrants and their children left Coney Island for more prosperous beaches; the slums expanded; crime and the fear of crime became as prevalent in Brooklyn as the light. The Coney Island of my childhood became part of the past, beyond recovery, depending for its existence upon the untrustworthy power of memory.

But the almost tidal pull of the past doesn't account in full for all those writers who were spawned in Brooklyn or were deeply touched as they passed through. One possibility is that the essential Brooklyn style is often an irresistible (for a writer) combination of toughness and lyricism. The tough guy myth had incredible power. On the streets, the kid who was "good with his hands" was respected, even honored. Most values were stoic. If you were poor, your pride was based on the ability to endure hard times without whining; the true tough guy didn't simply throw a punch, he could take one too. There were other tough guys among us, sallow-faced men with pistols and pinkie rings. They too inhabited a world of myth. I remember in my youth going to see the house where Al Capone grew up, thrilled that a guy from the neighborhood had made his way into the big world. A few blocks away was the restaurant where Joe Adonis ran the Brooklyn rackets with grace and style. One afternoon, when I was 10, I traveled with my father and his friends to the gym in Brownsville where a tough middleweight named Bummy Davis trained; it was full of hard-eyed Jewish hoods who had once been soldiers for Murder Inc. It was no accident that dozens of hard guys from street gangs in my neighborhood graduated into full membership in The Mob. We read about these people in the newspapers; we heard them discussed in the language of myth. So did the young hard guys. And so did many apprentice writers.

The tough guy style was tempered by the accidents of geography. In the heart of Brooklyn lie the 526 acres of Prospect Park, designed by Frederick Law Olmsted as a verdant refuge from the harder places of the city. Olmsted succeeded gloriously. The park is full of broad meadows, clusters of forest, hills and valleys, mysterious stone paths, stairways and monuments. If you came from tenements, as I did, the park was a theater for the imagination. You could be Pete Reiser, hammering triples down the first base line, or Bomba the Jungle Boy, searching the wilderness for the Giant Cataract. For many of us, the park remains the secret heart of Brooklyn, the first place in which we experienced the beauty of the world.

The other splendid accident was the beach. New York City is basically an archipelago, its boroughs lashed together by bridges and tunnels (only the Bronx is on the mainland). But only Brooklyn had the great beach at Coney Island. We knew that the Bronx had Orchard Beach and Queens had Rockaway, but they made movies about *our* beach, they wrote songs about it, they showed photographs of its dense crowds in the newspapers. For all of us, middle class or poor, the beach was another glorious fact, its throbbing sensuality a goad to the lyric impulse. Under the summer sun, we gazed at the immense variety of the human body. We fell in love with strangers. We plotted a thousand versions of the fall into sin. We found solace or relief in the chilly tides of the sea. On that beach, every weekend was an occasion for wonder, surprise, hedonism, failure, and sweet lies: the raw material of art.

In this book, you will encounter those poles of Brooklyn toughness and lyricism, along with their occasional merger. There is provincialism too, along with its twin, the romantic desire for escape and possibility. But somewhere in each text, stated or implied, is the presence of light. There is no Brooklyn without it.

Pete Hamill

THE

Brooklyn Reader

James Agee

James Agee, poet, novelist, and film critic, was raised in the Cumberland Mountains of Tennessee. He graduated from Harvard in 1932 and then moved to New York City. In the 1930s and 1940s he worked as a film critic for Fortune, Time, *and* The Nation *and wrote several film scripts, including* The African Queen. *Agee is best known for writing* Let Us Now Praise Famous Men, *an eight-week collaboration with photographer Walker Evans. Agee and Evans captured the lives of three rural Alabama families struggling through the Depression. Agee wrote two novels,* The Morning Watch *and his masterpiece,* A Death in the Family, *published posthumously.* "Southeast of the Island: Travel Notes" *was reprinted in* The Collected Short Prose of James Agee. "Southeast of the Island" *conveys Agee's belief in the lyricism of America and its people. The essay's style— with its repetitive rhythms and vivid imagery—is more poetry than prose. James Agee died in 1955.*

from Southeast of the Island: Travel Notes

City of homes and churches.
  —Whitman, writing of Brooklyn

One of the great waste places of the world.
  —Doughty, writing of Arabia

And blights with plagues the marriage hearse.
  —Blake, writing of London

Life is fundamentally composed of vegetable matter.
  —Obsolete textbook of biology

Watching them in the trolleys, or along the inexhaustible reduplications of the streets of their small tradings and their sleep, one comes to notice, even in the most urgently poor, a curious quality in the eyes and at the corners of the mouths, relative to what is seen on Manhattan Island: a kind of drugged softness or narcotic relaxation. The same look may be seen in monasteries and in the lawns of sanitariums, and there must have been some similar look among soldiers convalescent of shell shock in institutionalized British gardens where, in a late summer dusk, a young man could mistake heat lightnings and the crumpling of hidden thunder for what he has left in France, and must return to. If there were not Manhattan, there could not be this Brooklyn look; for truly to appreciate what one escapes, it must be not only distant but near at hand. Only: all escapes are relative, and bestow their own peculiar forms of bondage.

It is the same of the physique and whole tone and meter of the city itself. You have only to cross a bridge to know it: how behind you the whole of living is drawn up straining into verticals, tightened and badgered in nearly every face of man and child and building; and how where you are entering, even among the riverside throes of mechanisms and of tenements in the iron streets, this whole of living is nevertheless relaxed upon horizontalities, a deep taproot of stasis in each action and each building. Partly, it suggests the qualities of any small American city, the absorption in home, the casualness of the measuredly undistinguished: only this usual provincialism is powerfully enhanced here by the near existence of Manhattan, which has drawn Brooklyn of most of what a city's vital organs are, and upon which an inestimable swarm of Brooklyn's population depends for living itself. And again, this small-city quality is confused in the deep underground atomic drone of the intertextured procedures upon blind time of more hundreds on hundreds of thousands of compacted individual human existences than the human imagination can comprehend or bear to comprehend.

It differs from most cities in this: that though it has perhaps a "center," and hands, and eyes, and feet, it is chiefly no whole or recognizable animal but an exorbitant pulsing mass of scarcely discriminable cellular jellies and tissues; a place where people merely "live." A few American cities, Manhattan chief among them, have some mad magnetic energy which sucks all others into "provincialism"; and Brooklyn of all great cities is nearest the magnet, and is indeed "provincial": it is provincial as a land of rich earth and of this earth is an enormous farm, whose crop is far less "industrial" or "financial" or "notable" or in any way "distinguished" or "definable" than it is of human flesh and being. And this fact alone, which of itself makes Brooklyn so featureless, so little known, to many so laughable, or so ripe for patronage, this fact, that two million human beings are alive and living there, invests the city in an extraordinarily high, piteous and inviolable dignity, well beyond touch of laughter, defense, or need of notice.

Manhattan is large, yet all its distances seem quick and available. Brook-lyn is larger, seventy-one square miles as against twenty-two, but here you enter the paradoxes of the relative. You know, here: only a few miles from wherever I stand, Brooklyn ends; only a few miles away is Manhattan; Brooklyn is walled with world-traveled wetness on west and south and on north and east is the young beaverboard frontier of Queens; Brooklyn comes to an end: but actually, that is, in the conviction of the body, there seems almost no conceivable end to Brooklyn; it seems, on land as flat and huge as Kansas, horizon beyond horizon forever unfolded, an immeasurable proliferation of house on house and street by street; or seems as China does, infinite in time, in patience, and in population as in space.

The collaborated creature of the insanely fungoid growth of fifteen or twenty villages, now sewn and quilted edge to edge, and lacking any center in remote proportion to its mass, it is perhaps the most amorphous of all modern cities; and at the same time, by virtue of its arterial streets, it has continuities so astronomically vast as Paris alone or the suburbs south of Chicago could match: on Flatbush Avenue, DeKalb, Atlantic, New Lots, Church, any number more, a vista of low buildings and side streets of glanded living sufficient to paralyze all conjecture; simply, far as the eye can strain, no end of Brooklyn, and looking back, far as the eye can urge itself, no end, nor imaginable shore; only, thrust upon the pride of heaven, the monolith of the Empire State, a different mode of life; and even this, seen here, has the smoky frailty of a half-remembered dream.

(Observing in subway stations, in any part of Brooklyn, not in an hour of rush but in the leisured evening, you see this; how, wherever there is a choice of staircases, one toward Manhattan, one away, without thought or exception they descend the staircase toward the Island. An imaginative designer would have foreseen this and would have omitted the alternatives entirely.)

(In Upper Flatbush, already two miles deep inland from the bridges,

4

a young man of Manhattan asked a druggist how she might get into certain territory well south of there. Without thought of irony he began, "Oh. You want to go to Brooklyn.")

The center of population of the largest city in history is near the intersection of ———— and ———— Streets, in Brooklyn. That it should be in this borough of "being" rather than in that of doing and bragging seems appropriate to the point of inevitability. So does this: that when the fact was ascertained, and Manhattan news-swallows skimmed over to get the Local Angle, the replies were so fully intelligent that they had to be treated as a joke. Informed of his good fortune one said "So?", another said "So well?"; a landlady to be sure, said she'd have to tell her roomers about it that night, but gave evidence of no special emotion.

More homes are owned in Brooklyn than in any other Borough; there are more children per adult head; it is a great savings-bank town; there are fewer divorces; it is by and large as profoundly domesticated, docile and "stable" a population as one could conceive of, outside England. The horror of "unsuccessful" marriages—unsuccessful, that is, as shown by an open or legal break; the lethal effort of Carry On is thought well of—this horror is such that there is a special bank to which husbands come one day to deposit, estranged wives the next to be fertilized by this genteel equivalent of alimony. It seems significant of Brooklyn that it is probably the only city that has such a bank.

At the north brow of Prospect Park, where a vast number of these marriages are, in the medical sense, contracted and where, indeed, the whole sweep of infancy, childhood, and the descending discords of family life is on display, there stands a piece of statuary. From a way down Flatbush Avenue it suggests that cloven flame which spoke with Dante in hell but by a nearer view, it is a man and a nude woman in bronze, and their plump child, eager for the Park, and it represents the beauty and stability of Brooklyn, and of human, family life. The man and wife stand back to back, in the classical posture of domestic sleep. It is a thoroughly vulgar and sincere piece of work, and once one gets beyond the esthete's sometimes myopic scorn, is the infallibly appropriate creation of the whole heart of Brooklyn. Michelangelo would have done much less well.

5

$$* \quad * \quad *$$

All the neighborhoods that make up this city; those well known, and those which are indicated on no official map:

The Hill, for instance: the once supremely solid housing of Clinton Avenue, which are broken with a light titter of doctors' shingles; the two big homes which are become the L. I. Grotto Pouch and the Pouch Annex; or the boarded brownstone opposite the decrepitant bricks of the Adelphi Academy; or those blocks which have formed "protective associations" against the infiltration of Negroes:

Or Park Slope: the big Manhattan-style apartment buildings which now hem the Park, and on the streets of the upward slope, and on 8th Avenue, the bland powerful regiments of gray stone bays and the big single-homes, standing with a locked look among mature trees and the curious quietudes of bourgeois Paris: and these confused among apartment buildings and among parochial schools, and the yellow bricks of post-tenements, and the subway noises of "rough" children:

Or the Heights: the enormous homes and the fine rows, a steadily narrower area remains inviolable, the top drawer of Brooklyn, disintegration toward the stooping of the street the Squibb building: great houses broken apart for roomers; a gradual degeneration into artists and journalists, communists, bohemians and barbers, chiefly of Manhattan:

Or, among brownstones, between the last two-mile convergence of Fulton and Broadway, a swifter and swifter breakdown of the former middle classes, a steady thickening of Jews into the ultimacies of Brownsville and East New York:

Or that great range of brick and brownstone north of Fulton which in each two blocks falls upon more and more bad fortune: one last place, east of Fort Greene Park, the utmost magnificence of the brownstone style: and beyond-death at length in the Navy Yard district, the hardest in Brooklyn, harder even than Red Hook: (the hardest neighborhood in Brooklyn was a pinched labyrinth of brick and frame within a jump of Borough Hall, but the WPA cleared that one up:)

Or Eastern Parkway, the Central Park West of Brooklyn; in its first stretches near Prospect Park, the dwelling of the most potent Jews of the city; a slow then more swift ironing-out, and the end again in Brownsville:

Or Bay Ridge, and its genteel gentile apartment buildings, and the staid homes of Scandinavian seafarers:

Or Greenpoint and Williamsburg and Bushwick, the wood tenements, bare lots and broken vistas, the balanced weights and images of production and poverty; the headquarters of a municipal government as corrupt as any in the nation: everywhere the spindling Democratic clubs, the massive Roman churches; everywhere, in the eyes of men, in dark bars and on corners, knowledgeable appraising furtive light of hard machine politics; everywhere, the curious gas-lit odor of Irish-American democracy:

Or Flatbush: or Brighton: or Sheepshead Bay: or the negligible downtown: or the view, from the Fulton Street Elevated, of the low-swung and convolved sea of the living, as much green as roofs; or of Brooklyn's nineteenth century backyard life, thousands of solitaries, chips, each floated in his green eddy: or the comparable military attentions of the stoned dead, the stern hieroglyphs of Jews, the thousands of Gold Christs in the sun, the many churches focusing upon the frank secret stardemolished sky their steeplings and proud bulbs and triple crosses and sharp stars and squareflung roods moored high, light ballasted, among the harboring homes, ships pointing out the sun on a single wind: or the mother who walks on Division Avenue whose infant hexes her from his carriage in a gargoyle frown of most intense suspicion: or the street-writing on Park Slope: "Lois I have gone up the street. Don't forget to bring your skates": or the soft whistling of the sea off Coney Island: or the facade of the Academy of Music, a faded print of Boston's Symphony Hall: or the young pair who face each other astride a bicycle in Canarsie: or the lavender glow of brownstones in cloudy weather, or chemical brilliance of jonquils in tamped dirt: or the haloed Sunday hats of little girls, as exquisite as those of their elders are pathologic: or the scornful cornices of dishonored homes: or the shade-cord at whose end is a white home-crocheted Jewish star: or the hot-pants little Manhattan sweatshop girls who come to Tony's Square Bar to meet the sailors and spend a few bearable hours a week: or the

7

streaming of first-flight gentiles from Poly Prep into Williams and Princeton, the second flight into Colgate or Cornell: or of the Jews whose whole families are breaking their hearts for it from Boys High into Brooklyn College and Brooklyn Law, and the luckies of them into Harvard: or the finance editor of the *Eagle* who believes all journalists are gentlemen who are out of what he calls the Chosen, and who scabbed in the *Eagle* strike: or in the middle afternoon in whatever part of Brooklyn, the starlike amplitude of baby buggies and of strolling and lounging silent or soft-speaking women, the whole dwelling city as vacant of masculinity as most urgent war: or in his window above the banging of DeKalb Avenue late on a hot Saturday afternoon the grizzling skull-capped Jew who nods softly above the texts of his holiness, his lips moving in his unviolated beard, and who has been thus drowned in his pieties since early morning: or the grievings and the gracilities of the personalities at the zoo: or the bright fabric stretched of the confabulations of birds and children: or bed by bed and ward by ward along the sacred odors of the corridors of the twelve-street mass of the Kings County Hospital, those who burst with unspeakable vitality or who are floated faint upon dubiety or who wait to die: These the sick, the fainted or fecund, the healthful, the young, the living and the dead, the buildings, the streets, the windows, the linings of the ward nests, the lethal chambers of the schools, the fumed and whining factories, the pitiless birds, the animals, that Bridge which stands up like God and makes music to himself by night and by day: all in the lordly, idiot light, These are inhabitants of Brooklyn.

Woody Allen

Brooklyn native Allen Stewart Konigsberg was born in 1935. He began his career as a stand-up comedian and comedy writer and changed his name to Woody Allen. Allen moved on to films and plays in the late 1960s. The movie Annie Hall *was his first attempt at combining comedy and drama. Based on Allen's life,* Annie Hall *is the story of an angst-ridden Jewish man and his fey, WASP girlfriend. At several points in the film Allen's character flashes back to his Brooklyn childhood home, a house directly under Coney Island's Cyclone. Allen's films have become more serious in the last two decades, influenced by Swedish director Ingmar Bergman. Perhaps his most successful was* Hannah and Her Sisters, *a look at three sisters and their relationships with their husbands, lovers, parents, friends, and children. Allen's short fiction, much of it originally published in* The New Yorker, *has been collected in* Getting Even, Without Feathers, *and* Side Effects.

FROM *Side Effects*

*B*rooklyn: Tree-lined streets. The Bridge. Churches and cemeteries everywhere. And candy stores. A small boy helps a bearded old man across the street and says, "Good Sabbath." The old man smiles and empties his pipe on the boy's head. The child runs crying into his house. . . . Stifling heat and humidity descend on the borough. Residents bring folding chairs out onto the street after dinner to sit and talk. Suddenly it begins to snow. Confusion sets in. A vender wends his way down the street selling hot pretzels. He is set upon by dogs and chased up a tree. Unfortunately for him, there are more dogs at the top of the tree.

"Benny! Benny!" A mother is calling her son. Benny is sixteen but already has a police record. When he is twenty-six, he will go to the electric chair. At thirty-six, he will be hanged. At fifty, he will own his own dry-cleaning store. Now his mother serves breakfast, and because the family is too poor to afford fresh rolls, he spreads marmalade on the *News*.

Anatole Broyard

Anatole Broyard grew up in Brooklyn and was educated at Brooklyn College. He was a literary critic, essayist, and editor at the New York Times. *Broyard's work included* Aroused by Books; Men, Women and Other Climaxes; *and* Intoxicated by My Illness. *"Sunday Dinner in Brooklyn" is an excerpt from an unfinished novel that details the difference between Greenwich Village, home to "guitar players, folksingers, folk dancers, conga drummers, communists, anarchists, voyeurs, frotteurs, fairies, dogs, children, Negroes, sightseers, psychotics, anthropology professors, heroin pushers . . ." and Brooklyn, where everyone eats Sunday dinner at the same time. Broyard sees the difference between Manhattan and Brooklyn as symbolic of the difference between a child and his parents who share little but a feeling of incredulity that they could be related at all. Broyard died in 1991.*

Sunday Dinner IN Brooklyn

I took a roundabout route to the subway, and because I was going to Brooklyn the Village seemed to have at that moment all the charm of a Utrillo. It was only at times like this, in contrast to something else, that this neighborhood became attractive. Ugly in itself, it was a relief from certain kinds of beauty. To most of those like me who lived there, it was as inviting as a view of a squalid village would seem to a princess imprisoned in an ivory tower.

Since it was summer, the Italians were all outside on stoops and chairs or standing along the curb in their Sunday clothes, the old men in navy blue and the young men in powder blue suits, as though their generation was more washed out than the last. The mothers with their hair pulled back and their hands folded in their laps looked like Neanderthal madonnas, and they were dressed, of course, in black, since it was a miracle if someone in their families had not died within the year. The girls wore long pegged skirts which made their feet move incredibly fast. All of their movements seemed to be geared to this same tempo, and their faces were alert with the necessity of defending the one prize they had against mother and brother alike.

On the corner squatted their church—a huge casserole, fat, heavy, and plain as the women who prayed in it. Looking through the open doors as I passed, I saw the arches bending downward like a laborer under a heavy load. Even the bells of this church—presumably the voice of their god—were sour, and every Sunday morning I cursed them together with the priest who played some sort of chopsticks tune over and over on them.

On Thompson Street, a block and a half from where I lived, there was a stable, and here a horse's head poked through the window on the second floor. Above him, on the windowsill of the top floor, a geranium grew out of a rusty one-gallon can. Near the corner, a drunk slept in the sun against the wall of the Mills Hotel, and another drunk stood over him, holding out his hand, saying, "Shake, pal. Shake."

The waterless wading pond in the center of Washington Square, the bon's eye of the Village, was overflowing with guitar players, folksingers, folk dancers, conga drummers, communists, anarchists, voyeurs, frotteurs, fairies, dogs, children, Negroes, sightseers, psychotics, anthropology professors, heroin pushers, tea pushers, carriage pushers, lesbians, *New York Times* readers, people with portable radios, adenoidal girls looking for interesting boys, the uninteresting boys they would eventually wind up with, older girls between affairs, older boys on the lookout for younger girls, and so on. Where they stood, Fifth Avenue dribbled to its conclusion after penetrating Washington Arch.

Looking around, I didn't see any of my crew, so there was nothing else to do but head for the subway. At the entrance on Sixth Avenue and Waverly Place, I took a long breath like a deep-sea diver and went reluctantly underground.

The subway's roaring and screaming in the darkness, the passing under the river with the pressure in my ears—these were such a classical overture to going back home that I was weary of the joke. Riding the wrong way like that, I felt I had left Brooklyn for Manhattan only to discover on arriving that I had forgotten something I needed. Now,

13

retracing my steps, I found the ride an endless torture, as it always inexplicably is under these circumstances, although when I was going in the other direction the distance passed unnoticed.

Of course it was my mother and father I'd forgotten, and I'd do it all over again next time too, but by now I accepted this as in the nature of things. They could hardly forget me though, because they had my picture on the mantel next to the clock. It was ten years old, that picture, but they never asked for a new one, and I was convinced that this was the way they still saw me. Like a criminal, I might alter my appearance, but they were not to be fooled. Each time I arrived, I could see their moist eyes washing away my disguise.

I was holding a book open on my lap—I always carried a book to Brooklyn, as an amulet or charm, a definition of my delicate ego—but for all the reading I did I might just as well have put it into the seat of my pants. My mind kept dropping down the page like a marble in a pinball machine until I finally gave it up, conceding that no book could successfully compete with my favorite fiction, my mother and father.

The train stopped, and a man who had been sitting across from me got out. He had been occupying the seat next to the window, at a right angle to the wall. Now a woman placed alone on the seat parallel to the wall and in front of the one he had vacated, quickly changed to his empty seat. Whereupon a man sitting on the outside of the seat corresponding to the one she now occupied but on my side of the train, jumped up to take her former seat, and the man next to me on the seat parallel to the wall shifted to the seat at his left knee just vacated. All of this was done deadpan, but when I looked again at the woman to see how she was enjoying her new seat, I found her staring at me. She was sour and middle-aged, and her eyes, which were very small, were brooding deeply on me, full of a very personal distaste, as if she were imagining me as her own son. Something about me displeased the hell out of her—the way I was dressed, my haircut, or the expression on my face, which wasn't businesslike enough to spell security for her in her old age.

I didn't feel like answering this look, so I avoided her by staring myself at a man standing a few feet away from me. This man was very visibly chewing gum, and the movements of his bony jaws were so elaborate and so regular that they reminded me of printing presses. I noticed that he was studying himself in the window glass. Arresting his jaws in a position in which all the complications of structure were particularly conspicuous, he observed himself with the close and scientific attention of a Leonardo. Then the machine resumed its hypnotic movements. Now, shifting the gum this way and that, he worked out a wonderful variety of effects. Anyone watching him would have thought he was chewing over a problem. He began by taking it up languidly, indifferently, disarmingly, chewing with his front teeth, his mouth relaxed to the point where it was half open, when suddenly, without warning, he shifted the wad to the left side and began to work it over systematically between his molars. Very businesslike, he gave it an evenly paced pulverizing, and then, just before all the life ebbed out of it, he shifted it again to the center, where his teeth barely dented it, and his tongue turned it over and over in a revivifying massage.

As the train entered another station, without interrupting this ruminating, he stuck his hand through the rubber lip of the door in a Napoleonic attitude, and when the door drew back he flung his hand after it.

I could never chew gum like that, I was thinking, and then I saw the name of my own station through the open door and I jumped up and ran through it barely in time, absolutely confirming the lousy impression I had made on the sour-faced woman.

At the top of the stairs the sun hit me in the eye. It seemed to me that the sun was always shining in Brooklyn, drying clothes, curing rickets, evaporating puddles, inviting children out to play, and encouraging artificial-looking flowers in front yards. Against my will, it warmed over an ineffable melancholy in me. I felt that it was a great democratic source of central heating for this big house in which everyone lived together.

The streets were almost deserted, since everyone ate dinner at the same time in Brooklyn. I knew these streets so well I could have walked them with my eyes shut. There wasn't a tree I passed into which I hadn't thrown my knife, a wall against which I hadn't bounced my ball, a crack I hadn't avoided lest I break my mother's back. Now I saw them in slow motion; everything stood out in a kind of heavy-handed symbolism, as though I were the camera eye in an arty documentary film. When I was a boy, these streets had quickness and life for me, each detail daring me to do something, to match my wits, my strength, my speed, against them. Then I was always running. I saw things on the run and made my running commentary on them without breaking my stride, hurdling, skipping, dodging, but still racing forward . . . until one day I ran full tilt into myself and blocked my own path.

The scene was made even more sententious by the fact that it was Sunday. There was a tremendous vacuum left behind by God. In contrast to the kitchenlike intimacy of the church on Thompson Street— which in its ugliness succeeded in projecting its flock's image on the universe—the spiky shells on these blocks had a cold, punitive look, and seemed empty except for those few hours in the morning when people came with neutralized faces to pay their respects to a dead and departed deity.

From the corner, I could see my mother in the front yard. Her face was turned toward me, although I knew she couldn't see me at that distance. I had the feeling that wherever I was, her face was always turned toward me. Now she saw me, she was waving and talking. In a moment she would begin to shout. I was already smiling and gesticulating too. I modified my walk, making it playful. "Hello, Paul!" she was shouting. "How are you?" I was still too far to talk. I wanted to run, I always wanted to run those last few yards. I hated the last few steps, the final enormous gap, between us. Once we were close enough, like lovers in an embrace, we wouldn't be able to see each other so clearly.

I seized her by the shoulders and bent to kiss her. As usual, each of us offered a cheek. Quickly we turned our heads, and somehow miraculously avoided kissing each other on the lips, our heads turning just far enough so that each kissed the other with half a mouth in the middle of the cheek, making three or four smacks for good measure. My father was inside. He would have liked to come out too, but he felt he would be a spectacle, and besides he seemed to think that she ought to greet me alone, as though she were giving birth to me again.

He met me at the doorway, and we clogged up there, gesticulating

16

and embracing. We always gesticulated too much, we distrusted language and thoughts. And all the while we were shouting, as if we were singing an opera. "Take off your coat!" they were shouting. "Take off your tie!" Sometimes I almost expected them to ask for my belt and shoelaces, but I suppose they knew that, after all, there was no way of disarming the dagger of the mind.

"Wait, I'll make you a martini!" my father shouted, and he ran off into the kitchen. "Sit down!" my mother shouted. "Make yourself comfortable!" Shoving me into my father's chair, she pressed the button on the arm and I was suddenly in a horizontal position. She switched the radio to WQXR, and one of the more familiar symphonies poured out like coal out of a chute.

This chair had been a gift to my father on one of his birthdays. My mother was delighted by the idea of the button. I never liked it. It always struck me as uncanny. I felt myself straining in it, trying to keep my head up a little. My father came in with the martini. I saw that it was amber. He never thought to make himself one. Like a servant.

The martini was sweet. Suddenly I realized that I loved them very much. But what was I going to do with them?

"Here's the *Book Review,*" my mother said, handing me the paper. They both sat down, waiting for me to read it. How could I read it with them sitting there watching me as if I were performing a great feat? I was a spectacle, they assumed I didn't want to talk to them. I understood too that, in a way, they liked to believe I wasn't there just for a visit, and it was perfectly natural for me to be reading the *Book Review* of a Sunday afternoon.

I put the paper down, reassuring them that I'd read it later. We looked at each other for a moment, smiling. I felt that I was stretched out on a bier. Pressing the button, I allowed the back of the chair to come up. I smiled at my mother to show her I didn't mind the chair. I liked it, but I just felt like sitting up, I was such a bundle of energy.

"Well, how's everything, Paul?" she said. From the time I had been two years old, they had called me Bud, but somewhere in the last few years they began calling me Paul the way the outside world did. "Everything's fine," I said, realizing of course that they had no idea what that everything embodied. This vagueness was our tenderness. They'd have loved to know, but they were afraid of finding out something which might have offended not them, but me.

The dinner was ready. It was always ready when I arrived. Sometimes I had the fantasy of just walking by the house: my mother would be in the front yard, holding a box lunch in her hands. I would take the box without stopping. My face would be expressionless, hers grieving but controlled. My father would stand just inside the doorway. . . .

My mother brought in the roast and my father carved it with great concentration, as if he were carving out our destiny. He placed on my plate the portion he had always desired for me. My mother heaped potatoes, gravy, vegetables on my plate. "I know you like to eat," she said, smiling and heaping my plate still more. This was a fiction. I never ate heartily, but nevertheless I exclaimed, "You know me, Mom!"

Pretending I could scarcely wait, I attacked the roast with knife and fork, while my mother held back to observe this. "Home cooking," I mumbled around a mouthful, these two words speaking volumes to her. I wondered what she thought I ate every day, whether she ever speculated for a moment that I might have liked it better. As a matter of history, the first time I ate in the Automat, when I was about twelve, I discovered that my mother was not an especially good cook, and this had hurt me as much as anything in my childhood. I could hardly swallow the food for years after that, but practice makes perfect, and I had learned to chomp with the histrionic absorption of a movie hero on a picnic.

As we ate, we regressed in time, reingesting all the events that had separated us. We retraced our steps to the very beginning, and there, joining hands, we advanced again from the birth of the soft-eyed boy to my embarrassing and unassimilable prodigality there at the table. To their great surprise, it always came out the same. We always bumped up against the present. Each time we raised our eyes from the plate, we were startled to discover each other, so camouflaged by time. As soon as our eyes met, we jumped back, as from an abyss. In these encounters, we resembled two forever inhibited people who press against each other in the subway: both want the contact, but neither dares admit it.

It was like my friend Andrew's description of the first analyst he went to. This one was not a Freudian, he belonged to a group which held our difficulties to be "interpersonal," and so instead of having Andrew lie on a couch while he sat behind him, they faced each other across a table. There Andrew would lay out all the disgusting things he had done, avoiding the analyst's eye for fear of showing shame or triumph, but sneaking furtive glances now and then, while the analyst, on his side, had his hands full dissembling disapproval or any other sign which might conceivably have disturbed Andrew's flow. Occasionally, however, in darting about the room and briefly lighting on the table like flies, their eyes would collide, and in that split second shockingly copulate in a deep obscene surmise.

Our conversation consisted of answerable questions and unquestionable answers. As usual, my mother found that I looked thin. All my life, I had managed to stay thin as a reproach to her, and on her side, as if a mother's role were that of a fanatic taxidermist, she had done her best to stuff me. She asked me where I took my laundry. "Aren't the prices outrageous? And the way they boil your clothes in all that acid, a shirt doesn't last six months." She was working around to suggesting that I bring my laundry to her. Maybe those dirty shirts would tell her what she was so anxious, and so ashamed, to know. A smear of lipstick, a smell, a stain, might paint a Japanese picture.

My father discussed the last month's boxing matches. Since I occasionally watched televised bouts in a bar, this had become a regular gambit. With an old man's memory, which clings to things as a child clings to its mother, for fear of being abandoned, he recalled every blow. If I happened to disagree with him—by mistake, or because I wasn't following him—he revised his version accordingly. We fought those fights side by side.

When he wasn't talking about boxing, his remarks were designed to show me that he was a liberal, a man who understands. Yesterday he gave up his seat in the subway to a Negress. Jews are smart. Everybody does things without knowing why. Nobody can say who's right and who's wrong. There are two sides to every question.

I remembered him when he was ten feet tall and his every statement was a revelation of the absolute order of things. I tried to steer him around to himself, to push him gently back into his own indistinctly remembered convictions, but this only succeeded in panicking him. He tried to believe that the only difference between us was that I was "modern." He was going to be "modern" too, by denying everything he felt, and forgetting the few lessons life had taught him. He thought of my modernity as relentless and inescapable, a march of history which would let nothing—parents least of all—stand in its way.

My mother was smiling, and as I watched her over a forkful of mashed potatoes I realized that she was still pretty. I knew that smile from way back, I remembered how it had once outshone the sun in heaven. Only, it had had more of a Mona Lisa character then, an ambiguity that gave it a special quality of romance. Where was that romance now? I wondered. Which of us was unfaithful, and why? Each was caricatured by a love we didn't know how to express. Afraid to feel, we were condemned to think, and at the same time not to think. When—and how—had our oneness become three? What ingredient was added to my mixture to turn it to poison? What alchemy isolated my substance beyond their—and my—understanding? There we were, playing a painful game of blindman's buff. We began by bandaging our eyes; then the bandages had fallen away and we had realized that we were blind.

At last I judged that I had eaten enough, an exemplary amount. With all my blood and nerves busy in my stomach, I relaxed, I became flatulent with affection. My mother saw my face go blank and she beamed. Belly to belly, that was the only true way to talk.

My father was describing how, on the job, he had solved a problem that had stumped even the architect. He had just 'scribed a plumb line on the floor. "Well I'll be god-damned," the architect had said, "if old Pete hasn't gone and done it again!" As I listened to this story, I never doubted it for a moment, and I was proud of him. That was his reality, and in it he was still magnificent, just as my mother could calculate better than the Secretary of the Treasury, how much it would cost a newlywed couple to set up housekeeping. It was in these attitudes, like an old-fashioned photograph, that I thought of them most fondly, and although

I had long since exiled myself from that Garden of Eden, it was something I could not root out of my feelings. This homely love was my history. Like a navel, it was a reminder that I hadn't been struck fully formed from my own brow. I remember a story an Army doctor told me, about a Negro soldier whose belly was ripped open in a fight. They sewed him up in time and saved his life, but when they pulled off the adhesive tape, his belly button—he had the old-fashioned protruding kind—came away with it. When he saw what had happened, the soldier was beside himself, in the full sense of that expression, and they couldn't calm him down until the doctor sewed his belly button back on.

I knew how he felt. Although I liked to imagine myself unfettered by human history, faced only by free choices, exquisitely irresponsible, it was still comforting to know that I hadn't been born in a bad novel like most of the people who spent their evenings in Village bars. Although they too probably came from Brooklyn or the Bronx, I couldn't imagine them with families. They seemed to have risen spontaneously from rotting social tissues, the way flies were thought to generate in filth, or in a wound.

I admit that whenever I considered my parents for any length of time, I generally arrived at a feeling of incredulity there too, but at least this is some kind of an emotion, and after all, how else can you look at a mother and father who hatched you like a plot and then couldn't read their own writing? They, too, were inevitably incredulous, always wondering. I could see them right there in that moment struggling with this puzzle which was hidden in the back of their minds the way people you read about now and then in the newspapers hide their children in a closet or a windowless room for twenty years. Always, without realizing it, they were wondering what I was, whether to be proud of me or ashamed, whether my strangeness was genius, sickness, or simply evil, whether I had sold my soul like Faust or was still learning to walk, whether I was a hero or an abortion. In the familiar terms, I was a failure. I had neither money, fame, nor any immediate prospect of either. At least if I had been an idiot, lurching up and down the sidewalk in front of the house, they could have lavished all their pent-up love on my helpless heart, but as it was they were never sure.

21

My father was still talking about the job. He seemed very proud to have a hand in this particular building, which had been given a lot of publicity and which was apparently expected to become a world-famous monument on Broadway. As superintendent, he had a set of plans, and he brought them out for me to see. I recognized the name of a large low-priced clothing chain which sold standard stuff on installments. Feigning a show of interest, I studied the plans. Besides some very ill-adapted functionalist architecture, the building boasted two tremendous figures—a male and a female nude—above its façade, on either side of the store name like parentheses. They were over fifty feet high, my father assured me, and would be draped in neon lights. "They're like the Statue of Liberty on Broadway," he said, and I knew by the tone of his voice that he was quoting somebody. "What are they supposed to stand for?" I asked, in spite of the feeling I had that this question was all wrong. He looked at me, surprised and a little embarrassed. He was searching his mind for an answer, and although by now I didn't want an answer, I didn't know how to stop what I had started. I looked at the plans again. The figures were sexless, without even the pretense of drapery or a fig leaf. I knew what they stood for. The Statue of Liberty, since it was a French gift, may be presumed to have something under her robes, but these were American-made, this was the naked truth.

My father moved his lips as if to speak, but said nothing. In spite of myself again, I turned on him inquiringly, and he dropped his eyes. "It seems like a mighty big job, Pop," I said. "They must have a lot of confidence in you." "You said a mouthful," he said quickly, plainly relieved. "The architect himself asked for me."

Primitive tools—a saw, a hammer, nails, a square rule, a leveler—these were not enough. I looked at my father, at his innocent face which had been chiseled into homely, heart-rending lines by the simplest kind of considerations, at his jaw made square by practical decisions, his mouth made thin by everyday resolutions, his eyes kept clear and alert with estimations of length, breadth, and height . . . and it struck me then that his head might have been done by a sculptor with a warm feeling for texture and no talent for portraiture, a craftsman with no idea of art.

Suddenly I felt a mushrooming urge to blurt out something—I don't know what—"I think you're great, Pop" or "I'm with you" or "To hell with them all," and this made me very nervous, so nervous I could hardly sit still. In desperation, I abruptly decided to leave. With my mouth still full of lemon meringue pie, I announced apologetically that I had an unbreakable appointment for which I was already late. I had been on the point of calling them up, I improvised, for that very reason, but I felt that even a short visit was better than none. I would come again soon and we would have a nice long talk.

They immediately fell into a frenzy of reassurances. Talking both at once, drowning each other out, they assured me that I didn't have to give explanations to them, they certainly understood how busy I was, and they had not the most infinitesimal wish to interfere with these quintessential commitments. Perish the thought—perish, in fact, the mother and father who would interrupt for a thousandth of a second their son's glorious onrush toward his entelechy. . . .

Caught up in their extravagance, I reiterated my determination to come again soon with all the fervor of MacArthur vowing to return to the Philippines. I again congratulated my mother for having served up a truly historic feast and made ready to leave, avoiding my own eyes in the mirror as I knotted my tie.

My father left the room for a moment and reappeared in his coat. He would walk me to the subway, he said. I was on the point of protesting, but I knew I shouldn't, so I said, "O.K., Pop, let's go." I kissed my mother, and she walked out to the gate with us.

Closing the gate behind me, I said, "So long, Mom," and she answered, "So long, Bud," slipping unconsciously into my old nickname again. The sound of it moved me more than I would have thought possible, and I impulsively kissed her again before my father and I faded from her sight.

At the corner I looked back to see her still standing there, her features erased by distance, and I waved, although I knew she couldn't see me. To my astonishment, she waved back. I caught the movement of her arm in the corner of my eye just as I was turning my head. I couldn't believe I had actually seen it—I knew she couldn't see across the street without her glasses. I stopped and took a step back—she was gone. Had I imagined it? It seemed very important to me to find out, and then I realized that I believed she *knew* when I turned the corner, she *sensed* it. No, no, I expostulated with myself, she only knew how long it took us to reach the corner, and then she waved. . . .

"What's the matter?" It was my father, asking why I had stopped. "I was wondering how Mom could see this far," I said. "She just waved at us." "Yeah, she waves three, four times," he said indifferently, and we started off toward the subway again.

I was trying to dismiss a vague fear that he wouldn't stop at the subway entrance, that he would go all the way with me, then I reflected that he rarely came to visit me. My mother had never been to my place. "I can't climb all those steps," she would say, as if I lived on top of Parnassus. Once my father and I had walked, just as we were walking now, through the Village. He didn't remember the neighborhood very clearly—he said the last time he'd been there was before I was born—and he had looked around him like the sightseers who go through the streets in plastic-topped buses. On Fourth Street, we had passed a big fat lesbian dressed in men's clothes and with her hair cut like a man. My father favored her with a disapproving glance as she went by. "Put a dress on that bastard and he'd be a woman," he said, wholly unaware that it was.

A few minutes later, as we were walking through Waverly Place, he swept his arm over half a century's changes and said, "You know, this used to be all sportin' houses around here . . . ," and I could see that he was wondering how the simple, old-fashioned sportin' house—where you knew what you wanted and got what you paid for—had given way to this, had borne a brood of Hamlets and hermaphrodites whose sport was an ambiguous affair in which you never knew who was getting the f———ing or what unheard-of infections you risked in the bargain, and where you paid with your life. . . .

We had reached the subway entrance and I stopped, but he began to descend the steps. I seized him by the arm. "You don't have to walk me down, Pop," I said.

He was surprised. "That's all right," he said. "I haven't got anything else to do."

"Yeah, but what's the use of your breathing all those fumes and then having to come all the way up again?" I said, still holding his arm.

He was disappointed, I could see that he wanted to walk me down. "O.K., Pop," I said, letting go of his arm and starting down, "I guess a few steps don't faze you, do they?"

"No," he said, "I'm used to them," and we went down together and he came back up alone.

Truman Capote

Born in New Orleans, Truman Capote moved to New York in 1942 when he was 18. His first novel, Other Voices, Other Rooms, *was published to great critical acclaim six years later. Capote created a surreal, slightly sinister world in his early fiction, including* The Grass Harp *and the short-story collection* A Tree of Night. *In 1957 the set designer Oliver Smith invited Capote to visit his twenty-eight-room house in Brooklyn Heights. Capote wrote enviously, "There was a beautiful staircase floating upward in white, swan-simple curves to a skylight of sunny amber-gold glass. The floors were fine, the real thing, hard lustrous timber; and the walls! In 1820 when the house was built, men knew how to make walls— thick as buffalo, immune to the mightiest cold, the meanest heat." After that visit, Capote rented Smith's five-room basement apartment. It was in Brooklyn that Capote wrote* Breakfast at Tiffany's *and* In Cold Blood. *Capote left Brooklyn in the 1960s, but his tenure is immortalized in "A House on the Heights," published in his collection of essays,* The Dogs Bark. *Capote died in 1984 leaving an unfinished novel,* Unanswered Prayers.

A House on the Heights

I live in Brooklyn. By choice.

Those ignorant of its allures are entitled to wonder why. For, taken as a whole, it *is* an uninviting community. A veritable veldt of tawdriness where even the *noms des quartiers* aggravate: Flatbush and Flushing Avenue, Bushwick, Brownsville, Red Hook. Yet, in the greenless grime-gray, oases do occur, splendid contradictions, hearty echoes of healthier days. Of these seeming mirages, the purest example is the neighborhood in which I am situated, an area known as Brooklyn Heights. Heights, because it stands atop a cliff that secures a sea-gull's view of the Manhattan and Brooklyn bridges, of lower Manhattan's tall dazzle and the ship-lane waters, breeding river to bay to ocean, that encircle and seethe past posturing Miss Liberty.

I'm not much acquainted with the proper history of the Heights. However, I *believe* (but please don't trust me) that the oldest house, the oldest still extant and functioning, belongs to our backyard neighbors,

27

Mr. and Mrs. Philip Broughton. A silvery-gray, shingle-wood Colonial shaded by trees robustly leafed, it was built in 1790, the home of a sea captain. Period prints, dated 1830, depict the Heights area as a cozy port bustling with billowed sails; and, indeed, many of the section's finer houses, particularly those of Federal design, were first intended to shelter the families of shipmasters. Cheerfully austere, as elegant and other-era as formal calling cards, these houses bespeak an age of able servants and solid fireside ease; of horses in musical harness (old rose-brick carriage houses abound hereabouts; all now, naturally, transformed into pleasant, if rather doll-pretty, dwellings); invoke specters of bearded seafaring fathers and bonneted stay-at-home wives: devoted parents to great broods of future bankers and fashionable brides. For a century or so that is how it must have been: a time of tree-shrouded streets, lanes limp with willow, August gardens brimming with bumblebees and herbaceous scent, of ship horns on the river, sails in the wind, and a country-green meadow sloping down to the harbor, a cow-grazing, butterflied meadow where children sprawled away breezy summer afternoons, where the slap of sleds resounded on December snows.

Is that how it was? Conceivably I take too Valentine a view. However it be, my Valentine assumes the stricter aspect of a steel engraving as we mosey, hand in hand, with Henry Ward Beecher, whose church once dominated the spiritual life of the Heights through the latter half of the last century. The great Bridge, opened in 1883, now balanced above the river; and the port, each year expanding, becoming a more raucous, big-business matter, chased the children out of the meadow, withered it, entirely whacked it away to make room for black palace-huge warehouses tickly with imported tarantulas and reeking of rotten bananas.

By 1910 the neighborhood, which comprises sly alleys and tucked-away courts and streets that sometimes run straight but also dwindle and bend, had undergone fiercer vicissitudes. Descendants of the Reverend Beecher's stiff-collared flock had begun removing themselves to other pastures; and immigrant tribes, who had first ringed the vicinity, at once infiltrated en masse. Whereupon a majority of what remained of genteel old stock, the sediment in the bottom of the bottle, poured forth from their homes, leaving them to be demolished or converted into eyesore-seedy rooming establishments.

So that, in 1925, Edmund Wilson, allowing a paragraph to what he considered the dead and dying Heights, disgustedly reported: "The pleasant red and pink brick houses still worthily represent the generation of Henry Ward Beecher; but an eternal Sunday is on them now; they seem sunk in a final silence. In the streets one may catch a glimpse of a solitary well-dressed old gentleman moving slowly a long way off; but in general the respectable have disappeared and only the vulgar survive. The empty quiet is broken by the shouts of shrill Italian children and by incessant mechanical pianos in dingy apartment houses, accompanied by human voices that seem almost as mechanical as they. At night, along unlighted streets, one gives a wide berth to drunkards that sprawl out across the pavement from the shadow of darkened doors; and I have known a dead horse to be left in the road—two blocks from the principal post office and not much more from Borough Hall—with no effort made to remove it, for nearly three weeks."

Gothic as this glimpse is, the neighborhood nevertheless continued to possess, cheap rents aside, some certain appeal that brigades of the gifted—artists, writers—began to discover. Among those riding in on the initial wave was Hart Crane, whose poet's eye, focusing on his window view, produced *The Bridge.* Later, soon after the success of *Look Homeward, Angel,* Thomas Wolfe, noted prowler of the Brooklyn night, took quarters: an apartment, equipped with the most publicized icebox in literature's archives, which he maintained until his "overgrowed carcass" was carried home to the hills of Carolina. At one time, a stretch of years in the early forties, a single, heaven knows singular, house on Middagh Street boasted a roll call of residents that read: W. H. Auden, Richard Wright, Carson McCullers, Paul and Jane Bowles, the British composer Benjamin Britten, impresario and stage designer Oliver Smith, an authoress of murder entertainments—Miss Gypsy Rose Lee, and a Chimpanzee accompanied by Trainer. Each of the tenants in this ivory-tower boardinghouse contributed to its upkeep, lights, heat, the wages of a general cook (a former Cotton Club chorine), and all were present at the invitation of the owner, that very original editor, writer, *fantaisiste,* a gentleman with a guillotine tongue, yet benevolent and butter-hearted, the late, the justly lamented George Davis.

Now George is gone, and his house too; the necessities of some absurd civic project caused it to be torn down during the war. Indeed, the war years saw the neighborhood slide to its nadir. Many of the more substantial old houses were requisitioned by the military, as lodgings, as jukebox canteens, and their rural-reared, piney-woods personnel treated them quite as Sherman did those Dixie mansions. Not that it mattered; not that anyone gave a damn. No one did; until, soon after the war, the Heights commenced attracting a bright new clientele, brave pioneers bringing brooms and buckets of paint: urban, ambitious young couples, by and large midrung in their Doctor–Lawyer–Wall Street–Whatever careers, eager to restore to the Heights its shattered qualities of circumspect, comfortable charm.

For them, the section had much to offer: roomy big houses ready to be reconverted into private homes suitable for families of old-fashioned size; and such families are what these young people either had made or were making at stepladder rates. A good place to raise children, too, this neighborhood where the traffic is cautious and the air has clarity, a seaside tartness; where there are gardens for games, quiet stoops for amusing; and where, above all, there is the Esplanade to roller-skate upon. (Forbidden: still the brats do it.) While far from being a butter-flied meadow, the Esplanade, a wide terracelike walk overlooking the harbor, does its contemporary best to approximate that playing pasture of long-gone girls and their brothers.

So, for a decade and longer, the experiment of reviving the Heights has proceeded: to the point where one is tempted to term it a fait accompli. Window boxes bloom with geraniums; according to the season, green foliated light falls through the trees or gathered autumn leaves burn at the corner; flower-loaded wagons wheel by while the flower seller sings his wares; in the dawn one occasionally hears a cock crow, for there is a lady with a garden who keeps hens and a rooster. On winter nights, when the wind brings the farewell callings of boats outward bound and carries across rooftops the chimney smoke of evening

30

fires, there is a sense, evanescent but authentic as the firelight's flicker, of time come circle, of ago's sweeter glimmerings recaptured.

Though I'd long been acquainted with the neighborhood, having now and then visited there, my closer association began two years ago when a friend bought a house on Willow Street. One mild May evening he asked me over to inspect it. I was most impressed; exceedingly envious. There were twenty-eight rooms, high-ceilinged, well proportioned, and twenty-eight workable marble-manteled fireplaces. There was a beautiful staircase floating upward in white, swan-simple curves to a skylight of sunny amber-gold glass. The floors were fine, the real thing, hard lustrous timber; and the walls! In 1820, when the house was built, men knew how to make walls—thick as a buffalo, immune to the mightiest cold, the meanest heat.

French doors led to a spacious rear porch reminiscent of Louisiana. A porch canopied, completely submerged, as though under a lake of leaves, by an ancient but admirably vigorous vine weighty with grape-like bunches of wisteria. Beyond, a garden: a tulip tree, a blossoming pear, a perched black-and-red bird bending a feathery branch of forsythia.

In the twilight, we talked, my friend and I. We sat on the porch consulting martinis—I urged him to have one more, another. It got to be quite late, he began to see my point: Yes, twenty-eight rooms *were* rather a lot; and yes, it seemed only *fair* that I should have some of them.

That is how I came to live in the yellow brick house on Willow Street.

Often a week passes without my "going to town," or "crossing the bridge," as neighbors call a trip to Manhattan. Mystified friends, suspecting provincial stagnation, inquire, "But what do you *do* over there?" Let me tell you, life can be pretty exciting around here. Remember Colonel Rudolf Abel, the Russian secret agent, the biggest spy ever caught in America, head of the whole damned apparatus? Know where they nabbed him? Right here! Smack on Fulton Street! Trapped him in a building between David Semple's fine-foods store and Frank Gambuzza's television-repair shop. Frank, grinning as though he'd done the

31

job himself, had his picture in *Life;* so did the waitress at the Music Box Bar, the colonel's favorite watering hole. A peevish few of us couldn't fathom why our pictures weren't in *Life* too. Frank, the Music Box Bar girl—they weren't the only people who knew the colonel. Such a gentlemanlike gentleman: one would never have *supposed* . . .

I confess, we don't catch spies every day. But most days are supplied with stimulants: in the harbor some exotic freighter to investigate; a bird of strange plumage resting among the wisteria; or, and how exhilarating an occurrence it is, a newly arrived shipment at Knapp's. Knapp's is a set of shops, really a series of storerooms resembling caverns, clustered together on Fulton near Pineapple Street. The proprietor—that is too modest a designation for so commanding a figure—the czar, the Aga Khan of these paradisaic emporiums is Mr. George Knapp, known to his friends as Father.

Father is a world traveler. Cards arrive: he is in Seville, now Copenhagen, now Milan, next week Manchester, everywhere and all the while on a gaudy spending spree. Buying: blue crockery from a Danish castle. Pink apothecary jars from an old London pharmacy. English brass, Barcelona lamps, Battersea boxes, French paperweights, Italian witch balls, Greek icons, Venetian blackamoors, Spanish saints, Korean cabinets; and junk, glorious junk, a jumble of ragged dolls, broken buttons, a stuffed kangaroo, an aviary of owls under a great glass bell, the playing pieces of obsolete games, the paper moneys of defunct governments, an ivory umbrella cane sans umbrella, crested chamber pots and mustache mugs and irreparable clocks, cracked violins, a sundial that weighs seven hundred pounds, skulls, snake vertebrae, elephants' hoofs, sleigh bells and Eskimo carvings and mounted swordfish, medieval milkmaid stools, rusted firearms and flaking waltz-age mirrors.

Then Father comes home to Brooklyn, his treasures trailing after him. Uncrated, added to the already perilous clutter, the blackamoors prance in the marvelous gloom, the swordfish glide through the store's Atlantic-depth dusk. Eventually they will go: fancier *antiquaries,* and anonymous mere beauty lovers, will come, cart them away. Meanwhile, poke around. You're certain to find a plum; and it may be a peach. That paperweight—the one imprisoning a Baccarat dragonfly. If you want it, take it now: tomorrow, assuredly the day after, will see it on Fifty-seventh Street at quintuple the tariff.

Father has a partner, his wife, Florence. She is from Panama, is handsome, fresh-colored and tall, trim enough to look well in the trousers she affects, a woman of proud posture and, vis-à-vis customers, of nearly eccentric curtness, take-it-or-go disdain—but then, poor soul, she is under the discipline of not being herself permitted to sell, even quote a price. Only Father, with his Macaulayan memory, his dazzling ability to immediately lay hold of any item in the dizzying maze, is so allowed. Brooklyn-born, waterfront-bred, always hatted and usually wearing a wet cold cigar, a stout, short, round powerhouse with one arm, with a strutting walk, a rough-guy voice, shy nervous sensitive eyes that blink when irritation makes him stutter, Father is nevertheless an aesthete. A tough aesthete who takes no guff, will not quibble over his evaluations, just declares, "Put it down!" and, "Get it Manhattan half the money, I give it yuh free." They are an excellent couple, the Knapps. I explore their museum several times a week, and toward October, when a Franklin stove in the shape of a witch hut warms the air and Florence serves cider accompanied by a damp delicious date-nut bread she bakes in discarded coffee cans, never miss a day. Occasionally, on these festive afternoons, Father will gaze about him, blink-blink his eyes with vague disbelief, then, as though his romantic accumulations were closing round him in a manner menacing, observe: "I got to be crazy. Putting my heart in a fruitcake business like this. And the *investment*. The money alone! Honest, in your honest opinion, wouldn't you say I'm crazy?"

Certainly not. If, however, Mrs. Cornelius Oosthuizen were to beg the question—

It seems improbable that someone of Mrs. Oosthuizen's elevation should have condescended to distinguish me with her acquaintance. I owe it all to a pound of dog meat. What happened was: the butcher's boy delivered a purchase of mine which, by error, included hamburger meant to go to Mrs. O. Recognizing her name on the order slip, and having often remarked her house, a garnet-colored château in mood remindful of the old Schwab mansion on Manhattan's Riverside Drive,

I thought of taking round the package myself, not dreaming to meet the fine lady, but, at most, ambitious for a moment's glance into her fortunate preserve. Fortunate, for it boasted, so I'd had confided to me, a butler and staff of six. Not that this is the Height's sole *maison de luxe:* we are blessed with several exponents of limousine life—but unarguably, Mrs. O. is *la regina di tutti.*

Approaching her property, I noticed a person in Persian lamb very vexedly punching the bell, pounding a brass knocker. "God damn you, Mabel," she said to the door; then turned, glared at me as I climbed the steps—a tall, intimidating replica of frail unforbidding Miss Marianne Moore (who, it may be recalled, is a Brooklyn lady too). Pale lashless eyes, razor lips, hair a silver fuzz. "Ah, *you.* I know you," she accused me, as behind her the door was opened by an Irish crone wearing an ankle-length apron. "So. I suppose you've come to sign the petition? Very good of you, I'm sure." Mumbling an explanation, muttering servile civilities, I conveyed the butcher's parcel from my hands to hers; she, as though I'd tossed her a rather rotten fish, dangled it gingerly until the maid remarked, "Ma'am, 'tis Miss Mary's meat the good lad's brought."

"Indeed. Then don't stand there, Mabel. Take it." And, regarding me with a lessening astonishment that I could not, in her behalf, reciprocate: "Wipe your boots, come in. We will discuss the petition. Mabel, send Murphy with some Bristol and biscuit. . . . Oh? At the dentist's! When I *asked* him *not* to tamper with that tooth. What hellish nonsense," she swore as we passed into a hatrack-vestibule. "Why didn't he go to the hypnotist, as I told him? Mary! Mary! Mary," she said when now appeared a friendly nice dog of cruel pedigree: a spaniel cum chow attached to the legs of a dachshund, "I believe Mabel has your lunch. Mabel, take Miss Mary to the kitchen. And we will have our biscuits in the Red Room."

The room, in which red could be discerned only in a bowl of porcelain roses and a basket of marzipan strawberries, contained velvet-swagged windows that commanded a pulse-quickening prospect: sky, skyline, far away a wooded slice of Staten Island. In other respects, the room, a heavy confection, cumbersome, humorless, a hunk of Beidermeier pastry, did not recommend itself. "It was my grandmother's bedroom; my father preferred it as a parlor. Cornelius, Mr. Oosthuizen, died here. Very suddenly: while listening at the radio to the Roosevelt person. An attack. Brought on by anger and cigars. I'm sure you won't ask permission to smoke. Sit down. . . . Not there. There, by the window. Now here, it *should* be here, somewhere, in this drawer? Could it be upstairs? Damn Murphy, horrid man always meddling with my— No, I have it: the petition."

The document stated, and objected to, the plans of a certain minor religious sect that had acquired a half-block of houses on the Heights which they planned to flatten and replace with a dormitory building for the benefit of their Believers. Appended to it were some dozen protesting signatures; the Misses Seeley had signed, and Mr. Arthur Veere Vinson, Mrs. K. Mackaye Brownlowe—descendants of the children in the meadow, the old-guard survivors of *their* neighborhood's evilest hours, those happy few who regularly attended Mrs. O.'s black-tie-sitdowns. She wasted no eloquence on the considerable merit of their complaint; simply, "Sign it," she ordered, a Lady Catherine de Bourgh instructing a Mr. Collins.

Sherry came; and with it an assembly of cats. Scarred battlers with leprous fur and punch-drunk eyes. Mrs. O., motioning toward the least respectable of these, a tiger-striped marauder, told me, "This is the one you may take home. He's been with us a month, we've put him in splendid condition, I'm sure you'll be devoted. Dogs? What *sort* of dogs have you? Well, I don't approve the pure breeds. Anyone will give *them* a home. I took Miss Mary off the street. And Lovely Louise, Mouse and Sweet William—my dogs, all my cats, too, came off the streets. Look below, there in the garden. Under the heaven tree. Those markings: graves are what you see, some as old as my childhood. The seashells are goldfish. The yellow coral, canaries. That white stone is a rabbit; that cross of pebbles: my favorite, the first Mary—angel girl, went bathing in the river and caught a fatal chill. I used to tease Cornelius, Mr. Oosthuizen, told him, ha-ha, told him I planned to put him there with the rest of my darlings. Ha-ha, he wasn't amused, not at all. So, I mean to say, your having dogs doesn't signify: Billy here has such spirit, *he* can hold his own. No, I insist you have him. For I can't keep him much longer, he's a disturbing influence; and if I let him loose, he'll run back to his bad old life in the St. George alley. I wouldn't want *that* on my conscience if I were you."

Her persuasions failed; in consequence our parting was cool. Yet at Christmas she sent me a card, a Cartier engraving of the heaven tree protecting the bones in its sad care. And once, encountering her at the bakery, where we both were buying brownies, we discussed the impudent disregard her petition had received; alas, the wreckers had wrecked, the brethren were building. On the same occasion, she shame-on-you informed me that Billy the cat, released from her patronage, had indeed returned to the sinful ways of the St. George alley.

The St. George alley, adjoining a small cinema, is a shadowy shelter for vagrants: wino derelicts wandered over the bridge from Chinatown and the Bowery share it with other orphaned, gone-wild creatures; cats, as many as minnows in a stream, who gather in their greatest numbers toward nightfall; for then, as darkness happens, strange-eyed women, not unlike those black-clothed fanatics who haunt the cat arenas in Rome, go stealing through the alley with caressing hisses and sacks of crumbled salmon. (Which isn't to suggest that Mrs. O. is one who indulges in this somehow unhealthy hobby: regarding animals, her actions, while perhaps a bit overboard, are kindly meant, and not untypical of the Heights, where a high percentage of the pet population has been adopted off the streets. Astonishing, really, the amount of lost strays who roam their way into the neighborhood, as though instinct informed them they'd find someone here who couldn't abide being followed through the rain, but would, instead, lead them home, boil milk and call Dr. Wasserman, Bernie, our smart-as-they-come young vet whose immaculate hospital resounds with the music of Bach concertos and the barkings of mending beasts.)

Just now, in connection with these notes, I was hunting through a hieroglyphic shambles I call my journal. Odd, indeed the oddest, jottings—a majority of which conceal from me their meanings. God knows what "Thunder on Cobra Street" refers to. Or "A diarrhea of platitudes in seventeen tongues." Unless it is intended to describe a most tiresome local person, a linguist terribly talkative in many languages though articulate in none. However, "Took T&G to G&T" does make sense.

The first initials represent two friends, the latter a restaurant not far away. You must have heard of it, Gage & Tollner. Like Kolb's and Antoine's in New Orleans, Gage & Tollner is a last-century enterprise that has kept in large degree its founding character. The shaky dance of its gaslight chandeliers is not a period-piece hoax; nor do the good plain marble-topped tables, the magnificent array of gold-edged mirrors, seem sentimental affectations—rather, it is a testament to the seriousness of the proprietors, who have obliged us by letting the place stay much as it was that opening day in 1874. One mightn't suppose it, for in the atmosphere there is none of the briny falderal familiar to such aquariums, but the specialty is seafood. The best. Chowders the doughtiest down-easter must approve. Lobsters that would appease Nero. Myself, I am a soft-shelled-crab aficionado: a plate of sautéed crabs, a halved lemon, a glass of chilled Chablis—most satisfactory. The waiters, too, dignified but swift-to-smile Negroes who take pride in their work, contribute to the goodness of Gage & Tollner; on the sleeves of their very laundered jackets they sport military-style chevrons awarded according to the number of years each has served; and, *were* this the Army, some would be generals.

Nearby, there is another restaurant, a fraction less distinguished, but of similar vintage and virtually the same menu: Joe's—Joe being, by the way, an attractive young lady. On the far fringes of the Heights, just before Brooklyn becomes Brooklyn again, there is a street of Gypsies, with Gypsy cafés (have your future foretold and be tattooed while sipping tankards of Moorish tea); there is also an Arab-Armenian quarter sprinkled with spice-saturated restaurants where one can buy, hot from the oven, a crusty sort of pancake frosted with sesame seed— once in a while I carry mine down to the waterfront, intending to share with the gulls; but gobbling as I go, none is ever left. On a summer's evening a stroll across the bridge, with cool winds singing through the steel shrouds, with stars moving about above and ships below, can be intoxicating, particularly if you are headed toward the roasting-pork, sweet-and-sour aromas of Chinatown.

Another journal notation reads: "At last a face in the ghost hotel!"

Which means: after months of observation, in all climates at all hours, I'd sighted someone in a window of a haunted-seeming riverfront building that stands on Water Street at the foot of the Heights. A lonely hotel I often make the destination of my walks: because I think it romantic, in aggravated moments imagine retiring there, for it is as secluded as Mt. Athos, remoter than the Krak Chevalier in the mountains of wildest Syria. Daytimes the location, a dead-end Chiricoesque piazza facing the river, is little disturbed; at night, not at all: not a sound, except foghorns and a distant traffic whisper from the bridge which bulks above. Peace, and the shivering glow of gliding-by tugs and ferries.

The hotel is three-storied. Sunstruck scraps of reflected river-shine, and broken, jigsaw images of the bridge waver across the windows; but beyond the glass nothing stirs: the rooms, despite contradictory evidence, milk bottles on sills, a hat on a hook, unmade beds and burning bulbs, appear unoccupied: never a soul to be seen. Like the sailors of the *Marie Celeste,* the guests, hearing a knock, must have opened their doors to a stranger who swallowed them whole. Could it be, perhaps it *was,* the stranger himself that I saw?—"At last a face in the ghost hotel!" I glimpsed him just the once, one April afternoon one cloudless blue day; and he, a balding man in an undershirt, hurled up a window, flexed hairy arms, yawned hugely, hugely inhaled the river breeze—was gone. No, on careful second thought, I will never set foot in that hotel. For I should either be devoured or have my mystery dispelled. As children we are sensitive to mystery: locked boxes, whisperings behind closed doors, the what-thing that lurks yonder in the trees, waits in every stretch between street lamps; but as we grow older all is too explainable, the capacity to invent pleasurable alarm recedes: too bad, a pity—throughout our lives we ought to believe in ghost hotels.

Close by the hotel begins a road that leads along the river. Silent miles of warehouses with shuttered wooden windows, docks resting on the water like sea spiders. From May through September, *la saison pour la plage,* these docks are diving boards for husky ragamuffins—while perfumed apes, potentates of the waterfront but once dock-divers themselves, cruise by steering two-toned (banana-tomato) car concoctions. Crane-carried tractors and cotton bales and unhappy cattle sway above the holds of ships bound for Bahia, for Bremen, for ports spelling their names in oriental calligraphy. Provided one has made waterfront friends, it is sometimes possible to board the freighters, carouse and sun yourself: you may even be asked to lunch—and I, for one, am always quick to accept, embarrassingly so if the hosts are Scandinavian: they always set a superior table from larders brimming with smoked "taste thrills" and iced aquavit. Avoid the Greek ships, however: very poor cuisine, no liquor served except ouzo, a sickly licorice syrup; and, at least in the opinion of this panhandler, the grub on French freighters by no means meets the standards one might reasonably expect.

The tugboat people are usually good for a cup of coffee, and in wintry weather, when the river is tossing surf, what joy to take refuge in a stove-heated tug cabin and thaw out with a mug of the blackest Java. Now and again along the route minuscule beaches occur, and once, it was around sunset on a quiet Sunday, I saw on one of them something that made me look twice, and twice more: still it seemed a vision. Every kind of sailor is common enough here, even saronged East Indians, even the giant Senegalese, their onyx arms afire with blue, with yellow tattooed flowers, with saucy torsos and garish graffiti (Je t'aime, Hard Luck, Mimi Chang, Adios Amigo). Runty Russians, too—one sees them about, flap-flapping in their pajamalike costumes. But the barefooted sailors on the beach, the three I saw reclining there, profiles set against the sundown, seemed mythical as mermen: more exactly, mermaids—for their hair, striped with albino streaks, was lady-length, a savage fiber falling to their shoulders; and in their ears gold rings glinted. Whether plenipotentiaries from the pearl-floored palace of Poseidon or mariners merely, Viking-tressed seamen out of the Gothic North languishing after a long and barberless voyage, they are included permanently in my memory's curio cabinet: an object to be revolved in the light that way and this, like those crystal lozenges with secretive carvings sealed inside.

After consideration, "Thunder on Cobra Street" does become decipherable. On the Heights there is no Cobra Street, though a street exists that suits the name, a steep downhill incline leading to a dark sector of the dockyards. Not a true part of the Heights neighborhood, it lies, like a serpent at the gates, on the outmost periphery. Seedy hangouts, beer-sour bars and bitter candy stores mingle among the eroding houses, the multifamily dwellings that architecturally range from time-blackened brownstone to magnified concepts of Mississippi privy.

Here, the gutters are acrawl with Cobras; that is, a gang of "juvenile" delinquents: COBRA, the word is stamped on their sweatshirts, painted, sometimes in letters that shine with a fearful phosphorescence, across the backs of their leather jackets. The steep street is within their ugly estate, a bit of their "turf," as they term it; an infinitesimal bit, for the Cobras, a powerful cabala, cast owning eyes on acres of metropolitan terrain. I am not brave—*au contraire;* quite frankly, these fellows, may they be twelve years old or twenty, set my heart thumping like a sinner's at Sunday meeting. Nevertheless, when it has been a matter of convenience to pass through this section of their domain, I've compelled my nerves to accept the challenge.

On the last venture, and perhaps it will remain the last, I was carrying a good camera. The sun was unseen in a sky that ought to either rumble or rain. Rackety children played skip-rope, while a lamppost-lot of idle elders looked on, dull-faced and drooping: a denim-painted, cowboy-booted gathering of Cobras. Their eyes, their asleep sick insolent eyes, swerved on me as I climbed the street. I crossed to the opposite curb; then *knew,* without needing to verify it, that the Cobras had uncoiled and were sliding toward me. I heard them whistling; and the children hushed, the skip-rope ceased swishing. Someone—a pimpled purple-birthmark bandit-masked the lower half of his face—said, "Hey, yuh, Whitey, lemmeseeduhcamra." Quicken one's step? Pretend not to hear? But every alternative seemed explosive. "Hey, Whitey, hey, yuh, takemuhpitchawantcha?"

Thunder salvaged the moment. Thunder that rolled, crashed down the street like a truck out of control. We all looked up, a sky ripe for storm stared back. I shouted, "Rain! Rain!" and ran. Ran for the Heights, that safe citadel, that bourgeois bastion. Tore along the Esplanade—where the nice young mothers were racing their carriages

40

against the coming disaster. Caught my breath under the thrashing leaves of troubled elms, rushed on: saw the flower-wagon man struggling with his thunder-frightened horse. Saw, twenty yards ahead, then ten, five, then none, the yellow house on Willow Street. Home! And happy to be.

Shirley Chisholm

A member of the House of Representatives from 1969 to 1983, Shirley Chisholm was the first black woman elected to Congress. She campaigned for the Democratic presidential nomination in 1972. Born in Brooklyn, Chisholm graduated from Brooklyn College and Columbia University. Until her election to the New York Assembly in 1964 she worked on child welfare issues. This is an excerpt from her autobiography, Unbought and Unbossed, *published in 1970.*

Back to Brooklyn

When Mother brought Muriel, Odessa, and me back to Brooklyn, it was March 1934. I remember that year that the newspapers were full of pictures and stories about the Dionne quintuplets, who were born a few months after we returned.

All three of us were frightened by the cold. Mother, Father, and Selma were living at 110 Liberty Avenue in Brownsville. It was an unheated, four-room, cold-water railroad flat. Like the cars on a train, the rooms were in a line and you had to go through one to reach the next one. You came into the kitchen, went on through two bedrooms, and arrived at the parlor in the back. But the only heat came from a coal stove in the kitchen and none of it got to the back room, so the parlor was closed and forgotten all winter. Some days when Mother went to Belmont Market we children used to stay in bed most of the day to keep warm. To this day, I'm still afraid of the cold.

Brownsville in the 1930s was a heavily Jewish neighborhood of

43

run-down tenements, some up to ten stories tall with twenty or more apartments. Today we would probably call it a "ghetto." Its residents then would have laughed at the word. Some of them were first-generation Jews from central and eastern Europe, and they knew the difference. They had come from real ghettos.

Most of our playmates and many of Mother's and Father's neighbors were, of course, white and Jewish. Mother's sense of humor appealed to her white friends; they would roar at the imitation of their dialect. The other women often gathered around her bench in the park when she took us there in good weather. Because she was English-speaking and could give advice about bills and other legal pitfalls of city life, she became a kind of neighborhood oracle and leader.

The city was so different from the island, apart from the terrible cold. I kept getting lost. When Mother sent me on short errands, I got mixed up at the corners. Once I had to go to a store about ten blocks away, and she gave me careful written directions. I found my way there and back without trouble, but a few weeks later when I had to go again, I got lost. A store I had relied on as a landmark had moved away. Things didn't change that way in Barbados. The village shoemaker's shop, for example, had been in the same place for generations. I couldn't get used to keeping on the sidewalk, either. When it was crowded, I would take to the street, and Mother would scold, "Shirley, you gonna get killed someday."

The movies in Brooklyn were one of our first great discoveries. Mother usually managed to give us each ten cents to go on Saturdays. The screen was so big; we had never seen anything like it in the islands. We stayed through show after show, long past suppertime, sometimes for twelve or thirteen hours, until Mother came for us with a strap. The manager got to know her. "They're up front in the middle, Mrs. St. Hill," he told her. Mother would herd us home, scolding all the way.

She was thoroughly British in her ideas, her manners and her plans for her daughters. We were to become young ladies—poised, modest, accomplished, educated, and graceful, prepared to take our places in the world. Later Mother and Papa bought a piano, a luxury they could not afford even though it was only twenty-five dollars and was not in the

44

best repair. I went to piano lessons for nine years. When I began to show progress, they made an even greater sacrifice; they bought a new piano on time.

My father was working then as a helper in a big cake bakery. I idolized him, his good looks, his extensive vocabulary, and his intelligence. A tall, thin, handsome man with white hair (it turned in his early twenties), brown skin, and a straight, Grecian nose, he would have been a brilliant scholar if he had been able to go to college. He was an omnivorous reader. Even during the Depression, he always bought two or three newspapers a day. Mother never understood his spending the money; she thought he could get all the news from one. Papa read everything within reach. If he saw a man passing out handbills, he would cross the street to get one and read it. The result was that, although he only finished the equivalent of fifth grade, he seemed to know a little about almost everything.

A tireless talker, he had dozens of friends whom he brought home in the evenings for the sake of their conversation. Papa never smoked or drank, but he kept whiskey for his friends. Mother scolded him over that: "That's all they come for, Charles, you know you can't afford to entertain the way you want to. And you never know when to tell them to go." Mother was upset, not only at the cost of the whiskey with which Papa was so liberal, but also at the fact that we girls had to undress and go to bed in the next room while the men sat around the table in the kitchen. Lying in bed, we could hear them talk about the islands and their politics. Papa and his friends traded story after story showing how Britain was oppressing the colonial peoples of the world. He would speak scornfully of "the divine right of kings."

Papa was a Garveyite, too, a follower of Marcus Garvey, the Jamaican who originated many of the ideas that characterize today's militant black separatists. Garvey used to write and speak against "the mulatto leader," W. E. B. Du Bois, and the "light element of Negroes"—his phrase for the National Association for the Advancement of Colored People—who, he said, believed in miscegenation and an end to the race problem through racial mixing. Garvey declared in the 1920s that "black is beautiful" and called on blacks to preserve their racial purity

45

by becoming separate. His goal was to unite American blacks and return them to Africa, where they would become equals of any man, in an independent isolation. I think this appealed to my father because he, too, was a very proud black man. He instilled pride in his children, a pride in ourselves and our race that was not as fashionable at that time as it is today.

Much of the kitchen-table talk had to do with unions. Papa belonged to the Confectionery and Bakers International Union, and there was nothing he was more proud of than being a union man. He brought labor newspapers home and read from them to his friends. When he was elected a shop steward at the bakery, you would have thought he had been made a king. He had to have his shoes shined and wear a tie when he went to union meetings. It was the first time in his life he had been given the recognition his talents deserved.

Dinner together every night was an inflexible rule in our family. The table had to be set when Papa got there. We waited for him to say a blessing before anything was passed. Then he would lead the conversation, telling Mother about the events of his day and asking the children the inevitable question, "What did you learn in school?" It was no idle query; he wanted an answer. Papa harped on the theme, "You must make something of yourselves. You've got to go to school, and I'm not sending you to play either. Study and make something of yourselves. Remember, only the strong people survive in this world. God gave you a brain; use it."

Sometimes Papa would hold forth on his idol—hardly too strong a word—Marcus Garvey. He seemed almost to worship Garvey and was particularly proud of the fact that he was a West Indian, too. Papa believed America had treated Garvey wrongly, and as a result he talked negatively about the country. "America's got a lot to learn," Papa often proclaimed. When any organization had a Marcus Garvey tribute, he would dress up and go. Sometimes he took me, and there I heard my first black nationalist oratory—talk of race pride and the need for unity, despite any differences, because, the speakers stressed, "we have a common enemy."

My aunt Violet and her husband, Clement Jones, lived about fifteen minutes away. Aunt Violet and her four children had come back to Brooklyn with Mother and her girls, and we usually visited each other on weekends. On Saturdays, these two poor women would sometimes pack lunches and take their combined broods of seven active children by bus or train to Jones Beach, Coney Island, or some other spot for a picnic. Papa seldom went; he usually had to work on Saturdays.

School had been a setback for me at first. When we left Barbados, I had just been promoted to the sixth form, so I expected to be put in the sixth grade in Brooklyn. At P.S. 84 on Glenmore Avenue, the teachers were satisfied with my reading and writing ability, but horrified by my ignorance of American history and geography. They put me in grade 3-B, with children two years younger than I was. Bored, I became a discipline problem. I carried rubber bands in the pocket of my middy blouse and snapped them at the other children; I became expert at making spitballs and flicking them when the teacher's back was turned. Luckily someone diagnosed the trouble and did something about it. The school provided me with a tutor in American geography and history for a year and a half, until I caught up with and passed my age-grade level.

My sisters and I and the other black children were a minority at P.S. 84, but we were not much concerned about it. Blacks from the islands and the growing number from the South would in a few years reverse the racial makeup of the neighborhood, and the change would be accompanied by mounting bad feeling, but at that time the race line was not drawn in the same way it is today. As I remember it, the school was about 80 percent white, mostly Jewish children; all the teachers were white, and nearly all were Jewish. We were not particularly conscious of that fact, either.

On Saturdays, my sisters and I often sat on our fire escape and giggled at the Jewish neighbors going in and out of the synagogue. Mother punished us when she caught us at it. She was a deeply religious person and would not hear of our making fun of anyone's religion. Other children made fun of us because Mother enforced churchgoing on her daughters—three times every Sunday. They would chant, "Here come the St. Hill girls!" as Mother, Odessa, Muriel, Selma, and I walked to

11:00 A.M. services, 2:30 P.M. Bible service, and 7:30 P.M. services at the English Brethren Church. It was a small, Quaker-like sect that Mother belonged to. "You're going to grow up to be good Christians," she would tell us firmly, leading us past our playmates' jeers.

There was no formal service and no minister at the Brethren church. Benches were arranged in concentric circles in a large, bare room. Like a Quaker meeting, the service consisted largely of long silences. What we girls hated most was that we could never even whisper. A head brother would lead the congregation in an opening hymn, a cappella, because instruments were worldly and taboo. Then there would be silence until someone was moved by the spirit to preach or pray. When he was through, there were amens, and then more silence. In the middle, the head brother would lead another hymn. It was an hour and ten minutes of this morning and evening, with Bible study in the afternoon.

"The St. Hill girls" used to have to endure a lot of ridicule for the old-world way their parents controlled their lives. We were always the first ones to arrive at a party and the first to leave. If a party was at eight, we were there one minute early, in beautiful party dresses. However poor we were, Mother could always buy remnants at the market and make us dresses. Always, just as the party got going and I was starting to enjoy dancing, Odessa would come up with the self-righteous air of a girl who has a chance to tell her older sister what to do. "You remember what Mummy said. We've been here an hour and it's time to go home."

Whenever we left the house, Mother and Father always had a long list of dos and don'ts. As we got older, naturally we began to rebel. Our friends seemed to be having so much fun. Our parents were too old-fashioned. They didn't give us any freedom at all.

About 1936, we moved to 420 Ralph Avenue in Bedford-Stuyvesant. Their girls were getting bigger, and Mother and Father needed more room. The new apartment had only four rooms, too, but they were bigger and it was steam heated. It was over a candy store. The proprietor, our landlord, lived in back of the store downstairs and another black family lived upstairs.

"Bed-Stuy" was about 50 percent black in those days. After we moved there, I began to hear racial slurs and epithets for the first time—nigger, kike, Jew bastard, black son of a bitch. I was not used to black being used as a derogatory word.

Blacks were arriving in greater numbers from the South. But though their numbers were growing, there was not such thing as a black community. Most of the newcomers were passive and accommodating in the face of discrimination. They knew their place and stayed in it. They talked among themselves, but there was no racial consciousness, no leadership.

I finished grade school at P.S. 28, and then went to J.H.S. 178, which is still there. It is one of the schools in the Ocean Hill–Brownsville unit that is fighting to stay alive as an independent, locally controlled, and community-responsive school complex.

Those were the hardest years of the Depression. Dad had changed jobs and was working as a laborer in a burlap-bag factory. He had expected to gain several dollars a week by the move, but it turned out the work was not steady. Soon he was working as little as two days a week and bringing home sometimes no more than eighteen dollars. Mother had to do something she had always feared. She put a key on a string around my neck and went to work as a domestic for white families in Flatbush. Every noon I had to walk from junior high school to P.S. 28 and collect my sisters, take them home and feed them, and return to school. I was usually late getting back, but teachers knew why and made allowances. Lunch was usually a glass of milk and a bun. Every Thursday Mother gave me a quarter to go to a bakery and buy whatever was marked down as stale—bread, cake, or pie, enough for the week. She told us to go straight home at the end of the day, lock the door, and not open it for anyone until she got home. We sat in the front window, watching for the first glimpse of her. When she came in sight, we always screamed out in excitement, and the landlord downstairs would always shout, "Shut up!"

Papa's new job was a lot better, and when he worked, he came home at night exhausted. His hands were rough and callused from the tons of rough burlap he carried, and when he tried to read in the evening, he fell asleep over his book.

We had to read, too, even if we did not want to. We all had library cards and every other Saturday Mother took us to the library to check out the limit, three books each. Each of us had a dictionary, and our Christmas presents were books, often one of those endless "adventure" series such as Nancy Drew or Bobbsey Twins stories.

When I graduated from junior high school in 1939, I went to Girls' High School, one of Brooklyn's oldest schools, on Nostrand Avenue in Bedford-Stuyvesant. We had moved again while I was in high school—to 316 Patchen Avenue, where my father worked as the janitor so we had a six-room apartment free, and Mother could stay home again—and it was only a short walk to school. Many of the other students walked or rode there from the farthest parts of Brooklyn. The school was highly regarded. As the name indicates, it was all girls; about half of them were white, but the neighborhood by now was nearly all black.

Immigrants from the South were streaming to Brooklyn for jobs at the Brooklyn Navy Yard, the Long Island aircraft plants, and other growing defense industries. No one knew it then, but the present-day "inner city" (to use a white euphemism) was being created. Black workers had to crowd into neighborhoods that were already black or partly so, because they could not find homes anywhere else. Buildings that had four apartments suddenly had eight, and bathrooms that had been private were shared. White building inspectors winked at housing code violations and illegal rates of occupancy, white landlords doubled and trebled their incomes on slum buildings, and the white neighborhoods in other parts of town and in the suburbs stayed white. Today's urban ghettos were being born.

My family still kept me on a tight rein in my high school years. Mother knew to the minute when I should get home from school, and I had to be there on the dot or face a barrage of questions. My father remonstrated with Mother sometimes: "Ruby, you must remember these are American kids, not island kids. You are here in America." Mother was not impressed. We girls were allowed to go to school programs and occasional parties, but I never had a date, a regular date, in high school. In fact, I never had one in college.

The blessing of a high IQ combined with my good study habits (Mother and Father would not have stood for any other kind) kept me in the upper percentiles at school. I won a French medal; at a time when black students were seldom elected to offices, I was vice president of a girls' honor society, Junior Arista.

Frustration grew, naturally, as I saw my friends doing things I was forbidden to do. My rebellion took small forms. I began to play popular songs on the piano and started trying to play jazz by ear. When boys walked me home, I had them bring me to the door instead of leaving me on the corner. One night Mother opened the door and discovered me being kissed. She dragged me inside while the boy fled and began to lecture me: "I don't want you to carry on in the streets. Bring your friends home." But when I did, I was embarrassed. They had to leave by ten o'clock, and if they didn't, Mother took direct action. She came in the parlor in her nightgown and started pulling down the shades.

Mother always took the lead in handling social relationships, and Papa let her do so, perhaps because we were all girls. If we had been boys, perhaps he would have taken a greater hand. He felt sorry for us, I know, but he never intervened. Sometimes he would lecture Mother, trying to persuade her that she was an immigrant and should adapt more to the ways of her new country instead of trying to transplant all the values of the islands. Mother would not listen. "Charles," she would respond, "we've got to be strict on them if we want them to grow up to be something."

When I graduated from Girls' High in 1942, I drew several scholarship offers. I wanted to accept either one from Vassar or one from Oberlin. But my parents argued that they could not afford my room and board at an out-of-town school. I had to admit they were right, and in the fall I went to Brooklyn College.

Edwin Corle

Although born in Wildwood, New Jersey, in 1906, Edwin Corle wrote most of his books about the Southwest. His family moved to California when he was seventeen, and except for undergraduate studies at Yale, he remained a Westerner. Perhaps his best known work is Fig Tree John, a novel about a nineteenth-century Apache's relationship to whites. His other novels include People on the Earth; Listen, Bright Angel; and Three Ways to Mecca. Corle also wrote the nonfiction Desert Country and The Gila, River of the Southwest. "The Great Manta" was first published in The New Yorker in 1934 and was one of Corle's few stories set in the East. "It's the story of a Brooklyn doorman of alarmingly regular habits and his encounter with a giant devilfish. Edwin Corle died in 1956.

The Great Manta

*M*r. Gagus had a job. It was a good job, too. He said so and his wife said so. They were both very happy. Mr. and Mrs. Gagus lived in Brooklyn, almost as far out as New Lots, but not quite. They used the Van Siclen Avenue subway station.

One of the best things about the job was that Mr. Gagus didn't have to be at work until ten o'clock in the morning. Of course that meant he got home late at night, but even so, it was pretty nice to be able to start the business day at ten. There was something aristocratic about it. It gave him an air.

But in spite of that fact, Mr. Gagus had to get up at 7:30 every morning. It took him an hour to shave and dress and eat his breakfast. While he did these things, Mrs. Gagus packed his lunch. Occasionally in this interval he had time to glance at a newspaper, but usually he reserved that for his subway ride.

At 8:30, he left his tiny flat and walked along Livonia Avenue to the subway entrance. At 8:38, he boarded a Broadway–Seventh Avenue express. Then occurred his customary perusal of the affairs of the world at large, which lasted until 9:27, when he arrived at the Times Square subway station. Here he changed to a Broadway–Seventh Avenue local, and at 9:30 he left it at the Fiftieth Street subway station, where he ascended to the street. Eastward on Fiftieth Street he walked to Sixth Avenue and his establishment of business, arriving there more often than not (provided, of course, that the weather was fair) at 9:35. In bad weather, he might be as late as 9:38, but certainly never any later than that.

The first thing he did when he reached his place of business was to take off his suit and shirt and collar, tie, and shoes. These he placed in a locker. Then he put on a pair of trousers that resembled riding pants, but were not. They were marvelous trousers—a nice light blue with red stripes running down the sides. On his feet, he put a pair of black leather boots, and into the tops of the boots he tucked the legs of the trousers. Over his head he slipped a plain shirt of the type usually known as a sweatshirt. Over this he placed a white waistcoat with gold braid adorning its visible parts. Adjusting these garments with the skill of familiarity, he then took from a hanger a heavy coat with a cutaway tail. This coat was blue with red-and-white decorations, and the entire lining was a brilliant red. There were golden epaulets on the shoulders and several medals on the breast and a stiff brocade collar that fitted tightly under the chin. With the coat resting correctly on his back and shoulders and showing just the proper amount of waistcoat and none of the sweatshirt, he placed on his head a hat. This hat was all of a foot in height and was faced with black fur, adorned with a red plume and a gold band and a gold tassel. It was held in place by a strap under the chin and gave him an appearance of tremendous height and imperious dignity. He took a last look of self-inspection as he pulled a pair of white gloves onto his hands. It was 9:57. And, dressed as a captain of the Grenadier Guards of the First Empire, Mr. Gagus of Brooklyn, and doorman of the Greatest Picture Palace in the World, was ready to go to work. He would close the locker containing his own clothes, walk out of the building, and appear before it on the street at ten o'clock, on the job.

There wasn't much for him to do the first hour but look important and impressive and keep beggars away from the foyer. An occasional taxicab or private car would drive up and he would open the door, and close it after the occupant or occupants had got out. But by eleven o'clock the automobiles arrived with more frequency, and from then until two o'clock he was kept pretty well concentrated on the business of opening and closing automobile doors.

At two o'clock, after four hours on duty, he was relieved by Mr. Parkinson, whom he addressed below in the locker-room as Otto, but who, in public, was a captain of the Grenadier Guards, like himself. Mr. Gagus, turning over his duties to Mr. Parkinson, then retired to the locker room preparatory to eating his lunch—sandwiches, an apple, cheese, sweet chocolate, and coffee kept hot in a small thermos bottle. Before he could eat, he had first to remove his white gloves, his high fur hat, his dignified and decorated coat, and his gold-braided waistcoat. The trousers and the boots he was allowed to leave on if he was careful not to soil or scuff them, but if he wished to appear on the street, he had to change completely back to his own clothes. As this was a great nuisance and as he had no desire to walk anywhere after four hours on his feet, he almost invariably spent his relief period in his undress uniform. He ate and read and dozed, and sometimes he just sat.

At 6 P.M. Mr. Gagus, again attired in full regalia, relieved Mr. Parkinson. By 9 P.M. things began to get a little easier. Fewer and fewer automobiles arrived, though he was occasionally obliged to summon taxicabs for departing patrons. At 10 P.M., he had reached the end of his day's work.

Again he descended to the locker room, and again he took off the white gloves, the high fur hat, the dignified and decorated coat, the gold-braided waistcoat, and this time the plain sweatshirt, the black leather boots, and the red-striped trousers. All of these he placed in the locker in exchange for his own unimpressive clothes, and by 10:22 he was ready to walk west on Fiftieth Street. At 10:28, he entered the Fiftieth Street subway station. At 10:31, he transferred to an express at Times Square. At 11:20, he arrived at the Van Siclen Avenue subway station in Brooklyn. At 11:28, he unlocked the front door of his apartment building. At 11:29, he entered his tiny flat. At 11:35, he drank a cup of coffee and followed it with a supper of stew or vegetables or cold meat, or perhaps a bit of chicken and a piece of pie, and finished off with another cup of coffee. Mrs. Gagus might inquire as to whom he had this week, and he would laconically reply with a mouth full of meat, "John Barrymore," or "Katharine Hepburn," or "Will Rogers," or "Claudette Colbert," or some other name. Mrs. Gagus saw all of the big pictures at a neighborhood theater in Brooklyn, but Mr. Gagus, being in the business, never went to the movies at all.

Between 12 and 12:15, they went to bed. Then, at 7:30 the next morning, Mr. Gagus arose once more in order to get to work on time. It was good to have a job that began at ten o'clock in the morning, and that required him to wear such impressive garments and that made him an integral part of the greatest theater playing the greatest pictures in the greatest city for the greatest audiences in all this great world. He said so and his wife said so.

Then came The Great Manta.

At first Mr. Gagus wasn't concerned with it, didn't even notice it, and hadn't the remotest idea of what a manta was. But across Sixth Avenue from the Greatest Picture Palace in the World came this Great Manta and Mr. Gagus spent eight hours a day standing before it. The Great Manta—the largest devilfish ever exhibited, the most terrifying of marine monsters, and a barker with a line of wisecracks, who invited the public to come in and see it for ten cents, a thin dime, the tenth part of a dollar—was not at all out of place on Sixth Avenue, even directly across from the great cinema palace that provided a captain of the Grenadier Guards of the First Empire simply to open your carriage door. Sixth Avenue is an ambiguous street.

At first the attachés of the Greatest Picture Palace in the World were moved to smile and even laugh at this cheap Coney Island side-show attraction. Its price was enough to belittle it. Ten cents to see a big devilfish. Why, they were charging a top price of a dollar sixty-five to see Katharine Hepburn. The Great Manta was beneath them. But Sixth Avenue, a street of heterogeneous shops, has also a heterogeneity of people. Men stood before the flashy advertisements of The Great

Manta and read them. Of course at the beginning only a few men did so, but when four or five men stand still in New York and look at something, there is a crowd doing the same thing in a very few minutes. Then a few of the men went in, and before long most of the crowd managed to find a mere ten cents, and went in also. The Great Manta became a hit.

In time, the super-film with Katharine Hepburn left the Greatest Picture Palace in the World, and Anna Sten took her place in a super-super-production, but The Great Manta across the street stayed on. Four colossal, staggering, sensational super- and sometimes super-super-films went by, and still across the street The Great Manta stayed on.

Mr. Gagus, though he had no interest whatsoever in the fate of The Great Manta, could not help noticing this. A taxi-driver who had his stand near the entrance of the Greatest Picture Palace in the World once spoke to Mr. Gagus about it.

"Many people go see that damn thing?" he asked.

"Well, yes," admitted Mr. Gagus. "Quite a few."

And even as they looked over at this oddity, people were offering dimes to the ticket-seller and the barker was barking about The Great Manta, the largest devilfish ever exhibited, taken at the risk of a dozen lives. Usually he said it was the largest devilfish, but sometimes he made it the oldest, sometimes the meanest, occasionally the ugliest, and once in a while the heaviest. But always he came back to the point that it was the largest.

After some weeks of this, the thought, ever so casual, but nevertheless a thought, flickered through Mr. Gagus's mind to the effect that he had no idea what a great manta really looked like. The livid pictures outside the place were stirring but unsatisfying. He almost felt that he would like to see it. But the thought was so silly that he slammed a taxicab door a little harder than usual just to assert himself. Then one day, in his relief period in the locker-room, Mr. Gagus learned that Fritz, the assistant superintendent, and Joe, the first engineer, had both paid ten cents apiece to see The Great Manta.

"What's it like?" asked Mr. Gagus.

"Hell of a lookin' thing," said Joe.

57

"It is a great pig t'ing vot they got out of the ocean," said Fritz. Mr. Gagus nodded, but experienced no feeling of satisfaction.

A few days later, Mr. Gagus learned that his alternate, Mr. Parkinson, had, during his rest period, paid ten cents and visited The Great Manta. Mr. Gagus did not deign to discuss the subject at the time, but some hours later, when Captain of the Grenadier Guards Gagus replaced Captain of the Grenadier Guards Parkinson, Captain Gagus caught Captain Parkinson's eye and, nodding his head toward the opposite side of the street, Captain Gagus said quietly out of the corner of his mouth, "What's it like?" Captain Parkinson did not reply. His face grew serious, he shook his head ever so slightly, winked one eye and raised his eyebrows, and then, without a word, marched off to the locker-room.

And with the suspense at this high pitch, Mr. Gagus had to go to work for four hours, while across the street, when the roar of the "L" did not drown it out, came the rasping voice of the barker: "Here y' are, folks—step right up, one and all—the sensation of the age . . ."

At 10:22 that night, when Mr. Gagus walked west on Fiftieth Street to the Fiftieth Street subway station, he could still hear ringing in his ears "Step right up, folks—the sensation of the age," but he put it out of his mind and wondered what Mrs. Gagus would have ready for his supper.

At 11:35, he drank his first cup of coffee, and followed that with some pigs' knuckles and sauerkraut. And while he was eating with his mind on other things, Mrs. Gagus said, "Who do you have next week?"

"Oh, we got George Arliss."

"Oh, I like him," said Mrs. Gagus.

"And a Silly Symphony, too," added Mr. Gagus.

"My, my!" said Mrs. Gagus.

And at 12:15 they went to bed.

The days went by and Mr. Gagus continued his work. More and more of his casual acquaintances who worked at the Greatest Picture Palace in the World had succumbed to their instincts for romance and adventure and had gone to see The Great Manta. George Arliss and the Silly Symphony came and went. A musical talking-picture review with a blackface star and one hundred of the most beautiful girls in the world came to the Greatest Picture Palace in the World. In time it passed away and a foreign film, the greatest, naturally, that had ever been produced in Europe, took its place. The Great Manta stayed on. Every day, for four hours in the morning and four hours in the evening, Mr. Gagus heard the adjurations of the barker across the street and saw the crowds entering to see The Great Manta.

And as regularly as the earth turned, he stopped work at 10 P.M. And as regularly, at 10:22 he was ready to walk west on Fiftieth Street to the Fiftieth Street subway station. But hand in hand with regularity goes inevitability. Something had been going on in the environment of Mr. Gagus that made a reaction on his part inevitable. Through no really conscious control of his whatsoever, there came the inevitable night when, for the first time, he failed to walk west on Fiftieth Street at 10:22 P.M. Instead, without thinking much about it, and acting as if it were perfectly normal, he walked across Sixth Avenue and stopped at the ticket-seller of the attraction ballyhooed as The Great Manta. He paid ten cents and walked inside. Fifteen minutes later, he walked out. He had seen The Great Manta. He knew what it looked like. He was completely satisfied and he walked west on Fiftieth Street to the Fiftieth Street subway station.

That night it was 10:46 instead of 10:31 when he transferred to an express at Times Square. And it was 11:35 when he arrived at the Van Siclen Avenue station, instead of 11:20. It was 11:43 when he unlocked his front door, and 11:44 when he entered his tiny flat, and 11:50 when he drank his first cup of coffee. Over the supper of corned-beef hash, Mrs. Gagus commented that he was fifteen minutes late, and she wondered why.

"Stopped to see The Great Manta," he explained.

That meant nothing to Mrs. Gagus. Naturally, she inquired what it was. Mr. Gagus swallowed more coffee, and she asked again, "What is The Great Manta?"

Mr. Gagus paused and looked at his empty plate.

"It's a devilfish," he said finally.

"What's it look like?" asked Mrs. Gagus.

"Oh, funny-lookin' thing," he answered. "Kind of a big fish that they got out of the ocean."

"Huh," sniffed Mrs. Gagus, which meant she couldn't possibly see why anybody should ever want to waste time to go see a big fish that somebody had pulled out of the ocean.

And that night they went to bed at 12:30 instead of 12:15—all on account of a big fish. But Mrs. Gagus used her self-control and said nothing more about it. Next morning Mr. Gagus got up at 7:30 on schedule, so everything was back in order again. He shaved and dressed and ate his breakfast. While he did this, Mrs. Gagus packed his lunch. At 8:30, he left his tiny flat. At 8:38, he boarded a Broadway–Seventh Avenue express. . . .

Hart Crane

Hart Crane came from Ohio to New York as a young man and led a nomadic life in Greenwich Village. In 1924 he moved to a fourth-floor room in Brooklyn that had a majestic view of the Brooklyn Bridge. Mesmerized by the bridge, he wrote that it is "the most superb piece of construction in the modern world, I'm sure, with strings of lights crossing it like glowing worms as the Ls and surface cars pass each other going and coming." Crane rejected the cultural pessimism popularized by T. S. Eliot in The Wasteland *and wrote "To Brooklyn Bridge" as an affirmation of American culture. Despondent over what he considered literary failure, Crane committed suicide in 1932 at the age of thirty-three.*

To Brooklyn Bridge

How many dawns, chill from his rippling rest
The seagull's wings shall dip and pivot him,
Shedding white rings of tumult, building high
Over the chained bay waters Liberty—

Then, with inviolate curve, forsake our eyes
As apparitional as sails that cross
Some page of figures to be filed away;
—Till elevators drop us from our day . . .

I think of cinemas, panoramic sleights
With multitudes bent toward some flashing scene
Never disclosed, but hastened to again,
Foretold to other eyes on the same screen;

And Thee, across the harbor, silver-paced
As though the sun took step of thee, yet left
Some motion ever unspent in thy stride,—
Implicitly thy freedom staying thee!

Out of some subway scuttle, cell or loft
A bedlamite speeds to thy parapets,
Tilting there momently, shrill shirt ballooning,
A jest falls from the speechless caravan.

Down Wall, from girder into street noon leaks,
A rip-tooth of the sky's acetylene;
All afternoon the cloud-flown derricks turn . . .
Thy cables breathe the North Atlantic still.

And obscure as that heaven of the Jews,
Thy guerdon . . . Accolade thou dost bestow
Of anonymity time cannot raise:
Vibrant reprieve and pardon thou dost show.

O harp and altar, of the fury fused,
(How could mere toil align thy choiring strings!)
Terrific threshold of the prophet's pledge,
Prayer of pariah, and the lover's cry,—

Again the traffic lights that skim thy swift
Unfractioned idiom, immaculate sigh of stars,
Beading thy path—condense eternity:
And we have seen night lifted in thine arms.

Under thy shadow by the piers I waited;
Only in darkness is thy shadow clear.
The City's fiery parcels all undone,
Already snow submerges an iron year . . .

$\mathcal{A}$ $\mathcal{P}ainter$ ON A $\mathcal{P}lanet$ OF $\mathcal{B}lind$ $\mathcal{P}eople$

Joe Durso has been the greatest one-wall handball player for nearly a decade, but he's just as well known for his ferocious verbal assaults against his opponents. For both those reasons everybody wants to tear him down.

Today he's playing a pickup game against Abdul from Albania, a hotshot high schooler in New York City, where handball was once the preeminent adult participation sport. With his pencil mustache and cresting pompadour, Abdul comes off like another young Brooklyn stud on the rise. His mission: to whack Joe Durso and become Boss of All Handball Bosses.

This drama unfolds last summer on the municipal handball courts in Coney Island, where people drink lime rickeys and egg creams on the boardwalk, a knish toss from the center of the one-wall handball universe. Sea gulls whirl in crazy patterns overhead. In contrast to the urban rubble all about, the courts are as clean and white as altars. All the regulars are there to watch the match.

Durso, 35 years old at the time, is ultrafit and has male-model looks. At 6'1" he is the tallest champ ever in a sport in which close-to-the-ground guys are thought to have the edge—a concept backed up by the stature of most previous one-wall champs. Durso lets Abdul build an 8–2 lead and then, reluctantly, gets interested.

"Your death will be slow and excruciatingly painful," Durso taunts Abdul, beginning the torrent of facile abuse that is his trademark.

Durso leaps, meets a ball in midflight, seems to plunge to the right and then, with a feathery stroke, taps the ball to the left corner. It strikes the wall about two inches above the court, hangs there, and rolls out flat. Unplayable. Abdul can only stumble helplessly after it.

Durso does variations on this theme until the score is tied. The mocking smile never leaves his face. He doesn't sweat or even breathe hard.

"You can see he's crushed," Durso says, laughing. "He's demoralized. All he wants to do is crawl under the boardwalk and cry."

"He's disasterizing the kid," says Stevie the Judo Man, one of Durso's cronies. "I ain't storybooking it. Joe is the da Vinci of handball."

Durso grins wolfishly at Abdul. Crouching into a sidearm serve, he snaps the ball into the far right corner so hard that the challenger doesn't even run for it. His dominance assured, Durso starts creating three-dimensional aerial patterns composed of ball-hitting-wall, ball-riding-air-currents. The effect is breathtaking. Stars and trapezoids magically are drawn, only to vanish. Then come other, even more complex, shapes as Durso wills them. The blue ball is his paintbrush. The looming wall his canvas. Elaborate masterpieces are created, vanish and are recreated in seconds.

"I'm like Jackson Pollock, submerged in my own creation," Durso boasts loudly.

"Sounds like a rock star who cleans pools," cracks a spectator.

The fans gawk as Durso, stationary in the middle of the court, sends Abdul on futile chases along the perimeter. Durso lifts the ball, changes its velocity, drops it in front of himself and whams unreachable angle shots with either hand. He finally cracks Abdul's composure with an array of velvety underhand taps, and he finishes the game with a precise crosscourt push shot for his 21st point, a shot that leaves the Albanian gasping. Abdul stalks off the court, fuming.

"Did you see that?" Durso asks, laughing. "Was it godlike? Olympian? Tell me the truth. It's like I'm a gyroscope! Spin me around and I never fall. Albert Einstein couldn't compute the physics of these shots. Nobody wants any part of me. It's pure pain."

Nobody laughs or applauds the world's foremost living one-wall player. Joe Durso has been trampling other players' egos on Surf Avenue for almost two decades, and as a result he is a man who inspires, at best, mixed emotions.

"He's head and shoulders above the players of today," says Howie Eisenberg, an eight-time one-wall national champion (six of those are doubles victories) and the former one-wall commissioner of the United States Handball Association. "There's no question that Joe Durso has been the best player for the last eight years or so."

Among Durso's detractors are many of the tanned Brooklyn oldies who haunt the courts to schmooze in the sun and the salt air. The menagerie includes Red Face Benjy, Pat the Butcher, Louie Shoes (he never plays in sneakers), Abe the Ganef (which translates from Yiddish as "thief," but implies a more or less lovable rascal). They tell you that handball by the sea is a healthy way of life. They tell you that Durso wouldn't last against the Depression-era players back in one-wall's golden age. They tell you that the way Durso behaves on the courts leaves a lot to be desired.

Morris Levitsky, the grizzled park historian who usually refs the money games, appraises Durso dourly. "Anybody involved with handball has a childish mind," says Levitsky.

A childish mind never stopped anyone from becoming a celebrity in America. But Durso—the holder of 17 national one-wall titles, including 10 singles titles, the last four in a row outdoors—is not a player in the wealth-and-fame department. In a mainstream sport he might be a legend, recommending orange juice and sneakers for a price, squiring starlets in and out of gossip columns. But this is *handball,* light-years off the sports-media and money loops. So Durso is stuck in Brooklyn, teaching math at David A. Boody Junior High, chatting up stray maidens on the boardwalk and performing arcane athletic wonders on the court while the world looks the other way.

Aficionados say handball is an elite sport, a game in which being ambidextrous is not merely an advantage, it is virtually a requirement. And it is the only game in which you *dive* headfirst on concrete. Like boxing, it's too painful for most people. If you get good at handball, you're in an elite within an elite.

If you get *great,* if you transcend the genre, you're a Steve Sandler, the king of one-wall handball from the late '60s to the mid-'70s. Sandler won *15* national singles titles. He was so feared then that he had to play many games one-handed, lefty, just to get a match. Or you're a Joe Durso.

That status won't get you recognized in airports. As far as can be determined, the Betty Ford Center is devoid of addicted millionaire handball players.

After the game with Abdul, free as usual of media pressure, Durso breaks for lunch with Stevie the Judo Man. Sniffing the salt air and the aroma of cotton candy, Durso swings his 11-year-old sports car up Surf Avenue. The streets are full of teenagers; they are horsing around and shouting boisterously, maybe even menacingly. Durso turns back and cruises past the bumper-car arcade, the roller coaster, the dingy pizza parlors and the dark bars. He stops at a light. Nearby is a run-down shooting gallery. For a buck, a visitor can shoot an array of small animals clanking in and out of range on unseen belts. Hit anywhere near the target and a metal coyote snaps his head back and howls, "Oww-wwwwooooooooo! Oww oww owwwwwwooooooooo!"

Durso looks at the coyote, perhaps sees something of himself in it, shudders and drives on.

He parks in front of Lulu's deli, in Brighton Beach. These days Brighton Beach is called Little Odessa. In the shadow of the elevated train tracks, where mobsters once carried tommy guns, hordes of Russian immigrants now troop in and out of stores carrying shopping bags filled with salamis as big as baseball bats, jars of pickled Danubian salad, loaves of crisp bread. On the sidewalk, a fiddler plays unfamiliar melodies.

"It's like I'm a painter on a planet of blind people," says Durso as he dips the end of a kasha knish in mustard. "My talent is almost like a curse. I achieved greatness in something that the world can't appreciate. The fact that I got supergreat just adds to the pathos. If I'm playing a guy who I know is unworthy, where's my motivation? If I play hard, I'm acknowledging that he's worthy for me to play against, which I can't do. Does McEnroe play pickup games in the park? Did Ali have street fights?"

Durso is shirtless, his torso bronzed. Some Russian girls in tight silk dresses eye him from the next table. He winks at them. They blush.

"While guys are just struggling to make points," he continues, "I'm way beyond that. I *know* I'm going to make points. It's *how* I make them. It's a whole new level of being. What makes what I do trivial is the fact that handball is not in the American consciousness. That makes *me* look trivial. No matter how good *I* get, I can't get good enough to overcome the fact that the sport is not well known. I guess I must have the need to be loved."

Back at the courts, Durso stands in front of the handball doyens and stretches out his arms.

"Who's the best who ever lived?" he asks. "Who towers over this game like the Colossus of Rhodes?"

The veterans snort and follow Durso with their eyes as he begins tracking a pretty blonde with a small white dog on a leash. In moments he is charming her, and she sways with laughter. The white dog nips at Durso's feet.

Rivalries are as bitter as those of a prison yard. The glory days of one-wall are long gone, and even then there was no money in it. But with thousands of concrete courts in playgrounds—plus a limitless supply of flat factory, warehouse, theater and garage walls—new blood always rises. Especially in black and Latino neighborhoods, where the game is having a resurgence. However, the ball of choice among the younger set is a racquetball—which is far easier on the palms than the smaller, harder handball. Durso is not so much of a purist that he refuses to play "big ball" handball.

Last summer, the comer was Buddy Gant, a spindly-legged black ace who dominated the courts on West Fourth Street in Greenwich Village, where the game is mostly big ball.

"When are you going to play Buddy?" a Surf Avenue handball maven asks Durso between cigar puffs. "I got large cash on the guy."

"They'll stick your Gold Card in the coffin with you," says Durso. "It won't be long now."

A kingdom, however small, must be defended. Especially if your identity exists solely within its borders. Durso has a law degree, but he has not yet passed the New York State Bar exam. Meanwhile, he spends his days at the handball courts—whipping two players at once using just his left hand and spotting them 10 points—checking out the women and lamenting the fame that has eluded him.

"Where else can I go?" he asks.

Even the old masters, the stars of yesteryear, can't shake the game. They've gone on to raise families, retire, move to other states. But in their minds, they never leave Surf Avenue. And come the end of May, many of them will probably be there physically as well. Unlike previous years when the national tournament stretched out over several weekends, this year it will be a frenetic four-day affair held over Memorial Day weekend.

After eviscerating a pair of sullen Puerto Rican boys in a two-on-one match, Durso leans against the wall and waxes philosophic. "The *point*," he says, "is that losing is a habit. I like to lose the least *amount* that I can. Which is paradoxical because I probably lose more than anybody in the park. Out of boredom. But I never lose when I don't want to lose."

"That's enough of him. Let's get on to something worthwhile," says Ruby Obert, a grinning, extremely fit white-haired gent in a warmup suit.

Durso's eyes pop, and his face contorts into half smile, half rage. "Tell us who you were," he says. "Who *were* you, Ruby?"

Obert, one of the best all-around doubles players who ever lived, is enshrined in handball's Hall of Fame out in Tucson. He and his brothers, Carl and Oscar, were dominating forces in the sport from the mid-'50s to the early '70s, collecting 92 championships among them—an impressive feat even after you take into account that three separate organizations (YMCA, AAU and USHA) awarded championships. Obert doesn't flinch at Durso's jibe.

"Joe," he shouts back, "you're the transcendental manifestation of a cerebral aberration."

"Look at me," cries Durso. He angrily punches a ball at the wall. "Do I look 35? Not an ounce of fat." Nodding in the direction of Obert, Durso says, "He wouldn't get a shot, the poor devil."

Obert, the unofficial mayor of these courts, is not about to back down: "Hey, Joe, can two of you beat one of you? Can you beat yourself with a 10-point lead? I gave Joe a hockey puck last week. He's still trying to open it. . . . That's a nice head you got on your shoulders, Joe. Too bad it's not on your neck."

"When I lose, it takes on epic proportions," says Durso, turning Obert's allusion neatly into a willing acceptance of his own mythic status.

Still, the obscurity of any handball championship has weighed heavily on players before Durso. Outside of New York, few states have one-wall courts. Great handballers like Joe Garber, Moe Orenstein and Vic Hershkowitz remain unknown, and even the legendary Sandler was once heard to say, "Being the game's best player gives me the right to sit in the Bowery with the bums."

An air of mourning seems to surround the sport and its partisans. For Durso, who has devoted his life to handball, the mourning has turned to bitterness.

"One reason is that he doesn't have competition to develop his game," says Eisenberg, who now plays three-wall along the beach in Venice, Calif. "You grow up wanting to be a handball champ, like I did, and then find out you picked the wrong sport."

The long foyer of Durso's apartment in the Bay Ridge section of Brooklyn is adorned with T-shirts from scores of handball tournaments. They hang from wire hangers like flags at half-mast. Durso walks down the hall on this summer afternoon, knocks lightly, then enters the bedroom where his 83-year-old grandmother, Geraldine Durso, lies propped up by pillows. She smiles radiantly when she sees him. A home nurse gives Joe the once-over as he fluffs up his grandmother's pillows.

"Do you love me, Grandma?" he asks.

"I love you, Joseph."

He closes the door softly behind him. "She's dying of bone cancer," he says. It is a simple statement of fact: in three months, Geraldine will be dead.

They lived together in the small apartment for many years. Geraldine was the light of Durso's life after he was a year old, when his parents sent him to live in Point Pleasant, N.J., with his grandparents. Durso has seen very little of his parents since then, and their absence hasn't made his heart grow fonder.

Durso's grandfather, also named Joseph, died when Durso was 10, and Geraldine moved back to Coney Island with her grandson. In excellent physical shape from exploring Point Pleasant's beaches, construction sites and boatyards, Durso played and ran outside from morning to night.

"I never hung around or watched TV, like kids do today," he says. "I really think I developed an extra-big heart muscle or something."

As for sports, Durso was attracted only to handball, a game in which he didn't have to rely on anyone else.

"I don't really look for the love of the audience," he says. "I don't expect the love of the audience. In the same way I never looked for or expected the love of my parents. I didn't look for it then, and I don't play for it now. In a way it's freed me so I don't have to obey the conventions. I do what I want. And if other people don't like it . . ."

Durso's room is decorated with trophies and framed photos of athletic male and female bodies. There are posters of David Bowie and Bruce Lee in action. Durso shows scrapbooks documenting his career.

"Do you like these?" he asks, proudly indicating several unpainted replicas of Greek statuary that he picked up for $20 apiece. On a VCR he plays a video pastiche he has made of Laurence Olivier doing Shakespeare, Bruce Lee demolishing foes, and Joe Durso in tournament play on the Surf Avenue courts. Durso studies the performances with equal intensity.

"Idealized form, that's what I'm into," he says. "That's what Olivier is, and Bruce Lee. And that's what I try to be. I can *transcend* that way. Bowie is an idealized rock musician. Ayn Rand had an idealized philosophy of how life should be. Conan the Barbarian is an idealized tough guy."

All of which leads to Durso's approach to handball.

"It's like the shadow world of Plato," Durso says. "There's somewhere an idea of the sublime volley, I try to reveal that. Ballet is supposed to be visual poetry. The visual beauty is pretty, and I try to be physically graceful. I'm not trying to make the *point* alone."

Durso looks around the small, cluttered room with its narrow bed, and suddenly seems sad.

"This game is all about *I'm better than you.* It's not like a painting where you're trying to communicate some principle. It's just *I'm better than you.* It's a childish, stupid thing. But people do it because they've got nervous energy or misplaced sexual tension. Maybe I have more than anyone else. It's an ego confrontation, I'm very good at that."

Durso is silent. He switches off the TV sound and watches images of himself with that long reach, scoring points. Leaping. Vaulting. Spinning. Then, as if responding to an inner signal, he softly goes down the hall to check on Geraldine.

Daniel Fuchs

"Love in Brooklyn" was first published in The New Yorker *in 1939 and collected in Daniel Fuchs's collection of stories and sketches* The Apathetic Bookie Joint. *New York native Daniel Fuchs was born in 1909 and wrote about Jewish life in his three early novels,* Summer in Williamsburg, Homage to Blenholt, *and* Low Company *(republished as* Three Novels *in 1961). Fuchs moved to Hollywood as a screenwriter and still lives there.*

$Love$ IN
$Brooklyn$

I was sitting in my usual seat at the lamppost in Owen D. Larkin Park, reading a newspaper while I waited for the Macy's Walking Club. This was the humorous name three girls I know gave themselves, because they all worked at Macy's department store. They were Ruth, Betty, and Gertrude. I always waited for Gertrude in the park, since I couldn't take her to a nightclub or someplace like that, and it wouldn't do for me to spend too much time at her home when her parents knew I was unable to consider marriage because of financial circumstances. Most young couples, I think, will understand how it happened that the scene of my meetings with Gertrude was usually out of doors, and I chose Owen D. Larkin Park because there at least you could sit down.

While I waited that day, Mrs. Rand, who was the mother of young Dr. Rand, came along and took a seat near me. She was a tidy little woman, very proud and happy since she was, after all, the mother of a doctor of medicine. To her it was not only an honor but the satisfaction of a lifetime, and she came to the park regularly every evening to feel superior over the rest of us.

"Grass and trees and fresh air from the river," she sighed, looking about her. "The park is just like a wilderness."

"This is no park, Mrs. Rand," I said, killing time. Owen D. Larkin Park in Brooklyn is really a small plaza, an odd triangular area which the streets left when they intersected haphazardly. To fill up the space, the city had planted some greenery and so it was a park. "Were you ever in Central Park?" I asked Mrs. Rand. "Or Bronx Park? They're something. They're parks."

"No, Mr. Peru," the doctor's mother said to me. "I don't travel hardly nowhere. My son the doctor, he don't like me to go in the hot, congested subways."

"I can appreciate the point of view," I said. "But this place is really nothing. Those others are real parks."

Mrs. Rand refused, as always, to be impressed, having no further room for admiration. It was enough for her that her son was "the doctor," and other glories seemed to her irrelevant and trifling.

"My son the doctor," she said, "once he went to Bermuda. A cruise he took."

Then suddenly she stopped, all warmth left her voice, and she turned her back. That meant, I knew, that she saw the Macy's Walking Club arriving, for she had taken a sharp dislike to Ruth. I suppose she had her reasons, even then. Gertrude and the other two girls were coming up the path and I rose to greet them.

The girls stopped and Gertrude settled down on an empty bench for a little chat with me. Betty took up an impatient position a little distance away and started whimpering, "I should like to inquire whether we're going to stay here all night or did we start for a walk in the first place?"

"Just a minute," Gertrude told her. "Let's rest for a while."

"No one takes my inclinations into consideration," Betty said. "I was putting curlers in my hair after supper. Ruth comes along and says hurry up, we're going for a walk. So, if we're walking, then let's walk. It's only logical."

Ruth had gone over and seated herself next to the doctor's mother. She took her knitting out of the bag she carried and started to work on it. Ruth was a well-developed girl, husky but not fat; a little coarse, Gertrude and I thought, but even so I didn't then understand why Mrs. Rand had to dislike her so intensely. When I think of it now, I suppose it must have been maternal instinct.

"How is the doctor?" Ruth asked Mrs. Rand. "I see him so seldom."

"The doctor is a busy man," Mrs. Rand replied. "He has to attend to his office hours, his clinic service, and the visits to the patients outside. He is occupied with serious things. He has no time for enjoyment or girls."

"Listen to her," Ruth said in her heavy, gross voice. "Somebody would imagine heavens knows what. Don't worry, Madam Doctor. I won't steal your baby and marry him."

"I assure you it don't worry me in the least," Mrs. Rand said. "Miracles don't happen every day in America."

"Does anybody listen to me?" Betty was wailing. "Does anyone consult my inclinations? Who am I?"

"My son the doctor," said Mrs. Rand, talking to nobody, "he isn't like all the other boys. He don't go running crazy the minute he sees a pair of silk stockings. He's a good boy. Big as he is, he minds what his mother says. He keeps his head on his practice."

By this time Ruth was ignoring the doctor's mother in a very elaborate way. She stood up with the knitting in her hands and measured it over her bust. "Three balls of wool I put into this sweater and it still isn't enough. My God, it's simply terrible. I'm getting fat as a horse." But the way she said it, it sounded like a direct insult to Mrs. Rand.

"I've been reading *Ulysses*," Gertrude said to me. Gertrude and I generally discussed literature, the new dance, modern art, and subjects like these. I liked Gertrude very dearly, I confess. She meant much to me, more than most girls do to their boy friends, for ours was a genuine intellectual companionship, and that, I believed then, was the soundest basis for a mixed relationship. A girl of Ruth's type, of course, could hardly understand this. She thought there was something peculiar about our friendship simply because it was maintained on a high level. We both tried to ignore her cynical comments.

"Oh, yes, *Ulysses*," I said. "By James Joyce."

"Don't you love his down-to-earth realism?" Gertrude asked. "Parts of the book are simply terrifying."

"There she sits talking James Joyce," Ruth said. "She's impossible. Listen, Gertrude, where does James Joyce get you?"

"I don't understand," Gertrude said to her. "Why do you feel it's necessary to say those things to me?"

"Don't mind her, Gertrude," I said.

"I don't like to see it," Ruth said. "It makes me feel bad to see one of my sex making a fool out of herself. Wake up, for pity's sakes, Gertrude, if it's only to do me a personal favor."

"There's enough trouble in the world as it is," Gertrude said. "Why should your own friends be nasty?"

"Don't pay attention to her," I said. "She just can't understand."

"Can I help it if I'm sensitive?" Gertrude asked. "All day I work at Macy's in ladies' unmentionables. Most of my day is spent in a cultural vacuum. I get so little out of life, why don't they let me enjoy an intellectual companionship in peace?"

"I'm only doing this for your benefit," Ruth said. "Don't think it's just to be nasty."

Gertrude and I moved down the row of benches for a little privacy, and I told her that she really should ignore Ruth, a girl who was of an altogether different type. There was no point in taking offense at her, since, to put it unkindly, she was ignorant.

"I know she's common and crude," Gertrude said. "I make the allowances. I tell myself not to let her make me worry. But I do!"

"Everybody does what they prefer," Betty wailed again. "Here Ruth sits knitting and now he goes off with Gertrude. But are my wishes ever taken into consideration? Oh, no!"

So we walked away some distance and talked of Proust and Joyce and the art of Mary Wigman. But not for long. Soon there was Ruth before us, insisting that they go on with their walk.

"Come," she said, "or Betty will break out in a rash. Besides, I don't like to see you wasting away your life on literature and philosophy."

"Oh, go away, Ruth," I said. "I didn't send for you."

"I don't want to seem just a little impatient," Betty whined. "But an hour ago did we start out on a walk, or was I mistaken?"

So Gertrude resigned herself and joined Ruth and Betty, and the three went on with their evening stroll.

Then it was that I first began to resent Ruth. She was a busybody, an interferer, an extrovert of an obnoxious sort, and I wished heartily she didn't take up so much of Gertrude's time.

Mrs. Rand was sitting quietly at her place near the lamppost, absorbed in her own thoughts. I sat down by her again. "Girls see a professional," she confided sadly, "they run like ants. Especially when it's a doctor of medicine."

"What have you got against Ruth?" I asked. I had my reasons for disliking the girl, that was true, but what offense had she given Mrs. Rand?

"You're a nice boy, Mr. Peru," she said to me. "I like you. But after all, what do you know about girls? What good will it do to talk to you?"

I remember I was somewhat offended then, but how right Mrs. Rand was.

It is, unfortunately, more understandable to me now than it was then, but from that evening which I have just described I had great difficulty in seeing Gertrude. She seldom came to the park and the Macy's Walking Club was broken up. One evening, about two weeks later, when I went to my usual seat at the lamppost, I saw Betty alone, reading a book, her hair done up in curlers. I asked her whether she knew where Gertrude was, and she said she hadn't seen her or Ruth in ages, not even at Macy's, for they worked in different departments. I should have sensed then that something was in progress. It worried me and I missed Gertrude's company, but it hardly occurred to me that the situation was growing serious.

Soon the doctor's mother came into the park for her evening visit. It made her happy to see Betty reading a book.

"That's nice," Mrs. Rand said, a mournful note in her voice. "Most modern girls today don't bother with books. All they got on their minds, they got boys."

"You're right," Betty said. "My God, you're right, Mrs. Rand. Take me. I won't pet, I won't neck. What happens? I got no boy friends."

"You should worry, young lady. You go the right way. Books are better than wild times."

She drifted away into her sad thoughts and Betty went back to her book. "You slave for your children," Mrs. Rand said, almost talking to herself. "You go through sickness and fire for them. Every day you're at the dispensary with them. You bring them up, make all the sacrifices so they can go to college and medical school. You finally live to see the day they become a doctor of medicine. And then what happens? A young, ignorant girl who has no heart, she steals him away."

So I sat in the park, with Betty reading and Mrs. Rand moping. I read my paper, wondering where Gertrude was and why I hadn't been seeing her. The minutes passed and I thought this would be another day and no Gertrude.

About nine o'clock Ruth walked into the park. She was all dressed up and said she had an important appointment. Mrs. Rand had always disliked her, but tonight she positively hated her. The doctor's mother turned her back and muttered angrily so that Ruth would make no mistake about her attitude.

"My goodness," Ruth said. "Am I a bad draft or something? The temperature here resembles the North Pole."

"Insinuations," Mrs. Rand muttered.

"My goodness," Ruth said, "what did I ever do to you in my young life?"

"No law says I must speak to everybody," Mrs. Rand said, still addressing no one.

"All right," Ruth said. "So I saw the doctor. I admit it. So what? We went to an ice-cream parlor and had a soda. So what's the crime in that?"

"I'm not talking to anybody in particular," Mrs. Rand said. "But my understanding is that decent, respectable girls don't wait in the streets to catch a professional."

"It was an accident, Mrs. Rand!" Ruth cried. "I was walking home in the street, so I met the doctor. I didn't wait for him on purpose. And supposing I did, I didn't hurt him. I didn't eat him up."

"Please!" Betty said, looking up from her book. "Have a heart! A person can't even concentrate in the park. It's a shame."

"Oh, shut up, Betty," Ruth said. "Who's asking you?"

"Please!" Betty said. "Just because you're angry, don't take it out on me!"

The doctor's mother maintained her icy reserve, waiting with insulting obviousness for Ruth to leave the park so that she could breathe the air again.

"Ruth," I said. I realized this was a bad moment to approach her, but I was anxious to know. "Did you see Gertrude today?"

"Who needs you?" she shot at me. "Listen, Peru, when you grow up and become a man, then come around."

"Now, that's unnecessary," I said. "Did you see Gertrude?"

"Let me tell you something, Peru," she said. "No man has the right to bother a girl unless he's in a position to support a wife. That's a motto."

I swallowed my pride and ignored her insult, for there was no sense, I thought then, in paying attention to a person of Ruth's type.

"Did you see Gertrude?" I asked again.

"Yes, I saw her!" she said. "I had lunch with her today and I went home with her after work. All I hope is that someday she gets some sense in her head. She's at the beauty parlor."

Ruth took one more angry look at Mrs. Rand and swept away to her appointment. I didn't like what Ruth had told me about her motto for girls and especially I didn't relish her association with Gertrude. It affected me unpleasantly to think that they were spending so much time together.

Mrs. Rand still kept quiet, noble and proud in her silence, and yet, it was clear to see, unhappy.

What was I to do? By this time I hadn't seen Gertrude for more than two weeks and I realized her feelings toward me must have undergone a radical change. What was more, I learned that Gertrude

82

and Ruth had grown inseparable. I couldn't understand this new fondness for Ruth and I somehow felt that this association could do me no good.

I could not buy Gertrude flowers. That wasn't customary among the people who lived near Owen D. Larkin Park in Brooklyn. Nor, as I mentioned in the beginning, did my financial circumstances make it possible for me to take Gertrude to a nightclub or the theater. I did the best I could and bought two tickets for a lecture on "The American Revolution and Eighteenth-Century Poetry." I thought this would be an attractive subject, but when I went to Gertrude's home to invite her, her mother wouldn't even let me go inside the house. She kept me in the hall, told me Gertrude wasn't at home, and closed the door. I went to Owen D. Larkin Park, hoping that Gertrude might pass by. I fingered the two tickets in my pocket and bought a newspaper to help me while away the time.

At the park were Betty and Mrs. Rand. The doctor's mother was completely wrapped in some private grief and every time Betty offered to say something, Mrs. Rand said, "Not interested!" I opened the paper and read, waiting.

"Sacrifices we make for the children," Mrs. Rand said.

"The way of life," Betty agreed with her.

Mrs. Rand took to nodding her head as if in great grief, and there I sat, waiting for Gertrude with two tickets in my pocket. But she did not come.

A half hour of waiting passed in this quiet way until suddenly the doctor's mother stood up as though she had been hit. The lines of her face became set in the classic, calm attitude of misery and she began to move out of the park slowly and tragically. I wondered what the matter was, and then I noticed Ruth had come along.

"Momma," said Ruth.

I could hardly recognize her. She was altogether changed in dress and in manner. She wore a simple black dress with a plain white collar and she seemed reserved. There was a strange air of dignity about her.

"Don't go away, Momma," she called to Mrs. Rand, and now, of course, I could understand the reason for that poor woman's sorrow. "I came for you. We're eating dinner, Momma. I haven't any spite. Come to dinner with me, please."

Mrs. Rand stopped. "Please don't call me Momma," she said in heartbroken tones. "You are not my child. You take my child away from me." And she moved away majestically.

"That's a fine way to treat an intended daughter-in-law," Ruth finally said to Betty and me.

"Well, under the circumstances," Betty said, "you must take her feelings into consideration. After all, she's his mother."

"I'm practically breaking my neck to be nice to her," Ruth cried. "I'm willing to go down on my hands and knees. What more can I do? I can't jump off the roof."

"Ruth," I said. I was impatient. I did not like to intrude at such a time but she was the only person who could help me. I had no choice. "Ruth, did you happen to see Gertrude?"

"Yes, I saw her," she snapped at me.

"I'd like to find her," I said. "I have two tickets for a lecture. Do you know where she is now?"

"Listen, Peru," she said, "am I an information booth? I can't be annoyed."

"Listen to her, listen to her," Betty said. "She can't be annoyed! All of a sudden she's very refined."

"Oh, I see. I'm not so popular now," Ruth said. "All you have to do to lose your popularity is to get engaged to a professional, especially a doctor of medicine."

Then Ruth and Betty scrapped around for a few minutes, the way girls do, until finally Ruth felt she had wasted enough time. She pulled on her black gloves and started to go out of the park.

"I'm late as it is," she said airily. "The doctor has to attend a professional function at nine-thirty. Believe me," she confided, "it's no bargain to be a doctor's wife. You've got to make up your mind to expect a crazy home existence."

She walked away, leaving Betty to stare helplessly and say, "Well! Well! Well!" Her sarcasm barely covered the burning envy in her, and after trying a few minutes to collect herself, she gave it up and said she was going to take in a movie. Her day had been ruined.

So I was all alone in the park now, sitting under the light of the lamppost, trying to read my newspaper. My head was full of premonitions. I could tell that Ruth knew where Gertrude was and that she just didn't want to tell me. Those two were fast friends and I didn't like it.

Later that night Gertrude did come into the park. She, too, was transformed, the general intention clearly being to avoid anything that might give her the appearance of one who had intellectual interests. It was a revelation. Her hair was waved and arranged in small curls over her neck; she had discarded her eyeglasses; and when she walked she had a new sort of swagger.

"Gertrude," I said, but I knew at once from the listless glance she gave me that our companionship was nearing its end. She had an engagement at the beauty parlor, she told me, and explained that she went now twice a week. I told her about the tickets and she said she was sorry, it was thoughtful of me, but a previous engagement prevented. That was peculiar, too, because I hadn't told her when the lecture would be given.

"What's the matter with you, Gertrude?" I asked. "You're so changed. Have I done anything to offend you?"

"Well, to be frank about it, I've decided to make a change," Gertrude said. "What was I getting out of life? All day I worked at Macy's in ladies' unmentionables. At night I soaked my feet in Epsom salts and discussed Marcel Proust and Joyce with you. When you stop to think about it from a certain viewpoint—from the feminine angle—you can't blame me if I think it's time to make a change."

"I still don't understand," I said. "It must be something Ruth's been telling you."

"Don't pick on Ruth," she said, and it hurt me to see how ardently she defended her new intimate. "She's not as bad as some people think. Take me. I was sensitive and refined, interested in intellectual matters. What happened? Nothing. Look at Ruth. You think she's common and ignorant. And I agree she hasn't an ounce of sensitivity. But what happens to her? She catches a doctor."

"Oh," I said. "I understand. I see."

"Don't think I'm hard and unfeeling about it," Gertrude said. "But after all, when all's said and done it boils down to this: at bottom every girl wants a husband. I can't continue fooling myself indefinitely."

"All right, Gertrude," I said, and I picked up my newspaper. "Naturally I can't blame you if that's the way you feel. I won't say a single word."

"I'm sorry," she said. "I'm really very sorry."

I said it was all right again and started to read the paper, pretending I was very much absorbed in it. And finally Gertrude left.

It was all Ruth's fault. She had talked Gertrude into this new philosophy on men and love, and also, I suppose, every normal girl would have felt desperate and unhappy when she discovered Ruth had caught the doctor. Betty had gone to the movies to forget the pain, and as for Gertrude, all she could do was to make a change in her life. That I was the person to be affected was only incidental. It was unfortunate for me that our companionship had come to an end, but I knew there was no use moping about it. That wouldn't help, and I applied myself conscientiously to the newspaper. Tomorrow, it said, would be fair, and I went on from that point to read the news.

Cristina Garcia

Raised in New York City, Cristina Garcia was born in Havana in 1958. She attended both Barnard and Johns Hopkins before becoming a correspondent for Time *magazine.* Dreaming in Cuban, *her first novel, was published in 1992 and greeted with critical acclaim. She lives in Los Angeles.*

FROM *Dreaming in Cuban*

Pilar

*T*he family is hostile to the individual. This is what I'm thinking as Lou Reed says he has enough attitude to kill every person in New Jersey. I'm at a club in the Village with my boyfriend, Max. I figure I have enough attitude to kill a few people myself, only it never works on the right ones.

"I'm from Brooklyn, man!" Lou shouts, and the crowd goes wild. I don't cheer, though. I wouldn't cheer either if Lou said, "Let's hear it for Cuba." Cuba. Planet Cuba. Where the hell is that?

Max's real name is Octavio Schneider. He sings and plays bass and harmonica for the Manichaean Blues Band, a group he started back in San Antonio, where he's from. They do Howlin' Wolf and Muddy Waters and lots of their own songs, mostly hard rock. Sometimes they do backup for this crazy bluesman, the Reverend Billy Hines, who keeps his eyes shut when he sings. Max says that the reverend was a storefront preacher who played the Panhandle years ago and is attempting a comeback. Max himself had a modest hit in Texas with "Moonlight on Emma," a song about an ex-girlfriend who dumped him and moved to Hollywood.

I met Max at a downtown basement club a few months ago. He came over and started speaking to me in Spanish (his mother is Mexican) as if he'd known me for years. I liked him right away. When I brought him around to meet my parents, Mom took one look at his beaded headband and the braid down his back and said, *"Sácalo de aquí."* When I told her that Max spoke Spanish, she simply repeated what she said in English: "Take him away."

Dad was cool, though. "What does your band's name mean?" he asked Max.

"The Manichaeans, see, were followers of this Persian guy who lived in the third century. They believed that hedonism was the only way to get rid of their sins."

"Hedonism?"

"Yeah, the Manichaeans liked to party. They had orgies and drank a lot. They got wiped out by other Christians, though."

"Too bad," my father said sympathetically.

Later, Dad looked up the Manichaeans in the encyclopedia and discovered that, contrary to what Max claimed, the Manichaeans believed that the world and all matter were created by nefarious forces, and that the only way to battle them was through asceticism and a pure life. When I told Max about this, he just shrugged and said, "Well, I guess that's okay, too." Max is a tolerant kind of guy.

I just love the way Lou Reed's concerts feel—expectant, uncertain. You never know what he's going to do next. Lou has about twenty-five personalities. I like him because he sings about people no one else sings about—drug addicts, transvestites, the down-and-out. Lou jokes about his alter egos discussing problems at night. I feel like a new me sprouts and dies every day.

I play Lou and Iggy Pop and this new band the Ramones whenever I paint. I love their energy, their violence, their incredible grinding guitars. It's like an artistic form of assault. I try to translate what I hear into colors and volumes and lines that confront people, that say, "Hey, we're here too and what we think matters!" or more often just "Fuck you!" Max is not as crazy about the Ramones as I am. I think he's more of a traditionalist. He has a tough time being rude, even to people who deserve it. Not me. If I don't like someone, I show it. It's the one thing I have in common with my mother.

Neither of my parents is very musical. Their entire record collection consists of *Perry Como's Greatest Hits,* two Herb Alpert & the Tijuana Brass albums, and *Alvin and the Chipmunks Sing Their Favorite Christmas Carols,* which they bought for me when I was a kid. Recently, Mom picked up a Jim Nabors album of patriotic songs in honor of the bicentennial. I mean, after Vietnam and Watergate, who the hell wants to hear "The Battle Hymn of the Republic"?

I used to like the Fourth of July okay because of the fireworks. I'd go down by the East River and watch them flare up from the tugboats. The girandoles looked like fiery lace in the sky. But this bicentennial crap is making me crazy. Mom has talked about nothing else for months. She bought a second bakery and plans to sell tricolor cupcakes and Uncle Sam marzipan. Apple pies, too. She's convinced she can fight Communism from behind her bakery counter.

Last year she joined the local auxiliary police out of some misplaced sense of civic duty. My mother—all four feet eleven and a half inches and 217 pounds of her—patrols the streets of Brooklyn at night in a skintight uniform, clanging with enough antiriot gear to quash another Attica. She practices twirling her nightstick in front of the mirror, then smacks it against her palm, steadily, menacingly, like she's seen cops do on television. Mom's upset because the police department won't issue her a gun. Right. She gets a gun and I move out of state fast.

There's other stuff happening with her. For starters, she's been talking with Abuelo Jorge since he died. He gives her business advice and tells her who's stealing from her at the bakery. Mom says that Abuelo spies on me and reports back to her. Like what is this? The ghost patrol?

90

Mom is afraid that I'm having sex with Max (which I'm not) and this is her way of trying to keep me in line.

Max likes Mom, though. He says she suffers from an "imperious disposition."

"You mean she's a frustrated tyrant?" I ask him.

"More like a bitch goddess," he explains.

Max's parents split up before he was born and his mother cleans motel rooms for minimum wage. I guess Mom must seem exotic by comparison.

But she's really not. Mom makes food only people in Ohio eat, like Jell-O molds with miniature marshmallows or recipes she clips from *Family Circle.* And she barbecues anything she can get her hands on. Then we sit around behind the warehouse and stare at each other with nothing to say. Like this is it? We're living the American dream?

The worst is the parades. Mom gets up early and drags us out on Thanksgiving Day loaded with plastic foam coolers, like we're going to starve right there on Fifth Avenue. On New Year's Day, she sits in front of the television and comments on every single float in the Rose Parade. I think she dreams of sponsoring one herself someday. Like maybe a huge burning effigy of El Líder.

Max flatters me but not in a sleazy way. He says he loves my height (I'm five feet eight inches) and my hair (black, down to my waist) and the whiteness of my skin. His mouth is a little sauna, hot and wet. When we slow-dance, he presses himself against me and I feel his hardness against my thighs. He says I would make a good bass player.

Max knows about Abuela Celia in Cuba, about how she used to talk to me late at night and how we've lost touch over the years. Max wants to go to Cuba and track her down, but I tell him what happened four years ago, when I ran away to Florida and my plans to see my grandmother collapsed. I wonder what Abuela Celia is doing right this minute.

Most days Cuba is kind of dead to me. But every once in a while a wave of longing will hit me and it's all I can do not to hijack a plane to Havana or something. I resent the hell out of the politicians and the generals who force events on us that structure our lives, that dictate the memories we'll have when we're old. Every day Cuba fades a little more inside me, my grandmother fades a little more inside me. And there's only my imagination where our history should be.

It doesn't help that Mom refuses to talk about Abuela Celia. She gets annoyed every time I ask her and she shuts me up quickly, like I'm prying into top secret information. Dad is more open, but he can't tell me what I really want to know, like why Mom hardly speaks to Abuela or why she still keeps her riding crops from Cuba. Most of the time, he's too busy refereeing the fights between us, or else he's just in his own orbit.

Dad feels kind of lost here in Brooklyn. I think he stays in his workshop most of the day because he'd get too depressed or crazy otherwise. Sometimes I think we should have moved to a ranch in Wyoming or Montana. He would have been happy there with his horses and his cows, his land, and a big empty sky overhead. Dad only looks alive when he talks about the past, about Cuba. But we don't discuss that much either lately. Things haven't been the same since I saw him with that blond bombshell. I never said anything to him, but it's like a cut on my tongue that never healed.

Mom has decided she wants me to paint a mural for her second Yankee Doodle Bakery.

"I want a big painting like the Mexicans do, but pro-American," she specifies.

"You want to commission *me* to paint something for *you?*"

"*Sí,* Pilar. You're a painter, no? So paint!"

"You've got to be kidding."

"Painting is painting, no?"

"Look, Mom, I don't think you understand. I don't *do* bakeries."

"You're embarrassed? My bakery is not good enough for you?"

"It's not that."

"This bakery paid for your painting classes."

"It has nothing to do with that, either."

"If Michelangelo were alive today, he wouldn't be so proud."

"Mom, believe me, Michelangelo would definitely *not* be painting bakeries."

"Don't be so sure. Most artists are starving. They don't have all the advantages like you. They take heroin to forget."

"Jesus Christ!"

"This could be a good opportunity for you, Pilar. A lot of important people come to my shop. Judges and lawyers from the courts, executives from Brooklyn Union Gas. Maybe they'll see your painting. You could become famous."

My mother talks and talks, but I block out her words. For some reason I think about Jacoba Van Heemskerck, a Dutch expressionist painter I've become interested in lately. Her paintings feel organic to me, like breathing abstractions of color. She refused to title her paintings (much less do patriotic murals for her mother's bakery) and numbered her works instead. I mean, who needs words when colors and lines conjure up their own language? That's what I want to do with my paintings, find a unique language, obliterate the clichés.

I think about all the women artists throughout history who managed to paint despite the odds against them. People still ask where all the important women painters are instead of looking at what they did paint and trying to understand their circumstances. Even supposedly knowledgeable and sensitive people react to good art by a woman as if it were an anomaly, a product of a freak nature or a direct result of her association with a male painter or mentor. Nobody's even heard of feminism in art school. The male teachers and students still call the shots and get the serious attention and the fellowships that further their careers. As for the women, we're supposed to make extra money modeling nude. What kind of bullshit revolution is that?

"Mira, Pilar. I'm asking you as a favor. You could paint something simple, something elegant. Like the Statue of Liberty. Is that too much to ask?"

"Okay, okay, I'll paint something," I say deliberately, deciding to play my last card. "But on one condition. You can't see it before the unveiling." This will get her, I think. She'll never agree to this in a million years. She's too much of a control freak.

"That's fine."

"What?"

"I said that's fine, Pilar."

I must be standing there with my mouth open because she pops a macaroon into it and shakes her head as if to say, "See, you always underestimate me." But that's not true. If anything, I overestimate her. It comes from experience. Mom is arbitrary and inconsistent and always believes she's right. It's a pretty irritating combination.

Shit. How did I get into this mess?

Our warehouse is only two blocks from the river, and the Statue of Liberty is visible in the distance. I'd been there once when I was a kid, before we settled in Brooklyn. Mom and Dad took me on a ferry and we climbed up behind Liberty's eyes and looked out over the river, the city, the beginning of things.

A Circle Line tour boat is rounding the tip of Manhattan, optimistic as a wedding cake. There's someone on the top deck with a pair of binoculars aimed at Brooklyn. I can imagine what the tour guide is saying: ". . . and on your left, ladies and gentlemen, is the borough of Brooklyn, former home of the Dodgers and the birthplace of famous 'It' girl Clara Bow. . . ." What they don't say is that nobody ever dies in Brooklyn. It's only the living that die here.

That night, I get to work. But I decide to do a painting instead of a mural. I stretch a twelve-by-eight-foot canvas and wash it with an iridescent blue gouache—like the Virgin Mary's robes in gaudy church paintings. I want the background to glow, to look irradiated, nuked out. It takes me a while to get the right effect.

When the paint dries, I start on Liberty herself. I do a perfect replication of her a bit left of center canvas, changing only two details: first, I make Liberty's torch float slightly beyond her grasp, and second, I paint her right hand reaching over to cover her left breast, as if she's reciting the national anthem or some other slogan.

The next day, the background still looks off to me, so I take a medium-thick brush and paint black stick figures pulsing in the air around Liberty, thorny scars that look like barbed wire. I want to go all the way with this, to stop mucking around and do what I feel, so at the base of the statue I put my favorite punk rallying cry: I'M A MESS. And then carefully, very carefully, I paint a safety pin through Liberty's nose.

This, I think, sums everything up very nicely. *SL-76.* That'll be my title.

I fuss with Liberty another couple of days, more out of nervousness than anything. I keep getting the feeling that Mom is going to spy on my work. After all, her record doesn't exactly inspire confidence. So, before I leave my studio, I set up a booby trap—two tight rows of paint cans on the floor just inside the door. Mom would trip on them if she managed to open the latch and come creeping around late at night. It would serve her right, too, show her that she can't go breaking her promises and invading my privacy anytime she damn well pleases.

I'm usually a heavy sleeper but these last nights every little noise makes me jump out of bed. I'd swear I heard her footsteps, or someone picking the lock on my studio. But when I get up to investigate, I always find my mother sound asleep, looking innocent the way chronically guilty people do sometimes. Then I go to the refrigerator, find something to eat, and stare at the cold stub of her cigar on the kitchen table. In the mornings, my paint cans remain undisturbed and there are no suspicious stains on any of Mom's clothing in the hamper. Jesus, I must really be getting paranoid.

Max helps me set the painting up in the bakery the night before the grand opening, and we drape it with sewn-together sheets. My mother, surprisingly, still hasn't even tried to get a glimpse of the work. I can tell she's proud of the blind faith she's placed in me. She's positively aglow in her magnanimity. When I come home that night, Mom shows me the full-page ad she took out in the *Brooklyn Express*:

95

Pete Hamill

Pete Hamill left high school after two years to become a sheet-metal worker in the Brooklyn Navy Yard. In 1952, at seventeen, he joined the Navy and went to college on the G.I. bill. Hamill started his career as a designer and graphic artist before changing to journalism. He has written for the New York Post *and the New York* Daily News. *In addition to magazine and newspaper articles, Hamill has written novels, screenplays, and short stories. This selection is excerpted from* The Gift *(1973), an autobiographical novella.*

FROM *The Gift*

_I_ awoke to a room flooded with an oblique winter sun. The blanket was pink wool, and itchy, except on the edges, where it was trimmed with sateen. I was used to the broad ceiling beams of barracks, open rows of bunk beds, the wide chill murmur of boot-camp mornings. Now I was in a room that had once been large and suddenly had shrunk, and my eyes played on the lone picture, two snow-white parrots in a Brazilian jungle.

The jungle had to be Brazil; I had figured that out one time in geography class, and I was probably wrong. But I knew that parrots had to mean South America, because they didn't have them in Africa. And lying there, gradually becoming familiar with the molding around the ceiling trimming the green walls, feeling safe, I thought of Bomba. *A jagged streak of lightning shot athwart the sky, followed by a deafening crash of thunder. The lurid glare revealed Bomba, the jungle boy, crouched in a hollow beneath the roots of an overturned tree.* It was from "Bomba the Jungle Boy in the Swamp of Death, or the Sacred Alligators of Abarago" by Roy Rockwood, and I had memorized those opening lines, sitting alone at the top of the stairs one summer, next to the roof door. Bomba lived in a South American jungle with a naturalist named Cody Casson; he didn't know his mother or father, and reading about him, about how old Casson had been injured in an accident, and how Bomba became the provider, how at fourteen he was as strong as men twice his age, I would inhabit that distant jungle, alone, fighting pumas, jaguars, snakes, storms and cannibals. I copied pictures out of the books, which were published by Cupples and Leon, and which my brother Tommy and I would buy in the used-book store on Pearl Street, and once, with a flat sheet of cork stolen from a factory, I carved a whole river system, marked with jungles, native villages, and the massive headwaters of the Giant Cataract. At the end of every book, Bomba got closer to discovering the secret of his vanished parents, whose names were Andrew and Laura Bartow, and I wandered the used-book shops trying to find the missing volumes in the series, the volumes that would tell the whole story about this white boy lost in the South American jungle. Each book would end with Bomba wondering about his mother, longing for her, crying alone in the jungle. I never did find the missing volumes.

I looked up and my brother Denis was staring at me. He was only two, a kid with square shoulders and huge wet brown eyes. He was standing beside a chair, tentative and puzzled.

"Hello, Denis."

He said nothing.

"Don't you remember me?"

Wordless, he turned and started to run, waddling as he went, heading for the kitchen. Everybody else was gone, including my father. I got up and went to my father's closet. An old pair of light-blue civilian trousers was hanging next to a zipper jacket. I pulled them on, then took a shirt out of his drawer. Above the bureau, brown and fading, was an old photograph of an Irish soccer team. There were fifteen players and two coaches, and there was a banner before them that said *St. Mary's.* One of the players was my father.

The year before, after dropping out of high school, I had worked for a year in the sheet-metal shop of the Brooklyn Navy Yard, and men there had told me how good my father had been, when he was young and playing soccer in the immigrant leagues. He was fierce and quick, they said, possessed of a magic leg, moving down those Sunday playing fields as if driven by the engines of anger and exile, playing hardest against English and Scottish teams, the legs pumping and cutting and stealing the ball; hearing the long deep roar of strangers, the women on the sidelines, the hard-packed earth, the ice frozen in small pools, the needle beer in metal containers, and the speak-easies later, drinking until the small hours, singing the songs they had learned across an ocean. Until one day, in one hard-played game, a German forward had come out of nowhere and kicked, and the magic leg had splintered and my father fell as if shot, and someone came off the bench and broke the German's jaw with a punch, and then they were pulling slats off the wooden fence to tie against the ruined leg and waiting for an hour and a half for the ambulance to come from Kings County Hospital while they played out the rest of the game. The players and the spectators were poor; not one of them owned a car. And then at the hospital, he was dropped in a bed, twenty-eight years old and far from home, and there were no doctors because it was the weekend. Across the room, detectives were questioning a black man whose stomach had been razored open in a fight; and the ceiling reeled and turned, his face felt swollen and choked, he remembered his father's white beard and lifting bricks in the mason's yard; remembered all that, and the trip down the hill that day with the clothes in the bag, dodging the British soldiers, heading for a certain place where a certain man would get him on the boat to Liverpool and then to America; remembered that, he said later, and remembered how the razored man died in silence, and there was no feeling in the magic leg. When the doctors finally showed up the next morning, the leg was bursting with gangrene, and they had to slice the soccer boot off with a knife, and in the afternoon they took the leg off above the knee. When he talked about it later, he never mentioned the pain. What he remembered most clearly was the sound of the saw.

"Fried, Peter, or scrambled?"

I went into the kitchen. My mother was at the stove. Denis stood in silence in a corner, staring at me. I went into the L-shaped bathroom, with the swan decals on the walls, and the pull-chain box up high near the ceiling. I closed the door and felt tight and comfortable as I started to shave. And I knew that he shaved there too, every morning, shaved, and washed his face hard with very hot water so that his skin was shiny and gleaming, and then combed his hair very tightly, so that it was slick, black, glossy. And I wondered if he ever stood there and thought about me.

I wondered whether he cursed the vanished leg, the terrible Sunday at Wanderers' Oval, and whether he was sorry because he never could do the things with me and Tommy that fathers were expected to do in America. He had never played baseball with us, or thrown us a pass with a football. We had never gone fishing, or wandered around Brooklyn on long walks, or gone on rides to the country, because he never learned to drive a car. He was a stranger to me, though we shaved at the same mirror, often with the same razor, and I had come to love him from a distance. I loved him when he would come home with his friends and sit in the kitchen drinking cardboard containers of beer, talking about fights, illustrating Willie Pep's jab on the light cord or throwing Ray Robinson's hooks into the wash on the kitchen line. I loved the hard defiance of the Irish songs, and I would lie awake in the next room listening to them, as they brought up the old tales of British malignance and murders committed by the Black and Tans and what the men in the trench coats did in the hours after midnight. But I didn't really know him, and I was certain he didn't know me. I had some bald facts: he had left school at twelve to work as a stonemason's apprentice, because there were eleven children in the family; he had been in Sinn Fein, and a policeman had been murdered, and he came on the run to America; for a while he struggled with night school at Brooklyn Tech, with my mother helping him with spelling. But I was seventeen and a half, and I still didn't know when they had married, whether my mother was pregnant with me at the time, whether they had been married at all. There were no anniversary parties, and no wedding pictures on the walls. I tried not to care. But he didn't know really how to deal with me, didn't know what to do when I asked for help, and in many ways he was still Irish and I was an American. But I loved the way he talked and the way he stood on a corner with a fedora and raincoat on Sunday mornings, the face shiny, the hair slick under the hat, an Irish dude waiting for the bars to open, and I loved the way he once hit a guy with a ball-bat because he had insulted my mother. I just never knew if he loved me back.

I sat down to eat, and then heard him coming up the stairs. He worked across the street in the Globe Lighting Company, which took most of the third floor of the Ansonia Clock Building, once the largest factory in Brooklyn, to us a dirty red-brick pile. He was a wirer, a member of Local 3 of the International Brotherhood of Electrical Workers; but basically he was just another pair of hands on the assembly line, and sometimes in the night he would come home, after working all day on those concrete floors, and he would take off the wooden leg, and the stump sock, and lie back on the bed, the flesh of the stump raw and blistered; I never heard him complain; he would just lie there, hurting, his hands touching the bedsheets as if afraid to touch the ruin of the leg, as if admitting pain would be some ultimate admission that the leg was gone forever and he was mortal and growing old. Before the war he worked at the Roulston's plant, down on Smith Street, a clerk, because the Irish came to America with good handwriting, as they called it; he would bring home mysterious bundles, sometimes wrapped in newspapers and tied with twine, containing canned food or packaged spaghetti, and he would hand them to my mother, always in silence, explaining nothing. He left Roulston's for the war plant, and then there were a couple of years after the war, made up of uncertainty, idleness, Rattigan's, the attempt to make something of the apartment on Seventh Avenue, where we had all moved in 1943; everything was always being painted, because the rumor was that fresh coats of paint would kill the eggs of the cockroaches; the kitchen table and the chairs were painted with Red Devil red, a coat a year, with newspapers spread out on the linoleum floors, and the walls were painted, and the closets; but the roaches still came, long and sleek and heavy with eggs, chocolate brown, dark blond, plump and long and sometimes wedge-shaped, invincible, insidious, silent; and there is a dream I still have about a cockroach that moves into my ear at night, and gnaws its way to my brain, chewing, silent, its feelers humming and tentative, moving around in the crevices, an inhabitant of my skull.

"Hello, Magee."

He was in the door, with the familiar rolling limp, wearing a lumberjack's coat and a flannel shirt, hatless, the hair slicked back, and I got up and went over to him, and he shook my hand. My mother was behind us, making American-cheese sandwiches while tomato soup heated in a saucepan.

"Hey, you look good," he said, and he stepped back.

"They feed you pretty good there," I said.

"They must," he said. He had the jacket off now, and was sitting down, reaching for a steaming cup of tea. Denis put his head on my father's lap, and he rubbed the boy's head.

"You hear about O'Malley?"

"No, what?"

"The son of a bitch is taking the Dodgers out of Brooklyn."

"Billy," my mother said. "The language . . ."

"They're goin' to California," he said. "Him and the other son of a bitch, Stoneham. In a couple of years . . ."

"I don't believe it."

"Tommy Holmes had it in the *Eagle*."

"What for? I mean, why are they goin' out there?"

"Because O'Malley is a greedy son of a bitch, that's why."

My mother had sliced the sandwich in quarters and placed it before him, and he started to eat. Denis wandered into the other room.

"The players oughtta go on strike," he said. "Just say they're staying, and to hell with O'Malley. Never would've happened with Branch Rickey. He was a man, Rickey. Loved baseball, too. Put together the best bloody farm system in history."

"Yeah."

"Archie Moore's fighting Maxim this week, title fight."

"Moore should flatten him."

"I don't know," he said. "Maxim's a clever guinea. And Jack Kearns

104

doesn't take any chances. Some manager, that Kearns. He managed Dempsey, you know. And Mickey Walker."

"But he can't break an egg with a punch, Maxim."

"He holds, and grabs ya, and it's hard to bang him. It's no cinch for Moore. He hasn't made the weight in two years."

"What did you think of the election?"

"I didn't like Stevenson."

"You mean you voted for a Republican?"

"Ike was a hell of a general," he said flatly. "Even if he looks like someone's aunt."

"He sounded pretty dumb, compared to Stevenson."

"He was a hell of a general," he said. There was a note of finality in the statement; I remember it as a moment when I realized he was changing, because there wasn't a general who ever lived that Billy Hamill could admire. He was an enlisted man for life. I picked up the light zipper jacket.

"Well, I'll see you later," I said.

"Right," he said, without looking up.

I went out, moving quickly down the stairs, trembling.

Spike Lee

Shelton Jackson Lee was born in Atlanta, Georgia, in 1957. While still a graduate student at New York University, Lee wrote and directed his first film, Joe's Bed-Stuy Barbershop: We Cut Heads, *featured at the New Directors Series in New York City in 1983. His next film,* She's Gotta Have It, *about a woman and her three lovers, was made in twelve days and earned critical praise. With the success of* She's Gotta Have It, *Lee got backing from Columbia Pictures for his next film,* School Daze. *He had an even bigger budget for* Do the Right Thing *and spent eight and a half weeks shooting it in Bedford-Stuyvesant. His production notes are a diary of that experience. Lee wrote, "*Do the Right Thing *is not about Black people in three-piece suits going to work, it was about Black underclass in Bed-Stuy, a community that has some of the highest unemployment, infant mortality, and drug-related homicide rates in New York City. We're talking about people who live in the bowels of the social-economic system, but still live with dignity and humor." Lee's subsequent films have included* Jungle Fever *and* Malcolm X, *and his company, Forty Acres and a Mule, is based in Brooklyn.*

FROM *Do* THE *Right Thing: Production Notes*

Do *the Right Thing* was my first union film. To keep our costs down, Universal suggested that we shoot the film with a nonunion crew someplace outside of New York, like Philadelphia or Baltimore. I'm sorry, Philly and Baltimore are great cities, but they just aren't Brooklyn. This film had to be shot in Brooklyn, if it was to be done at all. However, there was no way we could shoot a $6.5-million film in New York City without giving the film unions a piece of the action.

On every film, I try to use as many Black people behind the camera as possible. A major concern I had about shooting with an all-union crew was whether this would prevent me from hiring as many Blacks as I wanted. There are few minorities in the film unions, and, historically, film unions have done little to encourage Blacks and women to join their ranks.

Originally we planned to sign a contract with the International

Alliance of Theatrical State Employees (IATSE, or IA) because they have more Black members. They proved to be too expensive, so we entered into negotiations with the National Association of Broadcast Employees and Technicians (NABET). The negotiations with NABET lasted a month, but we were able to win some important concessions.

One concession was that NABET allowed us to hire a number of Blacks to work on the film who were not members of the union, including Larry Cherry, our hairstylist, my brother David Lee, the still photographer, and Darnell Martin, the second assistant cameraperson. (At the time, there were no Blacks in these union categories.) In addition, we were able to hire some nonunion people as trainees in the grip and electric departments. NABET agreed to consider granting union membership to these people if their work on the film proved satisfactory. Eventually they were admitted to the union.

We cut a similar deal with the Teamsters union, which is responsible for all the vehicles driven on a union shoot. The Teamsters have the right to determine how many drivers are assigned to a union production. At $1,500 to $2,000 per week per driver, this can eat a hole in your budget. The Teamsters allowed us to hire a small number of union drivers and use nonunion production assistants to supplement this group. Out of the five union drivers they assigned to the production, two were Black.

I wanted to film *Do the Right Thing* entirely on one block. Our location scout combed the streets of Brooklyn for two weeks and came back with a book of photos. One Saturday, Wynn Thomas, the production designer, and I visited all the locations suggested by our scout. It turned out the block that we chose was the first one he had looked at—Stuyvesant Street between Lexington and Quincy avenues, in the heart of the Bedford-Stuyvesant section of Brooklyn.

The block had everything that we needed: brownstones which weren't too upscale or too dilapidated. And, most importantly, it had two empty lots that faced each other, where we could build sets for the Korean market and Sal's Famous Pizzeria. Once we decided on the block, Wynn went to work designing the sets and supervising construction.

I think it was Monty Ross's idea to hire the Fruit of Islam, the security force of the Nation of Islam, the Black Muslim organization, to patrol the set. Cops really have no respect in Black communities in New York, especially not in Bed-Stuy, where cops have been convicted in the past on drug-trafficking charges. We knew we couldn't bring in a white security force, it had to be Black. And Black people who were respected in the community. All this led us to the Fruit of Islam.

It was obvious that crack was being sold on the block. One of the first things we did was let the crack dealers know they weren't welcome. We boarded up an abandoned building that was being used as a crack house and turned another into a location site. We managed to move the dealers off the block, but we weren't able to put them out of business. They just closed up shop and moved around the corner.

During preproduction, Universal asked me to recommend a film-maker to do the electronic press kit that the studio would use to promote the film. I recommended the veteran documentary filmmaker St. Clair Bourne. When I met with St. Clair to discuss the press kit, I asked him to consider directing a film about the making of *Do the Right Thing*. We were shooting in Bed-Stuy. We were taking over an entire city block for eight weeks. And we had hired the Fruit of Islam— Farrakhan's private security force—to patrol the set and to close two crack houses. Certainly, this needed to be documented. St. Clair got to work on the project immediately.

Casting for *Do the Right Thing* was on a much smaller scale than *School Daze*. Most of the major roles I had decided upon even before I completed the script. We held auditions in New York only, whereas for *School Daze*, we saw actors in Los Angeles, Atlanta, and New York. I wanted to cast white actors who feel comfortable around Black people. A white actor nervous about setting foot in Bed-Stuy wasn't gonna work for this film. The fact that Danny Aiello grew up in the South Bronx, and John Turturro in a Black neighborhood in Queens, made them ideal choices.

The first day of rehearsal the full cast met to read through the script, then I opened up the floor for discussion and suggestions. Paul Ben-jamin, who plays ML, one of the Corner Men, is a veteran actor whom

I've wanted to work with for a long time. Paul was the first actor to raise a question about the script. He was worried that it showed nothing but lazy, shiftless Black people. It seemed to Paul that no one in the film had a job, and that his character and the other Corner Men just hung out all day.

It was Rosie Perez (Tina), who had never acted before in her life, who answered Paul's question. Rosie grew up in Bed-Stuy and stayed with relatives there during the shoot. She went off on a ten-minute tirade about how people like the Corner Men actually exist and that Paul and everyone else should go to Bed-Stuy and take a look.

I told Paul that *Do the Right Thing* was not about Black people in three-piece suits going to work, it was about Black underclass in Bed-Stuy, a community that has some of the highest unemployment, infant mortality, and drug-related homicide rates in New York City. We're talking about people who live in the bowels of the social-economic system, but still live with dignity and humor. Paul and I talked about it the next day and he understood.

We spent the rest of the rehearsal week meeting in small groups to talk about characters. When the Corner Men met for their group rehearsal, they were having trouble getting their characters to mesh. I decided that we should take a trip to the location and read the dialogue there. We drove out to Stuyvesant Street and set up some chairs in the same spot where the Corner Men's scenes would be shot. Being on the set, in the community, made all the difference.

The fact this film takes place on one single day was a challenge for everyone involved. Continuity was a motherfucker. Especially for Ernest, who had to make two months' worth of footage look like it was shot on one day. For the most part, he had to rely on available light, since we spent most of our time outdoors.

Though this film is about young Black people in Brooklyn, Ruthe Carter, the costume designer, and I wanted to downplay the gold fad. Besides the gold teeth that Mookie and Buggin' Out wear, and Radio Raheem's knuckle rings (which are really brass), you don't see much gold in this film. I think it's crazy for young Black kids to spend money they don't have on gold jewelry. The kids pick it up from the rappers. I mean no disrespect to L. L. Cool J and Eric B. & Rakim, but this gold-chains-by-the-ton shit is ridiculous.

I knew I wanted my character Mookie to wear tight bicycle shorts underneath a pair of loose-fitting shorts. I got this from basketball players. Instead of wearing jock straps now, many are wearing bicycle pants beneath their uniforms. I like the look because of the contrast. So I had an idea for the bottom of my costume, but I was stumped on what to wear on top.

Cecil Holmes, one of the bigwigs in Black music at CBS Records, knows I'm a baseball fan and once gave me a Jackie Robinson jersey. The night before we started shooting, I was still undecided about my costume, then I remembered the jersey.

The jersey was a good choice. I don't think Jackie Robinson has gotten his due from Black people. There are young people today, even Black athletes, who don't know what Jackie Robinson did. They might know he was the first Black major leaguer, but they don't know what he had to bear to make it easier for those who came after him.

When you're directing a film, it takes over your life completely. You get up at the crack of dawn, shoot for twelve to fourteen hours (if you're lucky), watch dailies, grab something to eat before you go to bed, then you're up again at the crack of dawn.

The first week of production went well. I felt we could have been better organized in terms of communication between the assistant directors and other departments, but by the end of the week it all came together.

It rained on and off for three of the days of the first week, and we were forced to shoot an interior scene, one of our precious few cover sets. There was concern about using up our cover sets so early in the shoot, since we had less than five to last us the entire shoot. But there was nothing we could do about that except pray for good weather. Depending on the size of the scene, overcast days were potential problems for us as well. Creating the effect of sunshine on a cloudy day over an area the size of a city block was something our budget didn't allow for.

We had a budget for extras on *Do the Right Thing,* which was a first for me. With no money to pay extras on *School Daze,* we could never predict if we'd get the number needed for a given scene. But if you look at the film, I think we did a good job disguising how few extras we actually had.

We had two open calls for extras, one for members of the Screen Actors Guild, and one for nonunion actors. We also held a community open call at a church near the location, Antioch Baptist, which graciously served as our meal hall during the shoot.

We cast a core group of extras to play block residents and they worked the entire shoot. Additional extras were brought on for the big scenes. The first week of shooting we had a time coming up with a system of documenting the extras and background action scene by scene. We had to establish which core extras would be placed on various sides of the block, how long they would remain there, and how many new extras we should see in each scene. I didn't want to look at this film a year later and see the same two extras crossing through every shot. Again, this was a task made complicated by the fact that the film takes place in a 24-hour period, but was shot out of sequence.

One sequence that took forever to shoot was the johnny pump sequence, where Charlie (played by Frank Vincent) and his white convertible get drenched by the kids. We allotted two days to shoot it, but we should have been more generous because it ended up taking five.

The car had to be specially rigged to withstand all the water, and dried off between takes. And each time Frank got wet, he needed a wardrobe change. We used two cameras to film the kids playing in the hydrant. One was encased in underwater housing, and we used that camera to shoot the close-ups of the hydrant. The camera department had a lot fun with it. It was orange and looked like an old diver's mask.

It's a compliment to Wynn Thomas's design work that people off the street were constantly wandering into Sal's Famous Pizzeria and the Korean Market, unaware they were sets. We spent almost a straight week shooting inside Sal's Famous Pizzeria. With the heat from the lights, and the crew and actors packed into one room, it really got hot in there. As soon as a take was over, people rushed to turn on the air conditioner. During lunch break, crew members used the booths as beds and caught some shut-eye.

Despite the heat, we were able to get through these interior scenes pretty quickly. John Turturro exploded one day over the prop pizza. The property master didn't have enough pies on set for John and Richard Edson to actually cut them into slices. They were told to fake it. John went off. He refused to fake it because it suspended all his belief in the scene. He was right. We saw dailies the next night and had to reshoot all the fake cutting.

I was pleased with the way we staged the conversation about "niggers" vs. "Blacks" that Mookie and Pino have in the pizzeria. As it reads in the script, the scene could have been a yelling match. It works just as well as a simple conversation, and it manages to keep the same intensity. There is enough yelling and screaming in this movie as it is.

Pino and Mookie's scene sets up the racial-slur sequence. Jump-cut sequences featuring a group of characters speaking toward the camera have been a staple of each of my films so far. *She's Gotta Have It* has the Dogs, *School Daze* has Half-Pint's unsuccessful attempt to pick up girls, and *Do the Right Thing* has representatives of different ethnic groups slurring each other.

In the first two films, the camera remains static while the subjects talk. I wanted to vary this formula a bit in *Do the Right Thing,* so I had the camera move in quickly to the person speaking. It was Ernest's idea to have the final actor in the sequence, Mister Señor Love Daddy, come toward camera. We hooked up Love Daddy's chair to a trick wire so it looks like he's being propelled by magic.

The racial-slur sequence was meant to rouse emotions. It's funny the way people react to it. They laugh at every slur except the one directed at their ethnic group. While we were watching the dailies of Pino's slur of Blacks, a woman in the Kraft Services department started hissing at John. She couldn't separate John from his character and was less than courteous to him for the rest of the shoot.

Some of the best acting in the film happens in the scene where Pino asks his father to sell the pizzeria. Danny, John, and I tinkered with the dialogue while the crew was setting up for the shot. We finally got it down, but we still didn't have a clincher to end the scene. I was always on the lookout for ways to work Smiley into the film, since for the most part, he wasn't scripted. It hit me that we could end the scene by having Smiley knock on the pizzeria window and interrupt Danny and John's conversation.

Danny and John are sitting at a table in front of the pizzeria window. What makes that scene so great to me is that as Danny tells John about the neighborhood and why he has chosen to remain there, through the window you can see activity on the block. It lends visual support to Danny's speech.

Even if principal actors didn't have dialogue in a scene, we often used them in the background, walking down the street or hanging out, to give a sense that their characters really lived on the block. Most of the deals we made with our principals were for eight weeks of work—the entire shoot—so we could have them on standby for that very reason.

The climactic fight in the pizzeria was just as I envisioned it—a messy street fight, complete with choking and biting. It starts inside the pizzeria and ends up outside on the pavement. After Sal demolishes Radio Raheem's box with his baseball bat, we wanted to do a shot where Raheem would grab Sal by the neck, slam his face into the counter, and drag him the length of the counter.

Danny refused to do the shot. He felt it was slapstick and had been done a million times. Some cast members felt that Danny's refusal was a question of ego, of not wanting to be wasted that bad on-screen. I sat down with Eddie Smith, the stunt coordinator, Danny, Danny Jr., Aiello's son and stunt double, and Bill Nunn, to hear the opinions of all involved. I decided that Bill should pull Danny over the counter instead of giving him a "facial." Danny was still not totally satisfied, but we proceeded anyway.

The cast was spurred on by Danny's reluctance to cooperate with what we had planned for the fight scene. As if to compensate for Danny's lapse of team spirit, they worked extra hard to make the scene realistic. Everyone suffered their share of bruises, including Martin Lawrence (Cee) who took a nasty shot in the eye.

Good things come out of adversity. I think the compromise we came up with made for a better shot, and I'm grateful to Danny for standing his ground. There was no tension on my part because of our disagreement. I think Danny felt isolated from the cast for a while. But I noticed that in no time he was back to his usual habit of hugging on everyone. Conflicts are bound to crop up on a film shoot. There are always differences of interpretation.

The riot scene was more involved than anything I've done on film before. Just the sheer numbers of people and vehicles involved—from extras to special-effects coordinators, from cop cars and paddy wagons to fire trucks—made it a big deal.

In order to capture all the action in the scene, we had to burn the pizzeria in stages, starting with the interior and moving outside. A big concern was how many days the pizzeria would hold up under the fire. If the fire got out of hand or the set caved in before we finished shooting the riot, we'd be up shit's creek with no paddle. But things worked out and we were able to get all the shots we wanted without losing the pizzeria.

My most pressured moment as an actor on this film was definitely when I had to throw the garbage can through the pizzeria window. No one thought about this beforehand, but the window glass was almost one-quarter inch thick. Breaking glass that thick is no easy feat. I was throwing hard, but it took four or five takes before I could get the garbage can through the window. On one take it even bounced off like a rubber ball. I was on the spot: we were filming with a special crane that had to be sent back to the rental house the next day, and the sun was coming up. Finally we got the shot.

The first night we shot the firemen turning their hoses on the crowd, the water pressure wasn't forceful enough. The stuntmen were overacting to compensate for it. The whole effect was fake, so we redid the shot the following evening.

The script called for a number of stunts involving characters getting swept away by the force of the water. Ruby Dee and my sister Joie were to get hit by a blast of water and go flying down the street. I decided the scene was powerful enough without these stunts. I cut them and came up with a different way to end the scene. Ruby Dee is in the middle of the street screaming hysterically because of all the chaos around her. Da Mayor comforts her with a hug.

Sam Jackson pointed out to me that he had the honor of acting in the first scene we shot of *School Daze* (he played one of the local yokels), and in the last scene we shot of *Do the Right Thing* (Mister Señor Love Daddy wakes up the Block). I hope this means luck for both of us.

Most wrap days are joyous occasions, unless your film is a real bomb. I felt I had a lot to be thankful for when we wrapped *Do the Right Thing.* We had a relaxed, practically hassle-free shoot. We had shot an entire film for eight and a half weeks at one location. (What could be easier?) The block residents and the community of Bed-Stuy had given us full cooperation. And the dailies looked good.

A couple of hours before wrap, a bet was waged on the exact time, down to the minute, that we would complete our last shot. One of the drivers won the bet and a pool of forty-five dollars. We broke out the champagne. And after listening to the movie-unit cops grumble about permissions, we laid a plaque in front of We Love Radio Station that states that the film was shot on the block. We even put up a street sign renaming Stuyvesant Street "Do the Right Thing Avenue," but the wind blew it down, so it stays in my office now.

Bernard Malamud

Brooklyn is the setting for much of Bernard Malamud's work. The son of Russian-immigrant parents, Malamud often wrote of Jewish American life. The Assistant, *from which this excerpt is taken, dealt with a Jewish shopkeeper and his Italian American assistant and reflected Brooklyn's sometimes uncomfortable collision of cultures. Malamud's other work included* The Natural, A New Life, The Fixer, The Tenants, *and* Dubin's Lives. *Malamud died in 1986 at 72.*

---

*H*elen Bober and Louis Karp walked, no hands touching, in the windy dark on the Coney Island boardwalk.

Louis had, on his way home for supper that evening, stopped her in front of the liquor store, on her way in from work.

"How's about a ride in the Mercury, Helen? I never see you much anymore. Things were better in the bygone days in high school."

Helen smiled. "Honestly, Louis, that's so far away." A sense of mourning at once oppressed her, which she fought to a practiced draw.

"Near or far, it's all the same for me." He was built with broad back and narrow head, and despite prominent eyes was presentable. In high school, before he quit, he had worn his wet hair slicked straight back. One day, after studying a picture of a movie actor in the *Daily News,* he had run a part across his head. This was as much change as she had known in him. If Nat Pearl was ambitious, Louis made a

118

relaxed living letting the fruit of his father's investment fall into his lap.

"Anyway," he said, "why not a ride for old times' sake?"

She thought a minute, a gloved finger pressed into her cheek; but it was a fake gesture because she was lonely.

"For old times' sake, where?"

"Name your scenery—continuous performance."

"The Island?"

He raised his coat collar. "*Brr,* it's a cold, windy night. You wanna freeze?"

Seeing her hesitation, he said, "But I'll die game. When'll I pick you up?"

"Ring my bell after eight and I'll come down."

"Check," Louis said. "Eight bells."

They walked to Seagate, where the boardwalk ended. She gazed with envy through a wire fence at the large lit houses fronting the ocean. The Island was deserted, except here and there an open hamburger joint or pinball machine concession. Gone from the sky was the umbrella of rosy light that glowed over the place in summertime. A few cold stars gleamed down. In the distance a dark Ferris wheel looked like a stopped clock. They stood at the rail of the boardwalk, watching the black, restless sea.

All during their walk she had been thinking about her life, the difference between her aloneness now and the fun when she was young and spending every day of summer in a lively crowd of kids on the beach. But as her high school friends had got married, she had one by one given them up; and as others of them graduated from college, envious, ashamed of how little she was accomplishing, she stopped seeing them too. At first it hurt to drop people but after a time it became a not too difficult habit. Now she saw almost no one, occasionally Betty Pearl, who understood, but not enough to make much difference.

Louis, his face reddened by the wind, sensed her mood.

"What's got in you, Helen?" he said, putting his arm around her.

"I can't really explain it. All night I've been thinking of the swell

119

times we had on this beach when we were kids. And do you remember the parties? I suppose I'm blue that I'm no longer seventeen."

"What's so wrong about twenty-three?"

"It's old, Louis. Our lives change so quickly. You know what youth means?"

"Sure I know. You don't catch me giving away nothing for nothing. I got my youth yet."

"When a person is young he's privileged," Helen said, "with all kinds of possibilities. Wonderful things might happen, and when you get up in the morning you feel they will. That's what youth means, and that's what I've lost. Nowadays I feel that every day is like the day before, and what's worse, like the day after."

"So now you're a grandmother?"

"The world has shrunk for me."

"What do you wanna be—Miss Rheingold?"

"I want a larger and better life. I want the return of my possibilities."

"Such as which ones?"

She clutched the rail, cold through her gloves. "Education," she said, "prospects. Things I've wanted but never had."

"Also a man?"

"Also a man."

His arm tightened around her waist. "Talk is too cold, baby, how's about a kiss?"

She brushed his cold lips, then averted her head. He did not press her.

"Louis," she said, watching a far-off light on the water, "what do you want out of your life?"

He kept his arm around her. "The same thing I got—plus."

"Plus what?"

"Plus more, so my wife and family can have also."

"What if she wanted something different than you do?"

"Whatever she wanted I would gladly give her."

"But what if she wanted to make herself a better person, have bigger ideas, live a more worthwhile life? We die so quickly, so helplessly. Life *has* to have some meaning."

"I ain't gonna stop anybody from being better," Louis said. "That's up to them."

"I suppose," she said.

"Say, baby, let's drop this deep philosophy and go trap a hamburger. My stomach complains."

"Just a little longer. It's been ages since I came here this late in the year."

He pumped his arms. "Jesus, this wind, it flies up my pants. At least gimme another kiss." He unbuttoned his overcoat.

She let him kiss her. He felt her breast. Helen stepped back out of his embrace. "Don't, Louis."

"Why not?" He stood there awkwardly, annoyed.

"It gives me no pleasure."

"I suppose I'm the first guy that ever gave it a nip?"

"Are you collecting statistics?"

"Okay," he said, "I'm sorry. You know I ain't a bad guy, Helen."

"I know you're not, but please don't do what I don't like."

"There was a time you treated me a whole lot better."

"That was the past, we were kids."

It's funny, she remembered, how necking made glorious dreams.

"We were older than that, up till the time Nat Pearl started in college, then you got interested in him. I suppose you got him in mind for the future?"

"If I do, I don't know it."

"But he's the one you want, ain't he? I like to know what that stuck up has got beside a college education? I work for my living."

"No, I don't want him, Louis." But she thought, Suppose Nat said I love you? For magic words a girl might do magic tricks.

"So if that's so, what's wrong with me?"

"Nothing. We're friends."

"Friends I got all I need."

"What do you need, Louis?"

"Cut out the wisecracks, Helen. Would it interest you that I would honestly like to marry you?" He paled at his nerve.

She was surprised, touched.

"Thank you," she murmured.

"Thank you ain't good enough. Give me yes or no."

"No, Louis."

"That's what I thought." He gazed blankly at the ocean.

"I never guessed you were at all remotely interested. You go with girls who are so different from me."

"Please, when I go with them you can't see my thoughts."

"No," she admitted.

"I can give you a whole lot better than you got."

"I know you can, but I want a different life from mine now, or yours. I don't want a storekeeper for a husband."

"Wines and liquors ain't exactly pisher groceries."

"I know."

"It ain't because your old man don't like mine?"

"No."

She listened to the wind-driven, sobbing surf. Louis said, "Let's go get the hamburgers."

"Gladly." She took his arm but could tell from the stiff way he walked that he was hurt.

As they drove home on the Parkway, Louis said, "If you can't have everything you want, at least take something. Don't be so goddam proud."

Touché. "What shall I take, Louis?"

He paused. "Take less."

"Less I'll never take."

"People got to compromise."

"I won't with my ideals."

"So what'll you be then, a dried-up prune of an old maid? What's the percentage of that?"

"None."

"So what'll you do?"

"I'll wait. I'll dream. Something will happen."

"Nuts," he said.

He let her off in front of the grocery.

"Thanks for everything."

"You'll make me laugh." Louis drove off.

The store was closed, upstairs dark. She pictured her father asleep after his long day, dreaming of Ephraim. What am I saving myself for? she asked herself. What unhappy Bober fate?

Paule Marshall

Paule Marshall's parents emigrated from Barbados to Brooklyn. She grew up during the Depression and credits the overheard conversations of her mother and her mother's friends as the major influence in her writing. "I grew up among poets," she wrote of the group of women who gathered in her parents' basement kitchen after a hard day of cleaning other people's houses. Marshall graduated from Brooklyn College in 1953 and became a magazine writer and researcher. Her first novel, Brown Girl, Brownstones, was written on assignment in Barbados. Marshall is also the author of several collections of short stories, including Soul Clap Hands and Sing and Reena and Other Stories, and the novels The Chosen Place, The Timeless People, Praisesong for the Widow, and Daughters.

The Making of a Writer: from the Poets in the Kitchen

$\mathcal{S}$ome years ago, when I was teaching a graduate seminar in fiction at Columbia University, a well-known male novelist visited my class to speak on his development as a writer. In discussing his formative years, he didn't realize it but he seriously endangered his life by remarking that women writers are luckier than those of his sex because they usually spend so much time as children around their mothers and their mothers' friends in the kitchen.

What did he say that for? The women students immediately forgot about being in awe of him and began readying their attack for the question-and-answer period later on. Even I bristled. There again was that awful image of women locked away from the world in the kitchen with only each other to talk to, and their daughters locked in with them.

But my guest wasn't really being sexist or trying to be provocative or even spoiling for a fight. What he meant—when he got around to explaining himself more fully—was that, given the way children are (or were) raised in our society, with little girls kept closer to home and their mothers, the woman writer stands a better chance of being exposed, while growing up, to the kind of talk that goes on among women, more often than not in the kitchen; and that this experience gives her an edge over her male counterpart by instilling in her an appreciation for ordinary speech.

It was clear that my guest lecturer attached great importance to this, which is understandable. Common speech and the plain, workaday words that make it up are, after all, the stock-in-trade of some of the best fiction writers. They are the principal means by which characters in a novel or story reveal themselves and give voice sometimes to profound feelings and complex ideas about themselves and the world. Perhaps the proper measure of a writer's talent is skill in rendering everyday speech—when it is appropriate to the story—as well as the ability to tap, to exploit, the beauty, poetry and wisdom it often contains.

"If you say what's on your mind in the language that comes to you from your parents and your street and friends, you'll probably say something beautiful." Grace Paley tells this, she says, to her students at the beginning of every writing course.

It's all a matter of exposure and a training of the ear for the would-be writer in those early years of apprenticeship. And, according to my guest lecturer, this training, the best of it, often takes place in as unglamorous a setting as the kitchen.

He didn't know it, but he was essentially describing my experience as a little girl. I grew up among poets. Now they didn't look like poets—whatever that breed is supposed to look like. Nothing about them suggested that poetry was their calling. They were just a group of ordinary housewives and mothers, my mother included, who dressed in a way (shapeless housedresses, dowdy felt hats and long, dark, solemn coats) that made it impossible for me to imagine they had ever been young.

Nor did they do what poets were supposed to do—spend their days in an attic room writing verses. They never put pen to paper except to write occasionally to their relatives in Barbados. "I take my pen in hand hoping these few lines will find you in health as they leave me fair for the time being," was the way their letters invariably began. Rather, their day was spent "scrubbing floor," as they described the work they did.

Several mornings a week these unknown bards would put an apron and a pair of old house shoes in a shopping bag and take the train or streetcar from our section of Brooklyn out to Flatbush. There, those who didn't have steady jobs would wait on certain designated corners for the white housewives in the neighborhood to come along and bargain with them over pay for a day's work cleaning their houses. This was the ritual even in the winter.

Later, armed with the few dollars they had earned, which in their vocabulary became "a few raw-mouth pennies," they made their way back to our neighborhood, where they would sometimes stop off to have a cup of tea or cocoa together before going home to cook dinner for their husbands and children.

The basement kitchen of the brownstone house where my family lived was the usual gathering place. Once inside the warm safety of its walls the women threw off the drab coats and hats, seated themselves at the large center table, drank their cups of tea or cocoa, and talked. While my sister and I sat at a smaller table over in a corner doing our homework, they talked—endlessly, passionately, poetically, and with impressive range. No subject was beyond them. True, they would indulge in the usual gossip: whose husband was running with whom, whose daughter looked slightly "in the way" (pregnant) under her bridal gown as she walked down the aisle. That sort of thing. But they also tackled the great issues of the time. They were always, for example, discussing the state of the economy. It was the mid and late '30s then, and the aftershock of the Depression, with its soup lines and suicides on Wall Street, was still being felt.

Some people, they declared, didn't know how to deal with adversity. They didn't know that you had to "tie up your belly" (hold in the pain, that is) when things got rough and go on with life. They took their image from the bellyband that is tied around the stomach of a newborn baby to keep the navel pressed in.

They talked politics. Roosevelt was their hero. He had come along and rescued the country with relief and jobs, and in gratitude they christened their sons Franklin and Delano and hoped they would live up to the names.

If F.D.R. was their hero, Marcus Garvey was their God. The name of the fiery, Jamaican-born black nationalist of the '20s was constantly invoked around the table. For he had been their leader when they first came to the United States from the West Indies shortly after World War I. They had contributed to his organization, the United Negro Improvement Association (UNIA), out of their meager salaries, bought shares in his ill-fated Black Star Shipping Line, and at the height of the movement they had marched as members of his "nurses' brigade" in their white uniforms up Seventh Avenue in Harlem during the great Garvey Day parades. Garvey: he lived on through the power of their memories.

And their talk was of war and rumors of wars. They raged against World War II when it broke out in Europe, blaming it on the politicians. "It's these politicians. They're the ones always starting up all this lot of war. But what they care? It's the poor people got to suffer and mothers with their sons." If it was *their* sons, they swore they would keep them out of the Army by giving them soap to eat each day to make their hearts sound defective. Hitler? He was for them "the devil incarnate."

Then there was home. They reminisced often and at length about home. The old country. Barbados—or Bimshire, as they affectionately called it. The little Caribbean island in the sun they loved but had to leave. "Poor—poor but sweet" was the way they remembered it.

And naturally they discussed their adopted home. America came in for both good and bad marks. They lashed out at it for the racism they encountered. They took to task some of the people they worked for, especially those who gave them only a hard-boiled egg and a few spoonfuls of cottage cheese for lunch. "As if anybody can scrub floor on an egg and some cheese that don't have no taste to it!"

Yet although they caught H in "this man country," as they called America, it was nonetheless a place where "you could at least see your way to make a dollar." That much they acknowledged. They might even one day accumulate enough dollars, with both them and their husbands working, to buy the brownstone houses which, like my family, they were only leasing at that period. This was their consuming ambition: to "buy house" and to see the children through.

There was no way for me to understand it at the time, but the talk that filled the kitchen those afternoons was highly functional. It served as therapy, the cheapest kind available to my mother and her friends. Not only did it help them recover from the long wait on the corner that morning and the bargaining over their labor, it restored them to a sense of themselves and reaffirmed their self-worth. Through language they were able to overcome the humiliations of the workday.

But more than therapy, that freewheeling, wide-ranging, exuberant talk functioned as an outlet for the tremendous creative energy they possessed. They were women in whom the need for self-expression was strong, and since language was the only vehicle readily available to them they made of it an art form that—in keeping with the African tradition in which art and life are one—was an integral part of their lives.

And their talk was a refuge. They never really ceased being baffled and overwhelmed by America—its vastness, complexity and power. Its strange customs and laws. At a level beyond words they remained fearful and in awe. Their uneasiness and fear were even reflected in their attitude toward the children they had given birth to in this country. They referred to those like myself, the little Brooklyn-born Bajans (Barbadians), as "these New York children" and complained that they couldn't discipline us properly because of the laws here. "You can't beat these children as you would like, you know, because the authorities in this place will dash you in jail for them. After all, these is New York children." Not only were we different, American, we had, as they saw it, escaped their ultimate authority.

Confronted therefore by a world they could not encompass, which even limited their rights as parents, and at the same time finding themselves permanently separated from the world they had known, they took refuge in language. "Language is the only homeland," Czeslaw

Milosz, the emigré Polish writer and Nobel laureate, has said. This is what it became for the women at the kitchen table.

It served another purpose also, I suspect. My mother and her friends were after all the female counterpart of Ralph Ellison's invisible man. Indeed, you might say they suffered a triple invisibility, being black, female and foreigners. They really didn't count in American society except as a source of cheap labor. But given the kind of women they were, they couldn't tolerate the fact of their invisibility, their power-lessness. And they fought back, using the only weapon at their command: the spoken word.

Those late afternoon conversations on a wide range of topics were a way for them to feel they exercised some measure of control over their lives and the events that shaped them. "Soully-gal, talk yuh talk!" they were always exhorting each other. "In this man world you got to take yuh mouth and make a gun!" They were in control, if only verbally and if only for the two hours or so that they remained in our house.

For me, sitting over in the corner, being seen but not heard, which was the rule for children in those days, it wasn't only what the women talked about—the content—but the way they put things—their style. The insight, irony, wit and humor they brought to their stories and discussions and their poet's inventiveness and daring with language—which of course I could only sense but not define back then.

They had taken the standard English taught them in the primary schools of Barbados and transformed it into an idiom, an instrument that more adequately described them—changing around the syntax and imposing their own rhythm and accent so that the sentences were more pleasing to their ears. They added the few African sounds and words that had survived, such as the derisive suck-teeth sound and the word *yam*, meaning to eat. And to make it more vivid, more in keeping with their expressive quality, they brought to bear a raft of metaphors, parables, biblical quotations, sayings and the like:

"The sea ain' got no back door," they would say, meaning that it wasn't like a house where if there was a fire you could run out the back. Meaning that it was not to be trifled with. And meaning perhaps in a larger sense that man should treat all of nature with caution and respect.

"I has read hell by heart and called every generation blessed!" They sometimes went in for hyperbole.

A woman expecting a baby was never said to be pregnant. They never used that word. Rather, she was "in the way" or, better yet, "tumbling big." "Guess who I butt up on in the market the other day tumbling big again!"

And a woman with a reputation of being too free with her sexual favors was known in their book as a "thoroughfare"—the sense of men like a steady stream of cars moving up and down the road of her life. Or she might be dubbed "a free-bee," which was my favorite of the two. I liked the image it conjured up of a woman scandalous perhaps but independent, who flitted from one flower to another in a garden of male beauties, sampling their nectar, taking her pleasure at will, the roles reversed.

And nothing, no matter how beautiful, was ever described as simply beautiful. It was always "beautiful-ugly": the beautiful-ugly dress, the beautiful-ugly house, the beautiful-ugly car. Why the word *ugly,* I used to wonder, when the thing they were referring to was beautiful, and they knew it. Why the antonym, the contradiction, the linking of opposites? It used to puzzle me greatly as a child.

There is the theory in linguistics which states that the idiom of a people, the way they use language, reflects not only the most fundamental views they hold of themselves and the world but their very conception of reality. Perhaps in using the term *beautiful-ugly* to describe nearly everything, my mother and her friends were expressing what they believed to be a fundamental dualism in life: the idea that a thing is at the same time its opposite, and that these opposites, these contradictions make up the whole. But theirs was not a Manichaean brand of dualism that sees matter, flesh, the body, as inherently evil, because they constantly addressed each other as "soully-gal"—soul: spirit; gal: the body, flesh, the visible self. And it was clear from their tone that they gave one as much weight and importance as the other. They had never heard of the mind/body split.

As for God, they summed up His essential attitude in a phrase. "God," they would say, "don' love ugly and He ain' stuck on pretty."

Using everyday speech, the simple commonplace words—but always with imagination and skill—they gave voice to the most complex ideas. Flannery O'Connor would have approved of how they made ordinary language work, as she put it, "double-time," stretching, shading, deepening its meaning. Like Joseph Conrad they were always trying to infuse new life in the "old old words worn thin . . . by . . . careless usage." And the goals of their oral art were the same as his: "to make you hear, to make you feel . . . to make you *see.*" This was their guiding esthetic.

By the time I was 8 or 9, I graduated from the corner of the kitchen to the neighborhood library, and thus from the spoken to the written word. The Macon Street Branch of the Brooklyn Public Library was an imposing half-block-long edifice of heavy gray masonry, with glass-paneled doors at the front and two tall metal torches symbolizing the light that comes of learning flanking the wide steps outside.

The inside was just as impressive. More steps—of pale marble with gleaming brass railings at the center and sides—led up to the circulation desk, and a great pendulum clock gazed down from the balcony stacks that faced the entrance. Usually stationed at the top of the steps like the guards outside Buckingham Palace was the custodian, a stern-faced West Indian type who for years, until I was old enough to obtain an adult card, would immediately shoo me with one hand into the Children's Room and with the other threaten me into silence, a finger to his lips. You would have thought he was the chief librarian and not just someone whose job it was to keep the brass polished and the clock wound. I put him in a story called "Barbados" years later and had terrible things happen to him at the end.

I sheltered from the storm of adolescence in the Macon Street library, reading voraciously, indiscriminately, everything from Jane Austen to Zane Grey, but with a special passion for the long, full-blown, richly detailed 18th- and 19th-century picaresque tales: *Tom Jones, Great Expectations, Vanity Fair.*

But although I loved nearly everything I read and would enter fully into the lives of the characters—indeed, would cease being myself and become them—I sensed a lack after a time. Something I couldn't quite define was missing. And then one day, browsing in the poetry section, I came across a book by someone called Paul Laurence Dunbar, and opening it I found the photograph of a wistful, sad-eyed poet who to my surprise was black. I turned to a poem at random. "Little brown-baby wif spa'klin' / eyes / Come to yo' pappy an' set on his knee." Although I had a little difficulty at first with the words in dialect, the poem spoke to me as nothing I had read before of the closeness, the special relationship I had had with my father, who by then had become an ardent believer in Father Divine and gone to live in Father's "kingdom" in Harlem. Reading it helped to ease somewhat the tight knot of sorrow and longing I carried around in my chest that refused to go away. I read another poem. " 'Lias! 'Lias! Bless de Lawd! / Don' you know de day's / erbroad? / Ef you don' get up, you scamp / Dey'll be trouble in dis camp." I laughed. It reminded me of the way my mother sometimes yelled at my sister and me to get out of bed in the mornings.

And another: "Seen my lady home las' night / Jump back, honey, jump back. / Hel' huh han' an' sque'z it tight . . ." About love between a black man and a black woman. I had never seen that written about before and it roused in me all kinds of delicious feelings and hopes.

And I began to search then for books and stories and poems about "The Race" (as it was put back then), about my people. While not abandoning Thackeray, Fielding, Dickens and the others, I started asking the reference librarian, who was white, for books by Negro writers, although I must admit I did so at first with a feeling of shame—the shame I and many others used to experience in those days whenever the word *Negro* or *colored* came up.

No grade school literature teacher of mine had ever mentioned Dunbar or James Weldon Johnson or Langston Hughes. I didn't know that Zora Neale Hurston existed and was busy writing and being published during those years. Nor was I made aware of people like Frederick Douglass and Harriet Tubman—their spirit and example—or the great 19th-century abolitionist and feminist Sojourner Truth. There wasn't even Negro History Week when I attended P.S. 35 on Decatur Street!

What I needed, what all the kids—West Indian and native black

American alike—with whom I grew up needed, was an equivalent of the Jewish shul, someplace where we could go after school—the schools that were shortchanging us—and read works by those like ourselves and learn about our history.

It was around that time also that I began harboring the dangerous thought of someday trying to write myself. Perhaps a poem about an apple tree, although I had never seen one. Or the story of a girl who could magically transplant herself to wherever she wanted to be in the world—such as Father Divine's kingdom in Harlem. Dunbar—his dark, eloquent face, his large volume of poems—permitted me to dream that I might someday write, and with something of the power with words my mother and her friends possessed.

When people at readings and writers' conferences ask me who my major influences were, they are sometimes a little disappointed when I don't immediately name the usual literary giants. True, I am indebted to those writers, white and black, whom I read during my formative years and still read for instruction and pleasure. But they were preceded in my life by another set of giants whom I always acknowledge before all others: the group of women around the table long ago. They taught me my first lessons in the narrative art. They trained my ear. They set a standard of excellence. This is why the best of my work must be attributed to them; it stands as testimony to the rich legacy of language and culture they so freely passed on to me in the wordshop of the kitchen.

Vladimir Mayakovsky

Vladimir Mayakovsky was the preeminent poet of the early Soviet Revolution. From 1908 to 1910 he spent time in prison for his political activities. In 1913 at the age of twenty he published his first book of poems, Ya (I). Mayakovsky was jubilant at the success of the Revolution and wrote propaganda for the cause. "Brooklyn Bridge" was written during an extensive tour of the West that included Brooklyn. Disillusioned with Bolshevism, at odds with literary opponents, and despondent over a failed love affair, Mayakovsky killed himself in 1930.

$\mathcal{B}rooklyn$
$\mathcal{B}ridge$ [1]

$\mathcal{G}$ive, Coolidge,

a shout of joy!

I too will spare no words

                  about good things.

Blush

      at my praise,

             go red as our flag,

however

        united-states

              -of-

america you may be.

As a crazed believer

           enters

                a church,

    retreats

[1] This poem was written in 1925 during Mayakovsky's three-month stay in the United States.

into a monastery cell,

austere and plain;

so I,

in graying evening

haze,

humbly set foot

on Brooklyn Bridge.

As a conqueror presses

into a city

all shattered,

on cannon with muzzles

craning high as a giraffe—

so, drunk with glory,

eager to live,

I clamber,

in pride,

upon Brooklyn Bridge.

As a foolish painter

plunges his eye,

sharp and loving,

into a museum madonna,

so I,

from the near skies

bestrewn with stars,

gaze

at New York

through the Brooklyn Bridge.

New York,

heavy and stifling

till night,

has forgotten

its hardships

and height;

and only

the household ghosts

137

ascend
        in the lucid glow of its windows.
Here
        the elevateds
                drone softly.
And only
        their gentle
                droning
tell us:
        here trains
                are crawling and rattling
like dishes
        being cleared into a cupboard.
While
        a shopkeeper fetched sugar
from a mill
        that seemed to project
                        out of the water—
the masts
        passing under the bridge
looked
        no larger than pins.
I am proud
        of just this
                mile of steel;
upon it,
        my visions come to life, erect—
here's a fight
        for construction
                        instead of style,
an austere disposition
                        of bolts
                                and steel.

If
  the end of the world
                befall—
and chaos
        smash our planet
                        to bits,
and what remains
                will be
                        this
bridge, rearing above the dust of destruction;
then,
      as huge ancient lizards
                              are rebuilt
from bones
          finer than needles,
                              to tower in museums,
so,
   from this bridge,
                    a geologist of the centuries
will succeed
            in recreating
                          our contemporary world.
He will say:
            —Yonder paw
                        of steel
once joined
           the seas and the prairies;
from this spot,
               Europe
                      rushed to the West,
scattering
          to the wind
                      Indian feathers.

This rib
            reminds us
                        of a machine—
just imagine,
                would there be hands enough,
after planting
                a steel foot
                            in Manhattan,
to yank
        Brooklyn to oneself
                            by the lip?
By the cables
            of electric strands,
I recognize
            the era succeeding
                            the steam age—
here
    men
        had ranted
                    on radio.
Here
    men
        had ascended
                    in planes.
For some,
            life
                here
                    had no worries;
for others,
            it was a prolonged
                            and hungry howl.

From this spot,
                    jobless men
leapt
        headlong
                    into the Hudson.[2]
Now
        my canvas
                    is unobstructed
as it stretches on cables of string
                            to the feet of the stars.
I see:
        here
                stood Mayakovsky,
stood,
        composing verse, syllable by syllable.
I stare
        as an Eskimo gapes at a train,
I seize on it
                as a tick fastens to an ear.
Brooklyn Bridge—
yes . . .
        That's quite a thing!
(1925)

---

[2] *Hudson:* Mayakovsky confused the Hudson with the East River.

C a r s o n
M c C u l l e r s

Born in Georgia in 1917, Carson McCull-ers was educated at Columbia and the Juilliard School of Music. Her first novel, The Heart Is a Lonely Hunter, *won her instant acclaim. In the early 1940s she lived in a group house in Brooklyn Heights that included an impressive collection of residents—George Davis, literary editor of* Harper's Bazaar, *and W. H. Auden. Theatrical designer Oliver Smith, Anaïs Nin, Leonard Bernstein, Salvador Dalí, Benjamin Britten, and Christopher Isherwood were often visitors. For a while Richard Wright, his wife, and child lived on the parlor floor and the basement. McCullers's novels include* Reflections in a Golden Eye, The Ballad of the Sad Cafe, *and* The Member of the Wedding. *She died in 1967.*

Brooklyn Is My Neighborhood

$\mathcal{B}$rooklyn, in a dignified way, is a fantastic place. The street where I live has a quietness and sense of permanence that seem to belong to the nineteenth century. The street is very short. At one end, there are comfortable old houses, with gracious facades and pleasant backyards in the rear. Down on the next block, the street becomes more heterogeneous, for there is a fire station, a convent, and a small candy factory. The street is bordered with maple trees, and in the autumn the children rake up the leaves and make bonfires in the gutter.

It is strange in New York to find yourself living in a real neighborhood. I buy my coal from the man who lives next door. And I am very curious about the old lady living on my right. She has a mania for picking up stray, starving dogs. Besides a dozen of these dogs, she keeps a little green, shrewd monkey as her pet and chief companion. She is said to be very rich and very stingy. The druggist on the corner has told me she was once in jail for smashing the windows of a saloon in a temperance riot.

"The square of the hypotenuse of a right triangle is equal to—"

On coming into the corner drugstore in the evening, you are apt to hear a desperate voice repeating some such maxim. Mr. Parker, the druggist, sits behind the counter after supper, struggling with his daughter's homework—she can't seem to get on well in school. Mr. Parker has owned his store for thirty years. He has a pale face, with watery grey eyes and a silky little yellow mustache that he wets and combs out frequently. He is rather like a cat. And when I weigh myself, he sidles up quietly beside me and peers over my shoulders as I adjust the scale. When the weights are balanced, he always gives me a quick little glance, but he has never made any comment, nor indicated in any way whether he thought I weighed too little or too much.

On every other subject, Mr. Parker is very talkative. He has always lived in Brooklyn, and his mind is a ragbag for odd scraps of information. For instance, in our neighborhood there is a narrow alley called Love Lane. "The alley comes by its name," he told me, "because more than a century ago two bachelors by the name of DeBevoise lived in the corner house with their niece, a girl of such beauty that her suitors mooned in the alley half the night, writing poetry on the fence." These same old uncles, Mr. Parker added, cultivated the first strawberries sold in New York in their back garden. It is pleasant to think of this old household—the parlor with the colored-glass windows glowing in the candlelight, the two old gentlemen brooding quietly over a game of chess, and the young niece, demure on a footstool, eating strawberries and cream.

"The square of the hypotenuse—" As you go out of the drugstore, Mr. Parker's voice will carry on where he had left off, and his daughter will sit there, sadly popping her chewing gum.

Comparing the Brooklyn that I know with Manhattan is like comparing a comfortable and complacent duenna to her more brilliant and neurotic sister. Things move more slowly out here (the streetcars still rattle leisurely down most of the streets), and there is a feeling for tradition.

144

The history of Brooklyn is not so exciting as it is respectable. In the middle of the past century, many of the liberal intellectuals lived here, and Brooklyn was a hotbed of abolitionist activity. Walt Whitman worked on the *Brooklyn Daily Eagle* until his antislavery editorials cost him his job. Henry Ward Beecher used to preach at the old Plymouth Church. Talleyrand lived here on Fulton Street during his exile in America, and he used to walk primly every day beneath the elm trees. Whittier stayed frequently at the old Hooper home.

The first native of Brooklyn I got to know when first I came out here was the electrician who did some work at my house. He is a lively young Italian with a warm, quick face and a pleasant way of whistling opera arias while on the job. On the third day he was working for me, he brought in a bottle of bright homemade wine, as his first child, a boy, had been born the night before. The wine was sour and clean to the tongue, and when we had drunk some of it the electrician invited me to a little supper to be held a week later at his house on the other side of Brooklyn, near Sheepshead Bay. The party was a fine occasion. The old grandfather who had come over from Italy sixty years ago was there. At night, the old man fishes for eels out in the Bay, and when the weather is fine he spends most of the day lying in a cart in the backyard, out in the sun. He had the face of a charming old satyr, and he held the new baby with the casualness of one who had walked the floor with many babies in his day.

"He is very ugly, this little one," he kept saying. "But it is clear that he will be smart. Smart and very ugly."

The food at the party was rich, wholesome Italian fare—provalone, cheese, salami, pastries, and more of the red wine. A stream of kinsmen and neighbors kept coming in and out of the house all evening. This family had lived in the same house near the Bay for three generations, and the grandfather had not been out of Brooklyn for years.

Here in Brooklyn there is always the feeling of the sea. On the streets near the waterfront, the air has a fresh, coarse smell and there are many sea gulls. One of the most gaudy streets I know stretches between Brooklyn Bridge and the Navy Yard. At three o'clock in the morning, when the rest of the city is silent and dark, you can come suddenly on a little area as vivacious as a country fair. It is Sands Street, the place where sailors spend their evenings when they come here to port. At any hour of the night some excitement is going on in Sands Street. The sunburned sailors swagger up and down the sidewalks with their girls. The bars are crowded and there are dancing, music, and straight liquor at cheap prices.

These Sands Street bars have their own curious traditions also. Some of the women you find there are vivid old dowagers of the street who have such names as the Duchess or Submarine Mary. Every tooth in Submarine Mary's head is made of solid gold—and her smile is rich-looking and satisfied. She and the rest of these old habitués are greatly respected. They have a stable list of sailor pals and are known from Buenos Aires to Zanzibar. They are conscious of their fame and don't bother to dance or flirt like the younger girls, but sit comfortably in the center of the room with their knitting, keeping a sharp eye on all that goes on. In one bar, there is a little hunchback who struts in proudly every evening, and is petted by everyone, given free drinks and treated as a sort of mascot by the proprietor. There is a saying among sailors that when they die they want to go to Sands Street.

Cutting through the business and financial center of Brooklyn is Fulton Street. Here are to be found dozens of junk and antique shops that are exciting to people who like old and fabulous things. I came to be quite at home in these places, as I bought most of my furniture there. If you know what you are about, there are good bargains to be found— old carved sideboards, elegant pier-glasses, beautiful lazy Susans, and other odd pieces can be bought at half the price you would pay any- where else. These shops have a musty, poky atmosphere, and the people who own them are an incredible crew.

The woman from whom I got most of my things is called Miss Kate. She is lean, dark, haggard and she suffers much from cold. When you go into the junkshop, you will most likely find her hovering over a little coal stove in the back room. She sleeps every night wrapped in a Persian rug and lying on a green velvet Victorian couch. She has one of the handsomest and dirtiest faces I can remember.

Across the street from Miss Kate, there is a competitor with whom she often quarrels violently over prices—but she always refers to him as an "adela Menchen," and once when he was to be evicted for failure to pay the rent she put up the cash for him.

"Miss Kate is a good woman," this competitor said to me. "But she dislikes washing herself. She only bathes once a year, when it is summer. I expect she's just about the dirtiest woman in Brooklyn." His voice as he said this was not at all malicious; rather, there was in it a quality of wondering pride. That is one of the things I love best around Brooklyn. Everyone is not expected to be exactly like everyone else.

Alice McDermott

*Alice McDermott has been compared to
Anne Tyler and Mary Gordon. A native
of Long Island, she was influenced both
by her suburban upbringing in the
1960s and her Irish ancestry. She is the
author of dozens of short stories and three
novels:* The Bigamist's Daughter,
That Night, *and* At Weddings and
Wakes. *In this excerpt from* At Weddings and Wakes, *a mother and her
three children visit her stepmother and
three sisters in Brooklyn. The children's
favorite relative is Aunt May, an ex-nun
who introduces them to the mystery of
Brooklyn. McDermott now lives in
Bethesda, Maryland.*

FROM *At*
Weddings AND
Wakes

_____

What greeted them first, despite the noise and the grit and the heat of the sun, was olfactory: diesel fuel and cooking grease and foreign spices, tar and asphalt and the limp, dirty, metallic smell of the train that followed beneath their feet as they walked, blowing itself across their ankles at every subway grate. Then the sounds: language too quick to be sensible speech, so quick that those who spoke it, women and children and men, Puerto Ricans and Lebanese and Russians, perspired heavily with the effort. The traffic, of course, trucks and cabs and horns and somewhere at the soft bottom of these their mother's heels against the sidewalk. Then whatever their eyes could take in as they walked quickly along: fat women sitting on crates, talking and sweating, smiling as they passed, a policeman on a horse, a man with an apron pushing a silver cart full of bottles topped with green nipples and filled with bright red or orange or turquoise-blue water—pushing it in what seemed slow motion as he pulled his

149

feet from the quicksand of the road and, lifting his knees high, placed each foot, toes first, heavily back down again.

They hurried down three stone steps, following her into a narrow cavern with a sinking wooden floor and walls that seemed to be covered with flour. Here the light came from two narrow basement windows, and the heat—it was hotter than anyplace they'd ever been—from the huge brown stove between them, but once again it was the smell that first overtook the three: the warm, prickly rough-textured smell of the loaves of flatbread that the baker, who knew their mother by name, had known her it seemed in some secret lifetime, shoveled hot into a brown paper bag.

On the street she broke three pieces in the bag and handed it to them warm and floury, the inside full of stalactites of dough and air pockets like baked bubbles. "This is the kind of bread," she said, "that Christ ate at the Last Supper." And then finished the loaf herself, her gloves off, and her pace slowed just that much to tell them that she was home after all and as happy—she allowed them to walk a few paces ahead of her—as she'd ever be.

At the apartment the boy was sent up the wide steep stone steps to ring the bell until her sister's face appeared in a top-floor window. There was the flutter of the lace curtain, the two long, pale hands trying the sash, and then, palms turned toward them, the glass itself, until the window slid open just the two inches required to fit between it and the sill the single key in the thin white handkerchief. The children struggled to watch it the four stories it fell and then raced (the boy having returned from the door and the doorbell at a wide-legged run) to be the first to retrieve it from the courtyard or the basement stairs, from among the garbage cans and the baby carriages covered with old shower curtains and planks of wood.

Key in hand, they climbed the steps again and let themselves in through the double glass door framed in heavy wood, across a tiled vestibule that held the cool stone smell of a church, and then into the dim hallway where the air was brown with the reflection of the dark wooden floor and the staircase, with the odor of stewing beef and boiled onions. And yet it was cooler here, cooler than the last part of the morning that they had left on the sidewalk. They climbed the stairs behind their mother—following her example without being told to do so by holding their bare hands as she held her gloved one, just two inches above the wide dusty rail of the banister. One flight and across a narrow hallway with silent doors on either end, another flight, their mother's shoes tapping on each tread and the dull yellow light now passing through an opaque lozenge of white skylight. An identical hallway (voices from behind the far door, again those rushed incomprehensible syllables struck throughout with startling exclamations), another flight, the light growing stronger until it spread itself like a blurred hand over the tops of each of the children's smooth heads. Here on the fourth floor under the dulled and hazy light there was only a single door and the hallway on either side of it was filled with a clutch of cardboard boxes and paper bags. Boxes filled with shoes and Christmas decorations and scraps of material, bags stuffed with magazines and old hats, a clutter of stored and discarded knickknacks and bric-bracs (or so their mother called it) that drew the children to imagine every time some impossible rainy day when their shy request to go inspect the boxes in the hall would be met with something more benign than their mother's or their aunts' appalled consternation.

The single door gave off the purr and rattle that made it seem thick and animate to the children, with an internal life all its own. There was the scratch of the delicate chain, the metallic slither of its bolts, the tumble and click of its lock, and then, slowly, the creak of its hinges.

The face that appeared between the door and its frame was thinner than their mother's and so, for the children, offered no resemblance— despite the same pale blue eyes and light skin and narrow mouth that was, as was their mother's, fighting to resist a grin.

"Well, well," Aunt May said, as if she truly had not expected to see them there. "Here you are!" She smelled like a nun, had been one in fact, and although she wore a shirtwaist dress like their mother's (hers a darker print, small pink roses in lined rows against a navy background) she held herself like a nun as she bent to kiss them—held her bodice with the back of her hand as if to keep a crucifix from swinging into their heads, held back her skirt with the other as if, like a nun, she had veil and sleeve and bib and scapular and long skirt to keep from coming between them.

The children kissed her with the same perfunctory air with which they wiped their feet at the door or genuflected in church, and were delighted, always surprised and delighted, to hear her laugh as soon as the last of them had gone past her, to hear her laugh and hit her palms together and shudder for just one second with her pleasure, with what they easily recognized as her pleasure at seeing them.

Although their mother made these journeys to determine her own fate, to resolve each time her own unhappiness or indecision, they had also heard her say to their father as he drove them home (the decision, for that day at least, made once again), "I go there as much for May as for Momma."

Knowing the routine, the children passed through the narrow living room, across a narrow hallway that after their trek through the length of the subway train seemed cool and surprisingly steady, into, as if it were another subway car, the dining room with its imposing, romantic, highly polished table and eight regal chairs, and there, at the end of the room, before a window that looked out onto the back of identical buildings and a dazzling white line of sun-drenched sheets, in a large soft chair that was covered with terry-cloth but that somehow managed to overwhelm the authority of even the wide-armed end chairs and the broad glass bosom of the hutch, was Momma.

Even the children, whose idea of pretty involved curly ponytails and bangs and puffy silver-pink dresses, recognized that she was beautiful. White face and soft white hair as wide and imposing as a cloud, and eyes so dark they seemed to be made of some element that had nothing to do with any of the familiar elements that made up flesh and bone, lip and skin. Her eyes didn't change to see them, only her mouth smiled. They each kissed her soft, cold cheek and their mother, kissing her, too, offered the bag of Syrian bread so shyly that the children forgot instantly the confident way she had turned into the bakery and greeted the baker by name and ordered the very freshest bread he had—the way she had broken the bread inside the bag and told them, distributing it, This is the bread that Christ ate.

Aunt May was suddenly behind them. "Let me make some sandwiches with it while it's still warm."

Knowing the routine, the children followed her into the narrow kitchen and watched without a word as she took butter and ham from the refrigerator and then a large glass bottle of Coke. She poured the Coke into three tumblers and then placed one tumbler before each of them at the white metal table. Putting it down softly so there would be no click of glass and steel, glancing toward the door as she carefully restopped the bottle, and warning them, every time, with her fingers to her lips, to do the same.

They understood, and savored the soda because of it, that it was not their mother she was afraid of.

From the dining room came their mother's voice embarked, already, on its lament. They understood only that it involved the course of their parents' snagged and unsuitable happiness and that the day would be long. They ate their sandwiches, thick with butter, on a linen tablecloth in the dining room while Aunt May, keeping an eye on them, talked about the weather and the news.

When they were excused they took their comics from the coffee table in the living room, and passing through another narrow vestibule (there was a mouse hole in the corner of the woodwork in this one and a thin cupboard covered with a long piece of chintz), they entered the bright front bedroom, where the older boy and girl took each of the two window seats, the window in one still open the inch or so Aunt May had needed to slip the key underneath. The smallest child sat for a moment before the three mirrors at the dressing table, trying to gauge the distance between herself and the smallest, farthest reflection of a dark-haired little girl.

Inside, their mother had begun again to speak in the stifled and frustrated tone she used only here. The youngest child and her endless reflections got up from the chair, walked to the door beside the night table, and pressed her ear against it, then walked to the double bed (her sister watching her carefully) and, without removing her shoes, stretched out on the chenille spread.

Aunt May spoke and their mother said, "I'm not expecting wine and roses."

In a photograph on the tall dresser at the foot of the bed her mother stood on the stone steps they had climbed just an hour ago, with Momma and Aunt May (a nun then) on one side of her, Aunt Agnes and Aunt Veronica on the other. She was in her wedding dress, a tall veil and a white scoop of neckline, and an armload of long, white flowers crushed around her. Through the bedroom wall behind her the child imagined she could hear Aunt Veronica stirring in her small room, a room the girl had seen only once or twice despite the many hours she had spent in this apartment, a room, she recalled, with fabric walls and pillowed floors and dim light reflected off a glass dressing table covered with jewels, a draped bed, a draped chair, a smell of perfume and the starry-night pinch of alcohol. She listened but suspected the sounds she heard were imaginary, a product of her own wishfulness, for if the day was ever to move forward at any pace at all, Aunt Veronica would have to appear.

At their windows her brother and her sister peered down into the street, to the shadowed door of the candy store they might get Aunt May to take them to, to the deserted playground of another elementary school that was closed for the summer where they might run, shoot imaginary baskets, hop through the painted squares for potsy which were now burning white in the city sun. There was another row of stores beyond the school's back fence, signless, mostly nondescript storefronts where, they had been told at various times, mattresses were made, ladies' lace collars, bow ties, church bulletins.

Once, sitting here, they had passed an hour watching bales of something, paper or cotton, being pulled hand over hand, one bale after the other, up from the street and into a third-story window. And once, their chins buried into their chests and their foreheads flat against the glass, they had watched a man in broad daylight walk on wobbly rubber legs from one edge of the sidewalk below them to another until he fell, all in a heap, between the fenders of two cars, and then, after some minutes, pulled himself up, peered over his forearm and the trunk of the first car like a man at the edge of a pool, and then righted himself and began his snaking progress all over again.

But today there was no such luck and when they had watched long enough for it they returned once again to the comics on their knees.

154

In the dining room their mother said, "But who thinks of me?" Aunt May's reply was too soft for them to understand. "A little happiness," their mother said, and then said again, "I don't know. Some peace before I die. I don't know."

She didn't know. The children understood this much about her discontent, if nothing more. She didn't know its source or its rationale, and although she brought it here to Brooklyn twice a week in every week of summer and laid it like the puzzling pieces of a broken clock there on the dining-room table before them, she didn't know what it was she wanted them to do for her. She was feeling unhappy, she was feeling her life passing by. She hated seeing her children grow up. She hated being exiled from the place she had grown up in. She feared the future and its inevitable share of sorrow.

"The good things," they heard Aunt May tell her, and their mother replied that she'd counted the good things until she was blue in the face. Against the silence they heard the teacups being gathered and children shouting in the playground across the street.

Knowing the routine, they knew that when Aunt May next came into the room, holding her wrists in her hands although she no longer hid them under a nun's sleeves, it would be to tell them that Momma was coming in for her nap now, if they would please. And sure enough, just as the game outside was getting interesting, there she was with the old woman behind her, as white and broad as a god.

She was not their natural mother but the sister of the woman who had borne them and who had died with Veronica, the last. Momma had married the girls' father when Agnes, the oldest, was seven. He had died within that same year and so there had been no chance, the three children understood in their own adulthood, for any of the half-hearted and reluctant emotion that stepmothers are said to inspire to form between them: within the same year as her arrival she quickly became not merely a stranger to resent and accommodate but the only living adult to whom they were of any value.

The children stood as Momma moved into the room. She was a short woman but serious and erect and wide-bosomed and it wasn't until the very last month of her life that any sense of fragility entered her old age, and even then it entered so swiftly and with such force, her flesh falling away from her bones in three quick weeks, that it hardly seemed appropriate to call the result of such a ravaging fragile. (Seeing her sunk into her coffin, the cartilage of her nose and the bones of her cheeks and wrists pressing into her skin, the three children, teenagers by then, would each be struck with a shocking, a terrifying notion: she had not wanted to die; she had, even at ninety, fought furiously against it.)

They passed her one by one as she stood between the dresser and the foot of the bedstead, the same small smile she had worn when she greeted them still on her lips. When they were gone Aunt May quietly closed the door.

The living room was a narrow and windowless passthrough, a large green horsehair couch on one side and a sealed white fireplace on the other, before which stood the coffee table with its lace doily and ceramic basket of waxed flowers. There was another ancient, overstuffed chair in the corner beside it and a large brass bucket filled with magazines, which the children, in their routine, next went to. They were Aunt Agnes's magazines, just as every book and newspaper and record album in the place belonged to Agnes. They were the singularly most uninteresting magazines the children had ever seen: *New Yorker*s with more print than pictures and cartoons that were not funny. *Atlantic Monthly*s without even the nonsensical cartoons, *Fortune, Harper's.* There were a handfull of *Playbill*s and these the older girl took to read once again (she had read them last week) the biographies of the actors and actresses, and two *National Geographic*s for the boy, and, finally, a single limp copy of *Life* magazine that featured on its cover a formal portrait of President Kennedy edged in black and inside (the younger girl found the place immediately) a full-page photograph of Mrs. Kennedy in her black veil, a dark madonna that the younger girl studied carefully on the worn Oriental rug.

"I know you children are going to put all these magazines back," Aunt May said as she passed through to rejoin their mother in the kitchen.

"Yes," they said, and watched her pick her way through the slick magazines, her pale thin legs in the same thick stockings Momma wore, her feet in the same brown oxfords. In their secret hearts they wished to see her slip on one of the magazines, see her rise for one second into the air like a levitated woman (garters and bloomers showing) and then fall crashing back, their mother running in from the kitchen, Momma pulling open the bedroom door—the noise, the excitement, the drama swallowing up at least one long half hour of the long and endless afternoon.

She safely reached the end of the room and then turned to say, in a whisper, "How about in a minute or two we go across the street for a treat?"

And so they got their easy half hour, anyway. They thundered ahead of her down the stairs ("Careful, careful," she whispered, but smiling, admiring how many steps they could leap at each landing) and crossed with her, her hand on the two girls' shoulders, between two parked cars. They chose bags of pistachio nuts from the candy store that seemed to them to be the authentic version of the one in their own neighborhood where they had bought their comics that morning. Here the man who took their money had only two fingers on his left hand and a four-digit number burned into his arm and the accent with which he spoke was to the children a Brooklyn accent, a city accent, as were the accents of all the people on the street and most of the grandparents of their friends, as was Momma's brogue.

In the street again, Aunt May let them sit on the low wall of the schoolyard that was once again deserted as they ate their pistachios and tossed the bright red shells into the street. She was, the children understood, cracking and tossing and leaning back against the fence to stay in the school's shade, the one of their mother's sisters most determined to be happy and, although she treated joy as a kind of contraband, sneaking them glasses of Coke, bags of pistachios, folded dollar bills, showing the great pleasure she took in their company at brief moments when no one else was looking (as she was doing now, holding her pale face and flashing glasses to the sun, swinging her legs against the wall like a girl), she was for the most part successful.

Her fifteen years in the convent had included some part of each of the children's lives and each, even the youngest, had some memory of her in her wimple and veil and long robes, robes that she seemed to use like a magician's cape, pulling from them as if from thin air the prettiest gifts: gilt-edged holy cards, miniature glass rosaries, a ceramic baby Jesus that the younger girl could cup in her palm. Each had some memory of her small face smiling at them from the circle of her habit as she slipped them these gifts; each at some point had had the impression that the habit was a kind of disguise, something she used only to gain access to the places where these lovely things were kept—only so she could swipe them and hide them in her robes and then, smiling, present them to her sister's children when no one else was looking.

And then, some years ago, Momma had spent the night in their parents' room (their parents moving into the girls' room, the girls into their brother's, their brother to the couch, in what was an illogical but equitable arrangement sure to guarantee each member of the family equal discomfort). In the morning their father drove them all to a convent, a lovely old white house surrounded by gardens and woods. It was a beautiful day in late spring and the air there smelled of the sea. There were white garden swings, freshly painted, here and there throughout the woods and most of the paths led to small grottoes where the ceramic face of the Sacred Heart or the Blessed Mother, Saint Francis and Saint Anthony, hung from the trunk of a tree. The children rocked the swings and ran down the paths and once or twice with elaborate ceremony knelt down to pray while their father read the newspaper in the car and Momma and their mother visited inside the convent.

Just as they were growing tired, even of that holy, enchanted place, and had begun to look around for something else, they saw Momma and their mother and Aunt May coming down the white steps of the house. They didn't recognize her at first, her hair was curly and short, pale red, and she wore a loose black suit that they knew had belonged to their mother, but then the sun caught her glasses as she glanced up at the sky.

The three women were halfway to the car before their father saw them and then he hurried to put the paper down and get out to open the back door. When the three women had slid in, he shut the door with great gentleness and then, with some sudden impatience, called to the three children. They rode all the way to Brooklyn squeezed beside him in the front seat and only got out to rearrange themselves when they got to Momma's street. Aunt May touched their hair before she and Momma climbed the steps to the door, to what would become the rest of her life. She touched their hair and brushed their cheeks and pressed into the hands of each a damp dollar bill folded to the size of a Chiclet.

Henry Miller

Henry Miller's family moved to the Williamsburg section of Brooklyn from Manhattan when he was a baby. Miller wrote of his Brooklyn boyhood, "From five to ten were the most important years of my life. I lived in the street and acquired the typical American gangster spirit." After a brief stint in college, Miller hawked his poetry door-to-door, then took a job with Western Union Telegraph before leaving for Paris in 1930. His nine years in Paris were his most productive, and he wrote Tropic of Cancer, Black Spring, and Tropic of Capricorn. "The Fourteenth Ward" appeared in Black Spring. Miller wove autobiography, philosophy, humor, and sex in his work. By the end of his life in 1980, Miller was better known as an American expatriate than as a Brooklyn native. However, he proudly proclaimed himself a "patriot—of the Fourteenth Ward" and always insisted that he was "just a Brooklyn boy."

in the open
at is called
't matter
he ocean
er the
No
ays
i:

Λ

I am a patriot—of the Fourteenth Ward, Brooklyn, where I was raised. The rest of the United States doesn't exist for me, except as idea, or history, or literature. At ten years of age I was uprooted from my native soil and removed to a cemetery, a *Lutheran* cemetery, where the tombstones were always in order and the wreaths never faded.

But I was born in the street and raised in the street. "The post-mechanical open street where the most beautiful and hallucinating iron vegetation," etc. . . . Born under the sign of Aries which gives a fiery, active, energetic and somewhat restless body. *With Mars in the ninth house!*

To be born in the street means to wander all your life, to be free. It means accident and incident, drama, movement. It means above all dream. A harmony of irrelevant facts which gives to your wandering a metaphysical certitude. In the street you learn what human beings really

161

are; otherwise, or afterwards, you invent them. What is n[o]
street is false, derived, that is to say, *literature*. Nothing of w[hat]
"adventure" ever approaches the flavor of the street. It does[n't matter]
whether you fly to the Pole, whether you sit on the floor of t[he]
with a pad in your hand, whether you pull up nine cities one a[fter the]
other, or whether, like Kurtz, you sail up the river and go ma[d. No]
matter how exciting, how intolerable the situation, there are al[ways]
exits, always ameliorations, comforts, compensations, newspapers, re[li-]
gions. But once there was none of this. Once you were free, wild[,]
murderous. . . .

The boys you worshiped when you first came down into the street
remain with you all your life. They are the only real heroes. Napoleon,
Lenin, Capone—all fiction. Napoleon is nothing to me in comparison
with Eddie Carney, who gave me my first black eye. No man I have ever
met seems as princely, as regal, as noble, as Lester Reardon, who, by the
mere act of walking down the street, inspired fear and admiration. Jules
Verne never led me to the places that Stanley Borowski had up his sleeve
when it came dark. Robinson Crusoe lacked imagination in comparison
with Johnny Paul. All these boys of the Fourteenth Ward have a flavor
about them still. They were not invented or imagined: they were real.
Their names ring out like gold coins—Tom Fowler, Jim Buckley, Matt
Owen, Rob Ramsay, Harry Martin, Johnny Dunne, to say nothing of
Eddie Carney or the great Lester Reardon. Why, even now when I say
Johnny Paul the names of the saints leave a bad taste in my mouth.
Johnny Paul was the living Odyssey of the Fourteenth Ward; that he
later became a truck driver is an irrelevant fact.

Before the great change no one seemed to notice that the streets
were ugly or dirty. If the sewer mains were opened you held your nose.
If you blew your nose you found snot in your handkerchief and not your
nose. There was more of inward peace and contentment. There was the
saloon, the race track, bicycles, fast women and trot horses. Life was still
moving along leisurely. In the Fourteenth Ward, at least. Sunday mornings no one was dressed. If Mrs. Gorman came down in her wrapper
with dirt in her eyes to bow to the priest—"Good morning, Father!"
"Good morning, Mrs. Gorman!"—the street was purged of all sin. Pat

162

McCarren carried his handkerchief in the tailflap of his frock coat; it was nice and handy there, like the shamrock in his buttonhole. The foam was on the lager and people stopped to chat with one another.

In my dreams I come back to the Fourteenth Ward as a paranoiac returns to his obsessions. When I think of those steel-gray battleships in the Navy Yard I see them lying there in some astrologic dimension in which I am the gunnersmith, the chemist, the dealer in high explosives, the undertaker, the coroner, the cuckold, the sadist, the lawyer and contender, the scholar, the restless one, the jolt-head, and the brazen-faced.

Where others remember of their youth a beautiful garden, a fond mother, a sojourn at the seashore, I remember, with a vividness as if it were etched in acid, the grim, soot-covered walls and chimneys of the tin factory opposite us and the bright, circular pieces of tin that were strewn in the street, some bright and gleaming, others rusted, dull, copperish, leaving a stain on the fingers; I remember the ironworks where the red furnace glowed and men walked toward the glowing pit with huge shovels in their hands, while outside were the shallow wooden forms like coffins with rods through them on which you scraped your shins or broke your neck. I remember the black hands of the ironmolders, the grit that had sunk so deep into the skin that nothing could remove it, not soap, nor elbow grease, nor money, nor love, nor death. Like a black mark on them! Walking into the furnace like devils with black hands—and later, with flowers over them, cool and rigid in their Sunday suits, not even the rain can wash away the grit. All these beautiful gorillas going up to God with swollen muscles and lumbago and black hands. . . .

For me the whole world was embraced in the confines of the Fourteenth Ward. If anything happened outside it either didn't happen or it was unimportant. If my father went outside that world to fish it was of no interest to me. I remember only his boozy breath when he came home in the evening and opening the big green basket spilled the squirming, goggle-eyed monsters on the floor. If a man went off to the war I remember only that he came back of a Sunday afternoon and standing in front of the minister's house puked up his guts and then

163

wiped it up with his vest. Such was Rob Ramsay, the minister's son. I remember that everybody liked Rob Ramsay—he was the black sheep of the family. They liked him because he was a good-for-nothing and he made no bones about it. Sundays or Wednesdays made no difference to him: you could see him coming down the street under the drooping awnings with his coat over his arm and the sweat rolling down his face; his legs wobbly, with that long, steady roll of a sailor coming ashore after a long cruise; the tobacco juice dribbling from his lips, together with warm, silent curses and some loud and foul ones too. The utter indolence, the insouciance of the man, the obscenities, the sacrilege. Not a man of God, like his father. No, a man who inspired love! His frailties were human frailties and he wore them jauntily, tauntingly, flauntingly, like banderillas. He would come down the warm open street with the gas mains bursting and the air full of sun and shit and oaths and maybe his fly would be open and his suspenders undone, or maybe his vest bright with vomit. Sometimes he came charging down the street, like a bull skidding on all fours, and then the street cleared magically, as if the manholes had opened up and swallowed their offal. Crazy Willy Maine would be standing on the shed over the paint shop, with his pants down, jerking away for dear life. There they stood in the dry electrical crackle of the open street with the gas mains bursting. A tandem that broke the minister's heart.

That was how he was then, Rob Ramsay. A man on a perpetual spree. He came back from the war with medals, and with fire in his guts. He puked up in front of his own door and he wiped up his puke with his own vest. He could clear the street quicker than a machine gun. *Faugh a balla!* That was his way. And a little later, in his warmheartedness, in that fine, careless way he had, he walked off the end of a pier and drowned himself.

I remember him so well and the house he lived in. Because it was on the doorstep of Rob Ramsay's house that we used to congregate in the warm summer evenings and watch the goings-on over the saloon across the street. A coming and going all night long and nobody bothered to pull down the shades. Just a stone's throw away from the little burlesque house called The Bum. All around The Bum were the saloons, and Saturday nights there was a long line outside, milling and pushing and squirming to get at the ticket window. Saturday nights, when the Girl in Blue was in her glory, some wild tar from the Navy Yard would be sure to jump out of his seat and grab off one of Millie de Leon's garters. And a little later that night they'd be sure to come strolling down the street and turn in at the family entrance. And soon they'd be standing in the bedroom over the saloon, pulling off their tight pants and the women yanking off their corsets and scratching themselves like monkeys, while down below they were scuttling the suds and biting each other's ears off, and such a wild, shrill laughter all bottled up inside there, like dynamite evaporating. All this from Rob Ramsay's doorstep, the old man upstairs saying his prayers over a kerosene lamp, praying like an obscene nanny goat for an end to come, or when he got tired of praying coming down in his nightshirt, like an old leprechaun, and belaying us with a broomstick.

From Saturday afternoon on until Monday morning it was a period without end, one thing melting into another. Saturday morning already—how it happened God only knows—you could *feel* the war vessels lying at anchor in the big basin. Saturday mornings my heart was in my mouth. I could see the decks being scrubbed down and the guns polished and the weight of those big sea monsters resting on the dirty glass lake of the basin was a luxurious weight on me. I was already dreaming of running away, of going to far places. But I got only as far as the other side of the river, about as far north as Second Avenue and Twenty-eighth Street, via the Belt Line. There I played the Orange Blossom Waltz and in the entr'actes I washed my eyes at the iron sink. The piano stood in the rear of the saloon. The keys were very yellow and my feet wouldn't reach to the pedals. I wore a velvet suit because velvet was the order of the day.

Everything that passed on the other side of the river was sheer lunacy: the sanded floor, the argand lamps, the mica pictures in which the snow never melted, the crazy Dutchmen with steins in their hands, the iron sink that had grown such a mossy coat of slime, the woman from Hamburg whose ass always hung over the back of the chair, the courtyard choked with sauerkraut. . . . Everything in three-quarter time that goes on forever. I walk between my parents, with one hand in my mother's muff and the other in my father's sleeve. My eyes are shut tight, tight as clams which draw back their lids only to weep.

All the changing tides and weather that passed over the river are in my blood. I can still feel the slipperiness of the big handrail which I leaned against in fog and rain, which sent through my cool forehead the shrill blasts of the ferryboat as she slid out of the slip. I can still see the mossy planks of the ferry slip buckling as the big round prow grazed her sides and the green, juicy water sloshed through the heaving, groaning planks of the slip. And overhead the sea gulls wheeling and diving, making a dirty noise with their dirty beaks, a hoarse, preying sound of inhuman feasting, of mouths fastened down on refuse, of scabby legs skimming the green-churned water.

One passes imperceptibly from one scene, one age, one life to another. Suddenly, walking down a street, be it real or be it a dream, one realizes for the first time that the years have flown, that all this has passed forever and will live on only in memory; and then the memory turns inward with a strange, clutching brilliance and one goes over these scenes and incidents perpetually, in dream and reverie, while walking a street, while lying with a woman, while reading a book, while talking to a stranger . . . suddenly, but always with terrific insistence and always with terrific accuracy, these memories intrude, rise up like ghosts and permeate every fiber of one's being. Henceforward everything moves on shifting levels—our thoughts, our dreams, our actions, our whole life. A parallelogram in which we drop from one platform of our scaffold to another. Henceforward we walk split into myriad fragments, like an insect with a hundred feet, a centipede with soft-stirring feet that drinks in the atmosphere; we walk with sensitive filaments that drink avidly of past and future, and all things melt into music and sorrow; we walk against a united world, asserting our dividedness. All things, as we walk, splitting with us into a myriad of iridescent fragments. The great fragmentation of maturity. The great change. In youth we were whole and the terror and pain of the world penetrated us through and through. There was no sharp separation between joy and sorrow: they fused into one, as our waking life fuses with dream and sleep. We rose one being in the morning and at night we went down into an ocean, drowned out completely, clutching the stars and the fever of the day.

And then comes a time when suddenly all seems to be reversed. We live in the mind, in ideas, in fragments. We no longer drink in the wild outer music of the streets—we *remember* only. Like a monomaniac we relive the drama of youth. Like a spider that picks up the thread over and over and spews it out according to some obsessive, logarithmic pattern. If we are stirred by a fat bust it is the fat bust of a whore who bent over on a rainy night and showed us for the first time the wonder of the great milky globes; if we are stirred by the reflections on a wet pavement it is because at the age of seven we were suddenly speared by a premonition of the life to come as we stared unthinkingly into that bright, liquid mirror of the street. If the sight of a swinging door intrigues us it is the memory of a summer's evening when all the doors were swinging softly and where the light bent down to caress the shadow there were golden calves and lace and glittering parasols and through the chinks in the swinging door, like fine sand sifting through a bed of rubies, there drifted the music and the incense of gorgeous unknown bodies. Perhaps when that door parted to give us a choking glimpse of the world, perhaps then we had the first intimation of the great impact of sin, the first intimation that here over little round tables spinning in the light, our feet idly scraping the sawdust, our hands touching the cold stem of a glass, that here over these little round tables which later we are to look at with such yearning and reverence, that here, I say, we are to feel in the years to come the first iron of love, the first stains of rust, the first black, clawing hands of the pit, the bright circular pieces of tin in the streets, the gaunt soot-colored chimneys, the bare elm tree that lashes out in the summer's lightning and screams and shrieks as the rain beats down, while out of the hot earth the snails scoot away miraculously and all the air turns blue and sulphurous. Here over these tables, at the first call, the first touch of a hand, there is to come the bitter, gnawing pain that gripes at the bowels; the wine turns sour in our bellies and a pain rises from the soles of the feet and the round tabletops whirl with the anguish and the fever in our bones at the soft, burning touch of a hand. Here there is buried legend after legend of youth and melancholy, of savage nights and mysterious bosoms dancing on the wet mirror of the pavement, of women chuckling softly as they scratch themselves, of wild sailors' shouts, of long queues standing in front of the lobby, of boats brushing each other in the fog and tugs snorting furiously against the rush of tide while up on the Brooklyn Bridge a man is standing in agony, waiting to jump, or waiting to write a poem, or waiting for the blood to leave his vessels because if he advances another foot the pain of his love will kill him.

The plasm of the dream is the pain of separation. The dream lives on after the body is buried. We walk the streets with a thousand legs and eyes, with furry antennae picking up the slightest clue and memory of the past. In the aimless to and fro we pause now and then, like long, sticky plants, and we swallow whole the live morsels of the past. We open up soft and yielding to drink in the night and the oceans of blood which drowned the sleep of our youth. We drink and drink with an insatiable thirst. We are never whole again, but living in fragments, and all our parts separated by thinnest membrane. Thus when the fleet maneuvers in the Pacific it is the whole saga of youth flashing before your eyes, the dream of the open street and the sound of gulls wheeling and diving with garbage in their beaks; or it's the sound of the trumpet and flags flying and all the unknown parts of the earth sailing before your eyes without dates or meaning, wheeling like the tabletop in an iridescent sheen of power and glory. Day comes when you stand on the Brooklyn Bridge looking down into black funnels belching smoke and the gun barrels gleam and the buttons gleam and the water divides miraculously under the sharp, cutting prow, and like ice and lace, like a breaking and a smoking, the water churns green and blue with a cold incandescence, with the chill of champagne and burnt gills. And the prow cleaves the waters in an unending metaphor: the heavy body of the vessel moves on, with the prow ever dividing, and the weight of her is the unweighable weight of the world, the sinking down into unknown barometric pressures, into unknown geologic fissures and caverns where the waters roll melodiously and the stars turn over and die and hands reach up and grasp and clutch and never seize nor close but clutch and grasp while the stars die out one by one, myriads of them, myriads and myriads of worlds sinking down into cold incandescence, into fuliginous night of green and blue with broken ice and the burn of champagne and the hoarse cry of gulls, their beaks swollen with barnacles, their foul garbaged mouths stuffed forever under the silent keel of the ship.

One looks down from the Brooklyn Bridge on a spot of foam or a little lake of gasoline or a broken splinter or an empty scow; the world goes by upside down with pain and light devouring the innards, the sides of flesh bursting, the spears pressing in against the cartilage, the very armature of the body floating off into nothingness. Passes through you crazy words from the ancient world, signs and portents, the writing on the wall, the chinks of the saloon door, the cardplayers with their clay pipes, the gaunt tree against the tin factory, the black hands stained even in death. One walks the street at night with the bridge against the sky like a harp and the festered eyes of sleep burn into the shanties, deflower the walls; the stairs collapse in a smudge and the rats scamper across the ceiling; a voice is nailed against the door and long creepy things with furry antennae and thousand legs drop from the pipes like beads of sweat. Glad, murderous ghosts with the shriek of night-wind and the curses of warm-legged men; low, shallow coffins with rods through the body; grief-spit drooling down into the cold, waxen flesh, searing the dead eyes, the hard, chipped lids of dead clams. One walks around in a circular cage on shifting levels, stars and clouds under the escalator, and the walls of the cage revolve and there are no men and women without tails or claws, while over all things are written the letters of the alphabet in iron and permanganate. One walks round and round in a circular cage to the roll of drum-fire; the theater burns and the actors go on mouthing their lines; the bladder bursts, the teeth fall out, but the wailing of the clown is like the noise of dandruff falling. One walks around on moonless nights in the valley of craters, valley of dead fires and whitened skulls, of birds without wings. Round and round one walks, seeking the hub and nodality, but the fires are burned to ash and the sex of things is hidden in the finger of a glove.

And then one day, as if suddenly the flesh came undone and the blood beneath the flesh had coalesced with the air, suddenly the whole world roars again and the very skeleton of the body melts like wax. Such

169

a day it may be when first you encounter Dostoyevski. You remember the smell of the tablecloth on which the book rests; you look at the clock and it is only five minutes from eternity; you count the objects on the mantelpiece because the sound of numbers is a totally new sound in your mouth, because everything new and old, or touched and forgotten, is a fire and a mesmerism. Now every door of the cage is open and whichever way you walk is a straight line toward infinity, a straight, mad line over which the breakers roar and great rocs of marble and indigo swoop to lower their fevered eggs. Out of the waves beating phosphorescent step proud and prancing the enameled horses that marched with Alexander, their tight-proud bellies glowing with calcium, their nostrils dipped in laudanum. Now it is all snow and lice, with the great band of Orion slung around the ocean's crotch.

It was exactly five minutes past seven, at the corner of Broadway and Kosciusko Street, when Dostoyevski first flashed across my horizon. Two men and a woman were dressing a shop window. From the middle of the upper legs down the mannikins were all wire. Empty shoe boxes lay banked against the window like last year's snow. . . .

That is how Dostoyevski's name came in. Unostentatiously. Like an old shoe box. The Jew who pronounced his name for me had thick lips; he could not say Vladivostok, for instance, nor Carpathians—but he could say Dostoyevski divinely. Even now, when I say Dostoyevski, I see again his big, blubbery lips and the thin thread of spittle stretching like a rubber band as he pronounced the word. Between his two front teeth there was a more than usual space; it was exactly in the middle of this cavity that the word Dostoyevski quivered and stretched, a thin, iridescent film of sputum in which all the gold of twilight had collected— for the sun was just going down over Kosciusko Street and the traffic overhead was breaking into a spring thaw, a chewing and grinding noise as if the mannikins in their wire legs were chewing each other alive. A little later, when I came to the land of the Houyhnhnms, I heard the same chewing and grinding overhead and again the spittle in a man's mouth quivered and stretched and shone iridescent in a dying sun. This time it is at the Dragon's Gorge: a man standing over me with a rattan stick and banging away with a wild Arabian smile. Again, as if my brain

170

were a uterus, the walls of the world gave way. The name Swift was like a clear, hard pissing against the tin-plate lid of the world. Overhead the green fire-eater, his delicate intestines wrapped in tarpaulin; two enormous milk-white teeth champing down over a belt of black-greased cogs connecting with the shooting gallery and the Turkish baths; the belt of cogs slipping over a frame of bleached bones. The green dragon of Swift moves over the cogs with an endless pissing sound, grinding down fine and foreshortened the human-sized midgets that are sucked in like macaroni. In and out of the esophagus, up and down and around the scapular bones and the mastoid delta, falling through the bottomless pit of the viscera, gurgitating and exgurgitating, the crotch spreading and slipping, the cogs moving on relentlessly, chewing alive all the fine, foreshortened macaroni hanging by the whiskers from the dragon's red gulch. I look into the milk-white smile of the barker, that fanatical Arabian smile which came out of the Dreamland fire, and then I step quietly into the open belly of the dragon. Between the crazy slats of the skeleton that holds the revolving cogs the land of the Houyhnhnms spreads out before me; that hissing, pissing noise in my ears as if the language of men were made of seltzer water. Up and down over the greasy black belt, over the Turkish baths, through the house of the winds, over the sky-blue waters, between the clay pipes and the silver balls dancing on liquid jets: the infra-human world of fedoras and banjos, of bandannas and black cigars; butterscotch stretching from peg to Winnipeg, beer bottles bursting, spun-glass molasses and hot tamales, surf-roar and griddle sizzle, foam and eucalyptus, dirt, chalk, confetti, a woman's white thigh, a broken oar; the razzle-dazzle of wooden slats, the Meccano puzzle, the smile that never comes off, the wild Arabian smile with spits of fire, the red gulch and the green intestines. . . .

O world, strangled and collapsed, where are the strong white teeth? O world, sinking with the silver balls and the corks and the life-preservers, where are the rosy scalps? O glab and glairy, O glabrous world now chewed to a frazzle, under what dead moon do you lie cold and gleaming?

Marianne Moore

Brooklyn was poet Marianne Moore's home during the middle of her life. Born in St. Louis, Missouri, and educated at Bryn Mawr College, Moore moved to Brooklyn in 1931 and lived in the Fort Greene neighborhood for more than thirty years. "The Camperdown Elm" is typical of Moore's poetry, with its wit and natural imagery. Although she moved to Greenwich Village at the end of her life, Moore's memorial service in 1972 was held at the Lafayette Presbyterian Church, the Brooklyn church she devotedly attended twice a week.

The Camperdown Elm

Gift of Mr. A. G. Burgess to Prospect Park, Brooklyn, 1872.

I think, in connection with this weeping elm,
of "Kindred Spirits" at the edge of a rockledge
           overlooking a stream:
Thanatopsis-invoking tree-loving Bryant
conversing with Thomas Cole
in Asher Durand's painting of them
under the filigree of an elm overhead.

No doubt they had seen other trees—lindens,
maples and sycamores, oaks and the Paris
street-tree, the horse-chestnut; but imagine
their rapture, had they come on the Camperdown elm's
massiveness and "the intricate pattern of its branches,"
arching high, curving low, in its mist of fine twigs.
The Bartlett tree-cavity specialist saw it
and thrust his arm the whole length of the hollowness
of its torso and there were six small cavities also.

Props are needed and tree-food. It is still leafing;
still there. *Mortal* though. We must save it. It is
           our crowning curio.

173

Ernest Poole

Born in Chicago in 1880, Ernest Poole attended Princeton. After graduation he went to work in settlement houses in New York and wrote muckraking articles about the conditions in the sweat shops of the Lower East Side. Poole's first novel, The Harbor, from which this is excerpted, was published in 1915 and was a best-seller. The Harbor portrays proletarian America, a land of immigrants' dreams. Two years later Poole wrote His Family, which won a Pulitzer Prize. Many novels followed, some based on his visits to Russia, but none lived up to the promise of The Harbor. Poole died in 1950.

FROM *The Harbor*

$\mathcal{A}$s I walked home from church with my mother that day the streets seemed as quiet and safe as her eyes. How suddenly tempting it seemed to me, this quiet and this safety, compared to the place where I was going. For I had decided to run away from my home and my mother that afternoon, down to the harbor to see the world. What would become of me 'way down there? What would she do if I never came back? A lump rose in my throat at the thought of her tears. It was terrible.

"All the same I am going to do it," I kept thinking doggedly. And yet suddenly, as we reached our front steps, how near I came to telling her. But no, she would only spoil it all. She wanted me always up in the garden, she wanted me never to have any thrills.

My mother knew me so well. She had seen that when she read stories of fairies, witches and goblins out of my books to Sue and me, while Sue, though two years younger, would sit there like a little dark imp, her

175

black eyes snapping over the fights, I would creep softly out of the room, ashamed and shaken, and would wait in the hall outside till the happy ending was in plain view. So my mother had gradually toned down all the fights and the killings, the witches and the monsters, and much to my disappointment had wholly shut out the gory pirates who were for me the most frightfully fascinating of all. Sometimes I felt vaguely that for this she had her own reason, too—that my mother hated everything that had to do with the ocean, especially my father's dock that made him so gloomy and silent. But of this I could never be quite sure. I would often watch her intently, with a sudden sharp anxiety, for I loved my mother with all my soul and I could not bear to see her unhappy.

"Never on any account," I heard her say to Belle, "are the children to go down the street toward the docks."

"Yes, ma'am," said Belle. "I'll see to it."

At once I wanted to go there. The street in front of our house sloped abruptly down at the next corner two blocks through poorer and smaller houses to a cobblestone space below, over which trucks clattered, plainly on their way to the docks. So I could go down and around by that way. How tempting it all looked down there. Above the roofs of the houses, the elevated railroad made a sharp bend on its way to the Bridge, trains roared by, high over all the Great Bridge swept across the sky. And below all this and more thrilling than all, I caught glimpses of strange, ragged boys. "Micks," Belle sometimes called them, and sometimes, "Finian Mickies." Up here I had no playmates.

From now on, our garden lost its charms. Up the narrow courtway which ran along the side of the house I would slip stealthily to the front gate and often get a good look down the street before Belle sharply called me back. The longest looks, I found, were always on Sunday afternoons, when Belle would sit back there in the garden, close to the bed of red tulips which encircled a small fountain made of two white angels. Belle, who was bony, tall and grim, would sit by the little angels reading her shabby Bible. Her face was wrinkled and almost brown, her eyes now kind, now gloomy. She had a song she would sing now and then. "For beneath the Union Jack we will drive the Finians back"—is all I can remember. She told me of witches in the Scotch hills. At her touch horrible monsters rose in the most surprising places. In the bathtub, for example, when I stayed in the bath too long she would jerk out the stopper, and as from the hole there came a loud gurgle—"It's the Were-shark," Belle would mutter. And I would leap out trembling.

This old "Were-shark" had his home in the very middle of the ocean. In one gulp he could swallow a boy of my size, and this he did three times each day. The boys were brought to him by the "Condor," a perfectly hideous bird as large as a cow and as fierce as a tiger. If ever I dared go down that street and disobey my mother, the Condor would "swoop" down over the roofs, snatch me up in his long yellow beak with the blood of the last boy on it, and with thunder and lightning would carry me off far over the clouds and drop me into the Were-shark's mouth.

Then Belle would sit down to her Bible.

Sunday after Sunday passed, and still in fascinated dread I would steal quietly out to the gate and watch this street forbidden. Pointing to it one day, Belle had declared in awful tones, "Broad is the way that leadeth to destruction." But it was not broad. In that at least she was all wrong. It was in fact so narrow that a Condor as big as a cow might easily bump himself when he "swooped." Besides, there were good strong lamp-posts where a little boy could cling and scream, and almost always somewhere in sight was a policeman so fat and heavy that even two Condors could hardly lift him from the ground. This policeman would come running. My mother had said I must never be scared by policemen, because they were really good kind men. In fact, she said, it was foolish to be scared by anything ever. She never knew of Belle's methods with me.

So at last I had decided to risk it, and now the fearful day had come. I could barely eat my dinner. My courage was fast ebbing away. In the dining-room the sunlight was for a time wiped out by clouds, and I grew suddenly happy. It might rain and then I could not go. But it did not rain nor did anything I hoped for happen to prevent my plan. Belle sat down by the angels and was soon so deep in her Bible that it was

177

plain I could easily slip up the path. Sue never looked up from her sand-pile to say, "Stop Billy! He's running away from home!" With a gulp I passed my mother's window. She did not happen to look out. Now I had reached the very gate. "I can't go! I can't open the gate!" But the old gate opened with one push. "I can't go! There is no policeman!" But yes, there he was on my side of the street slowly walking toward me. My heart thumped, I could hardly breathe. In a moment with a frantic rush I had reached the nearest lamp-post and was clinging breathless. I could not scream, I shut my eyes in sickening fear and waited for the rushing of enormous wings.

But there came no Condor swooping.

Another rush—another post—another and another!

"What's the matter with you, little feller?"

I looked up at the big safe policeman and laughed.

"I'm playing a game," I almost shouted, and ran without touching another post two blocks to the cobblestone space below. I ran blindly around it several times, I bumped into a man who said, "Heigh there! Look out!" After that I strutted proudly, then turned and ran back with all my might up the street, and into our house and up to my room. And there on my bed to my great surprise I found myself sobbing and sobbing. It was a long time before I could stop. I had had my first adventure.

I made many Sunday trips after that, and on no one of them was I caught. For delighted and proud at what I had done I kept asking Belle to talk of the Condor, gloomily she piled on the terrors, and seeing the awed look in my eyes (awe at my own courage in defying such a bird), she felt so sure of my safety that often she would barely look up from her Bible the whole afternoon. Even on workdays over her sewing she would forget. And so I went "to destruction."

At first I stayed but a little while and never left the cobblestone space, only peering up into the steep little streets that led to the fearsome homes of the "Micks." But then I made the acquaintance of Sam. It happened through a small toy boat which I had taken down there with the purpose of starting it off for "heathen lands." As I headed across the railroad tracks that led to the docks, suddenly Sam and his gang appeared from around a freight car. I stood stock-still. They were certainly "Micks"—ragged and dirty, with holes in their shoes and soot on their faces. Sam was smoking a cigarette.

"Heigh, fellers," he said, "look at Willy's boat."

I clutched my boat tighter and turned to run. But the next moment Sam had me by the arm.

"Look here, young feller," he growled. "You've got the wrong man to do business with this time."

"I don't want to do any business," I gasped.

"Smash him, Sam—smash in his nut for him," piped the smallest Micky cheerfully. And this Sam promptly proceeded to do. It was a wild and painful time. But though Sam was two years older, he was barely any larger than I, and when he and his gang had gone off with my boat, as I stood there breathing hard, I was filled with a grim satisfaction. For once when he tried to wrench the boat from me I had hit him with it right on the face, and I had had a glimpse of a thick red mark across his cheek. I tasted something new in my mouth and spit it out. It was blood. I did this several times, slowly and impressively, till it made a good big spot on the railroad tie at my feet. Then I walked with dignity back across the tracks and up "the way of destruction" home. I walked slowly, planning as I went. At the gate I climbed up on it and swung. Then with a sudden loud cry I fell off and ran back into the garden crying, "I fell off the gate! I fell on my face!" So my cut and swollen lip was explained, and my trips were not discovered.

I felt myself growing older fast. For I knew that I could both fight and tell lies, besides defying the Condor.

In the next years, for weeks at a time my life was centered on Sam and his gang. How we became friends, how often we met, by just what means I evaded my nurse, all these details are vague to me now. I am not even sure I was never caught. But it seems to me that I was not. For as I grew to be eight years old, Belle turned her attention more and more to that impish little sister of mine who was always up to some mischief or other. There was the corner grocer, too, with whom I pretended to be staunch friends. "I'm going to see the grocer," I would say, when I heard Sam's cautious whistle in front of the house—and so presently I would join the gang. I followed Sam with a doglike devotion, giving up my weekly twenty-five cents instead of saving it for Christmas, and in return receiving from him all the world-old wisdom stored in that bullet-shaped head of his which sat so tight on his round little shoulders.

And though I did not realize it then, in my tense crowded childhood, through Sam and his companions I learned something else that was to stand me in good stead years later on. I learned how to make friends with "the slums." I discovered that by making friends with "Micks" and "Dockers" and the like, you find they are no fearful goblins, giants bursting savagely up among the flowers of your life, but people as human as yourself, or rather, much more human, because they live so close to the harbor, close to the deep rough tides of life.

Into these tides I was now drawn down—and it did me some good and a great deal of harm. For I was too little those days for the harbor.

Sam had the most wonderful life in the world. He could go wherever he liked and at any hour day or night. Once, he said, when a "feller" was drowned, he had stayed out on the docks all night. His mother always let him alone. An enormous woman with heavy eyes, I was in awe of her from the first. The place that she kept with Sam's father was called "The Sailor's Harbor." It stood on a corner down by the docks, a long, low wooden building painted white, with twelve tight-shuttered, mysterious windows along the second story, and below them a "Ladies' Entrance." In front was a small blackboard with words in white which Sam could read. "Ten Cent Dinners" stood at the top. Below came, "Coffee and rolls." Next, "Ham and eggs." Then "Bacon and eggs." And then, "To-day"—with a space underneath where Sam's fat father wrote down every morning still more delicious eatables. You got whiffs of these things and they made your mouth water, they made your stomach fairly turn against your nursery supper.

But most of our time we spent on the docks. All were roofed, and exploring the long dock sheds and climbing down into the dark holds of the square-rigged ships called "clippers," we found logs of curious mottled wood, huge baskets of sugar, odorous spices, indigo, camphor, tea, coffee, jute and endless other things. Sam knew their names and the names of the wonder-places they came from—Manila, Calcutta, Bombay, Ceylon. He knew besides such words as "hawser," "bulkhead," and "ebb-tide." And Sam knew how to swear. He swore with a fascinating ease such words as made me shiver and stare. And then he would look at me and chuckle.

"You think I'll go to hell for this, don't you," he asked me once. And my face grew hot with embarrassment, for I thought that he assuredly would.

I asked him what were heathen lands, and he said they were countries where heathen lived. And what were heathen? Cannibals. And what were they?

"Fellers that eat fellers," he said.

"Alive?" I inquired. He turned to the gang:

"Listen to the kid! He wants to know if they eat 'em alive!" Sam spat disgustedly. "Naw," he said. "First they roast 'em like any meat. They roast 'em," he added reflectively, "until their skin gets brown and bubbles out and busts."

One afternoon a carriage brought three travelers for one of the ships, a man, his wife and a little girl with shining yellow pig-tails. "To be et," Sam whispered as we stood close beside them. And then, pointing to some of the half-naked brown men that made the crew of the ship near by—"cannibals," he muttered. For a long time I stared at these eaters, especially at their lean brown stomachs.

"We're safe enough," Sam told me. "They ain't allowed to come ashore." I found this very comforting.

But what a frightful fate lay in store for the little girl with pig-tails. As I watched her I felt worse and worse. Why couldn't somebody warn her in time? At last I decided to do it myself. Procuring a scrap of paper I retired behind a pile of crates and wrote in my large, clumsy hand, "You look out—you are going to be et." Watching my chance, I slipped this into her satchel and hoped that she would read it soon. Then I promptly forgot all about her and ran off into a warehouse where the gang had gone to slide.

These warehouses had cavernous rooms, so dark you could not see to the ends, and there from between the wooden columns the things from the ships loomed out of the dark like so many ghosts. There were strange sweet smells. And from a hole in the ceiling there was a twisting chute of steel down which you could slide with terrific speed. We used to slide by the hour.

Outside were freight cars in long lines, some motionless, some suddenly lurching forward or back, with a grinding and screeching of wheels and a puffing and coughing from engines ahead. Sam taught me how to climb on the cars and how to swing off while they were going. He had learned from watching the brakemen that dangerous backward left-hand swing that lands you stock-still in your tracks. It is a splendid feeling. Only once Sam's left hand caught, I heard a low cry, and after I jumped I found him standing there with a white face. His left hand hung straight down from the wrist and blood was dripping from it.

"Shut up, you damn fool!" he said fiercely.

"I wasn't saying nothing," I gasped.

"Yes, you was—you was startin' to cry! Holy Christ!" He sat down suddenly, then rolled over and lay still. Some one ran for his mother, and after a time he was carried away. I did not see him again for some weeks.

We did things that were bad for a boy of my size, and I saw things that I shouldn't have seen—a docker crushed upon one of the docks and brought out on a stretcher dead, a stoker as drunk as though he were dead being wheeled on a wheelbarrow to a ship by the man called a "crimp," who sold this drunken body for an advance on its future pay. Sam told me in detail of these things. There came a strike, and once in the darkness of a cold November twilight I saw some dockers rush on a "scab," I heard the dull sickening thumps as they beat him.

And one day Sam took me to the door of his father's saloon and pointed out a man in there who had an admiring circle around him.

"He's going to jump from the Bridge on a bet," Sam whispered. I saw the man go. For what seemed to me hours I watched the Great Bridge up there in the sky, with its crawling processions of trolleys and wagons, its whole moving armies of little black men. Suddenly one of these tiny specks shot out and down, I saw it fall below the roofs, I felt

Sam's hand like ice in mine. And this was not good for a boy of ten.

But the sight that ended it all for me was not a man, but a woman. It happened one chilly March afternoon when I fell from a dock into water covered with grease and foam, came up spluttering and terrified, was quickly hauled to the dock by a man and then hustled by Sam and the gang to his home, to have my clothes dried and so not get caught by my mother. Scolded by Sam's mother and given something fiery hot to drink, stripped naked and wrapped in an old flannel night-gown and told to sit by the stove in the kitchen—I was then left alone with Sam. And then Sam with a curious light in his eyes took me to a door which he opened just a crack. Through the crack he showed me a small back room full of round iron tables. And at one of these a man, stoker or sailor I don't know which, his face flushed red under dirt and hair, held in his lap a big fat girl half dressed, giggling and queer, quite drunk. And then while Sam whispered on and on about the shuttered rooms upstairs, I felt a rush of such sickening fear and loathing that I wanted to scream—but I turned too faint.

I remember awakening on the floor, Sam's mother furiously slapping Sam, then dressing me quickly, gripping me tight by both my arms and saying,

"You tell a word of this to your pa and we'll come up and kill you!"

That night at home I did not sleep. I lay in my bed and shivered and burned. My first long exciting adventure was over. Ended were all the thrills, the wild fun. It was a spree I had had with the harbor, from the time I was seven until I was ten. It had taken me at seven, a plump sturdy little boy, and at ten it had left me wiry, thin, with quick, nervous movements and often dark shadows under my eyes. And it left a deep scar on my early life. For over all the adventures and over my whole childhood loomed this last thing I had seen, hideous, disgusting. For years after that, when I saw or even thought of the harbor, I felt the taste of foul, greasy water in my mouth and in my soul.

So ended the first lesson.

Norman Rosten

Norman Rosten spent his boyhood in Coney Island where his family rented locker space to bathers who came from other parts of the city to go to the beach. It was the 1920s and the Steeplechase and Luna Park, still in their heyday, were magic to a young boy. Rosten graduated from Brooklyn College and studied drama at the University of Michigan. In the early 1940s Rosten lived in the same converted brownstone as his college friend Arthur Miller. Unlike Miller, Rosten has remained in Brooklyn. He has published over half a dozen books of poetry, several plays, two books of nonfiction, and four novels, including Over and Out, Love in All Its Disguises, *and* Under the Boardwalk, *from which this is excerpted.*

FROM *Under* THE *Boardwalk*

*C*ome *to Coney!* The posters
called, and everybody listened. And they came. On summer weekends
a thousand people a minute spilled from the subway and trolley termi-
nals and down Surf Avenue, some to the beach, some to the pools, sailors
and girls waiting for evening, and the mystery of the place brocaded
with lights and real stars.

Beyond the Amusement Park, over the rim of spires and pennants,
just a block away, the mist was rising from the Atlantic, burning off
under a high sun. It was going to be a good hot weekend. Let it rain
Monday through Thursday, but Friday through Sunday let it stay clear
and blue—this was the prayer of the merchant, and he prayed all
summer long.

From the avenue right at the corner I could hear the early morning
barkers trying out their voices: hurry hurry a nickel a nickel hurry a
frank a root beer a nickel hurry potato chip fresh all fresh (fresh last

week) and corn hot fresh (really warm and soggy) try a ride it's a dime take the little girl along she'll love to be kissed hurry hurry . . .

It was all starting up again, that long humid day of a million people, and nobody seemed to mind the lies and the sweat, or notice the run-down houses and streets full of the poor.

The High-Striker bell began to clang. I watched a guy proving his strength to his girl: slamming down the wooden mallet on the rubber pad which sent the slug shimmying up the tight wire, past Weakling past Weak Sister past 1500 past 2000 past Muscle Man and Sally and Lover Boy and Hercules all the way to the top: BONG! A box of candy, a Kewpie doll, souvenir! I flexed my boy's muscle and longed for the day when I could reach Hercules. BONG for the girl, O for a BONG!

Across the horizon, the empty Ferris wheel towered, turning on its trial run. The outside gondolas kept an easy balance, while inside the wheel a series of looped overhead tracks allowed other gondolas to drop and swing in tight arcs, rocking until they gently came to rest. At night, a thousand, maybe ten thousand electric bulbs framed the wheel, and on a clear night, when the lights turned, it was as if the nearby stars were turning along with them, you couldn't be sure.

The rides were warming up. Every two or three minutes, a string of cars whooshed and clanked around the curve of the roller coaster, to disappear down the spidery tracks and drop into a dip of great delight before it sped upward again. Soon the screams of girls would be heard on the turns and drops, rising above the clatter of the cars. I knew the girls were locked in their seats and couldn't escape, and on the drops they would freeze and scream, and when you pulled them close they were too busy screaming to fight back if you held their breasts or slid a hand under their dress. I heard all kinds of stories about what went on down those drops but maybe they were lies, too.

You couldn't tell what was real in a place like this. Whenever you thought something was real, the music of a calliope would start up. It was one of the problems in living here. Maybe that's what the signs meant: Come to Coney!

Each morning as the sun's heat slowly glazed the streets, the garbage truck came by. Its side panels were about six feet high, forming an open box. Inside, the garbageman labored in dungarees, high boots, and a T-shirt. A handkerchief was tightly bound across his forehead, his hands covered with heavy asbestos gloves. The truck moved slowly along, as two other men dragged or rolled the refuse-laden cans from the curb into the street. With a rhythmic grunt-and-lift, together they heaved the can to the lip of the panel, where the man inside seized it, shifted it to his hip, and in a continuing movement spilled the contents into the boxed area. Then, without a pause, he flipped the empty can over the side where waiting hands received it, spinning it to the curb while a partner began rolling another loaded can toward the truck. Together, they repeated their lifting maneuver with a loud *Ho,* while the driver crept along at a slow steady pace.

By the time it reached our house, the truck was almost full, the mounds piled high in the corners. A foul odor, like a haze, hung over it. The man, standing higher now in the center, waist-deep in garbage, was covered with sweat while around his head an army of black flies buzzed. Large, heavy-winged, swarming above the stench, descending in waves, they settled on his arms as though to devour him whole, but the garbageman kept to his rhythm, taking the can, emptying it, tossing it back over the side. When finally the truck passed our house, a gang of waiting boys flung apple rings, chicken bones, even bottles into it, yelling at the figure balanced on the pile.

"Hey, stinky, here's more garbage!"

"Phew, you stink!"

"Get a horse!"

Someone always had balls of dried horse dung ready, and tossed them like grenades, taunting the man, who said nothing, who moved his glistening arms black with flies, until the truck reached the avenue.

I followed. It was time to do my work.

My job at this prenoon hour was to hawk bathers for the locker establishment in our house. In the summer season, we rented locker space to as many people we could squeeze into it. There were all kinds of "clubs," for example, ten boys and girls, sharing one room on weekends. My mother enjoyed the confusion. She would even allow part of our own apartment to be used if the demand was great. On some weekends we rented the garage (which was really a storeroom). One summer I slept in the hallway on a small folding-cot I carried around most of the time so I'd be sure of having something to lie on. On a holiday, relatives always came to visit and I'd sleep on the beach or under the boardwalk. It was like a camping trip without going any-where.

Our regular bath lockers (built in our basement because nothing much was going on in that empty basement and my mother liked to have things going on everywhere) could squeeze in over fifty people. Not that there were fifty lockers. My mother had a system of renting each locker several times a day, and hanging the clothes in a storeroom, so that at the end of the day nobody was sure whom he might find dressing in his locker. I remember a lot of screaming and giggling but nobody complained. My mother's place was always a sellout.

I didn't like my job, being thrust this way into a world of strangers, having to call out: *Lockers twenty-five cents hot and cold showers no waiting.* There was always waiting, and I hated to call out lies, but nobody seemed to mind. On a good morning I'd haul in maybe twenty-five and many more would come by themselves.

The avenue was full of suckers that morning, and I got about fifteen customers in less than an hour. I had all sorts of tricks such as grabbing the duffle bag while giving my pitch or if it was a young couple I'd speak my lines to the girl so that the boy would show he could make up his mind and it was easier to say yes. Most people liked yes better than no. My mother taught me these tricks, she made them up one every minute.

My work completed early, I decided to take a swim. I was already in my swim trunks. I raced barefoot over the hot pavement toward the beach a block away, stopping to cool my feet in patches of tree shade.

I had to dash under the boardwalk to get to the beach. Midway under it, I paused to catch my breath. A chill of apprehension touched me with the sudden cold air. A fetid odor rose up from the sand: it seemed to come from a subterranean source, born of sewage seeping in from the ocean and absorbed in the deepest layers of earth.

In this place of half light, sunlight flaked down through the boards, a pattern of gold running straight, then diagonally, then straight again. I chased the filtered light until it unraveled and ended at the concrete pillars. I played games with it: cutting it up, throwing sand on it, catching it in the air with my open mouth, or letting it tremble on my eyelids. Tired of that, I zigzagged between the pillars, my heart pounding, looking up through the thin spacings between the boards in search of ladies who left their underwear home, an Indian stalking his prey.

Under the boardwalk, for miles, stretched a fringe of corrugated metal and wire fence, entrances to locker houses, frayed billboards, rotting wood, and decayed boats alive with rats and mongrel dogs. Some of the Steeplechase rides skirted the area. You could hear, if you were close to the fence, the rustle of water where the gondola glided through the Tunnel of Love. Nearby, in the shadows, men and women loitered, silent, some holding hands, some clinging to each other, a man pressing a girl against the concrete pillar, a girl combing a man's hair, others watching, silent, waiting.

It was spooky under here. I leaped again into the blinding sun where the sand blazed at my feet and the edge of water rose and fell just a little ways ahead. I was glad to be out in the light again. I skipped over legs, arms, and heads, gathering myself for the plunge. The breakers roared in my ears. Skinny, my soul half-formed, I dived over a rim of foam and under the heaving wall of water.

The coolness enfolded me. My lungs ballooned with air. I became a fish, my glazed eyes open to the green world below. I saw glistening legs of swimmers, slow-motion thrashing legs, erotic and muffled in the sea-green meadow. How my heart hungered! I was a fish nibbling at weeds, nudging at limbs, swimming round and round those languorous girls like the ones in the bathing suit ads with their lips smiling and their legs together like fins.

Down I propelled to a colder level. In my ears boomed the faraway hiss of surf—all the way from Europe or Africa! I had no pain or cares, and overhead I knew the world waited with its flowering sun. I was far from my house and my mother's caution. In an instant, I saw my drowning death, the funeral route, my face unsmiling in the open casket. My mother weeping, my father stunned, cousins and uncles and aunts in dreadful black veils, all rushed past my eyes. They'd miss me, they'd suffer. O this power I had!

My feet kicked bottom sand. My lungs tired. I turned my stroke upward, the green became lighter, and I broke sunlight, gasping for air. I hung on to the rope, breathing hard. The shore seemed to retreat, grow small, the landscape beyond the boardwalk—Ferris wheel, parachute drop, loop-the-loop, Steeplechase—becoming a child's cutout.

With short quick strokes I swam to the shore, edging past a grapefruit rind that rode the wave with the ease of a yellow boat.

By now, at noon, the beach was almost filled. Of course, you never can fill up a beach, the whole idea of a beach is that no matter how crowded it gets you can always squeeze another thousand people in. People were stepping over other people, jumping over other people, calling or staring down at other people. Through this jumbled mass, more other people were maneuvering toward the water which you couldn't see because of the density of the crowd. Voices and sounds merged to a hum, the buzzing of an immense hive.

I lay facedown on the sand, my bones stretching in the heat, my head turned slightly in the crook of my arm where, as through a keyhole, I could steal forbidden glimpses of this world. Red, white, blue, green, yellow, umbrellas. A sudden kiss, a breast revealed, a hand at rest upon a thigh, a gently stroking motion. I watched and dreamed with eyes open.

Then, filtering through the hum, through the haze, a faint sound drifted to my ears. At first I thought it was someone singing. As the sound came closer, I recognized the chant of the pretzel man.

He moved carefully through the sun-baked sand, head bent forward, wearing sneakers, loose trousers, faded sport shirt, and a round straw skullcap. He was an old man, his skin weathered by sun and wind. Supported by rope which cut into his shoulders, a large basket of pretzels hung at his hip. The pretzels were mounted on sticks jutting vertically from the basket. Slowly, accurately, he stepped between the people sprawled everywhere, calling *Pretzels ten cents fresh pretzels.*

Close by, he set the basket on the sand. He wiped the sweat from his face, groaning softly. Then he sat down, took off his sneakers and shook

the sand out, thoughtfully, one sneaker at a time. He looked up at the sky. He reached for a small water flask from his pocket and drank. A group of kids rushed by, their heels kicking sand against the basket, and he yelled after them, "Hey, hey, watch out! Gangsters!"

I counted the pretzels on the sticks. I counted at least twenty-five. My mouth hungered. Maybe he'd drop one? A woman alongside of me turned toward him. "How much the pretzels?"

"Ten cents."

"For one?"

"Naturally. Would it be ten cents a dozen?"

"And three?"

"Thirty cents, lady."

"I saw three for a quarter on the boardwalk."

"On the beach it's ten cents."

"At the subway station it's even five cents."

"Go to the station then, if you please."

"Give me one," said the woman.

The pretzel man folded back the white cloth which covered part of the basket, removed one pretzel from the stick, and replaced the cloth. He accepted a coin, reached into his pocket, and made change.

The woman asked, "These are fresh?"

He answered firmly, "Baked fresh this morning."

My mouth was watering. I wondered, if he'd turn his back for a moment, whether I'd have the courage to slip a pretzel off the stick. He would hardly miss one pretzel. He suddenly stiffened and gave a little cry. My eyes followed his gaze. Coming down from the boardwalk stairs, at a slight trot, a policeman moved toward him. He swung the basket to his shoulder and started quickly toward the water.

As he passed me, I reached up and neatly picked a pretzel off the stick and, with the same motion, slid it under my shirt. I fell back to the sand. It was so easy I wanted to laugh—and practically in front of the cop, too! The pretzel smelled good, the pungent dough, the salt. But I wouldn't eat it right away. I wanted to see what would happen first.

I got up and followed the policeman. Onlookers were converging

191

toward him from all directions, anticipating an arrest or, better still, a brawl. The old man had broken into a run, the basket swinging perilously at his side. As he ran, he kicked off his sneakers, tossed away his shirt and, at the water's edge, setting the basket carefully down, he got out of his trousers. He wore swimming trunks underneath. With a mute look at the amused spectators, he plunged into the water, still wearing the straw skullcap, and swam out to the rope.

The policeman came up to the shore, waving his nightstick. "Come out, you!"

The pretzel man, puffing at the rope, bobbing up and down with the mild waves, called back, "What for?"

"I warned you yesterday to get off the beach."

"So I forgot."

"If I catch you around again, y'hear, I'll give you a summons."

"Ha, ha," the old man laughed wildly, adjusting his hat.

The crowd laughed. The policeman flicked his club impatiently. The pretzel man called out, "Come in here and give me a summons, ha, ha!" The policeman pointed at him with his nightstick, shouting, "Keep off the beach. Last warning!" He started to walk away. The voice from the water called after him, "It's against the law to eat, is that right? I have to make a living!" He pulled himself along the rope toward the shore, his voice shrill, "I have to make a living, tell that to the captain. Go put crooks in jail, I'm not a crook. I have a family, a sick wife . . ."

The policeman disappeared. Two kids ran up from nowhere, snatched pretzels off the stick, and darted away. The crowd laughed. The old man scrambled out of the water. He waved to the cop, "Catch them, catch the little gangsters!" He started chasing the kids, but soon gave up. He came back to the basket, reached for his trousers and put them over his dripping trunks; he found his shirt and his sneakers. He lifted the basket to his shoulder and peered into the crowd. "Come out, you little crooks! I know you're hiding!"

Several youths scooped up handfuls of sand and ran by with Indian whoops, tossing the sand over the pretzels. The old man kicked at them savagely. "Gangsters!" he shouted. Tears sprang to his eyes. He blew the

sand from the pretzels, shifted the weight of the basket more evenly on his shoulders, and started off.

I followed him along the beach. I was hungry, but now I couldn't eat the stolen pretzel. The old man kept a wary eye ahead and behind, stopping often to scan the beach for any sign of the law. I stopped when he did, jogged after him when he started up again. I figured if I got up close, I could slip the pretzel back on the stick. I closed in on him. As he was making a sale, I edged toward the basket, at the same time holding the pretzel ready. Suddenly he looked up and saw me. His body stiffened. "Here's one of them! You want to steal more?" And he lunged at me. I stepped back, and easily vanished in the crowd. I heard his voice. "Gangster, let me catch you, if I catch you . . . Where is he?"

I lay on the sand, breathing heavily. Soon he was calling again, going off, *Pretzels fresh a dime fresh every time.* I rose, and ran a wide circle ahead of him, then dropped to the sand, waiting for him to pass. The pretzel, heated by my body, grew sticky under my shirt. This time I wouldn't try to get it on the stick, but just run by and toss it into the basket.

Through a lattice of sprawled and passing figures, I watched him approach. He was coming in a straight line, but as he neared me he turned off in answer to a customer's shout. I figured this was a good time to do it.

I got up again, pressed toward him, swallowing, because I was hungry now, real hungry, and it was crazy not to eat the pretzel, but I couldn't eat it, I knew that, and wanted to get it out of my hands as soon as possible. I broke into a trot and swerved so that I would cut directly across his path.

I had just reached him, when he saw me again. His eyes lit up with surprise. He swung his arm, as if to strike me, and swung the basket behind him so I couldn't toss the pretzel into it. I continued my run past him and stopped helplessly a little way off.

"I'll catch you, wait!"

"Take your lousy pretzel," I yelled. "I don't want it."

"You want to steal, heh?"

"Listen, I don't want it. Here, take it." I held out the pretzel, looking very foolish with all the people watching, but all he did was to shout at me and curse me, so I moved off and disappeared again into the crowd. I watched him pass me, getting smaller and smaller until he was lost in the swirling hive, the sun-drenched day. The pretzel was now soggy from my sweat. I took one bite, then hurled it into the water.

I ran back to the house. I wanted to get the pretzel man out of my mind. Passing the locker room, I stuck my head into the shower, and the ladies clucked and screamed like a bunch of chickens.

I felt better already.

Irwin Shaw

Irwin Shaw's commercial success has eclipsed his earlier work. Born in 1913, Shaw began writing serials for radio and later, scripts for Hollywood. He first attracted attention with his antiwar play Bury the Dead *in 1936. His next play,* The Gentle People: A Brooklyn Fable, *dealt with the threat of fascism. "Borough of Cemeteries" originally appeared in the* New Yorker, *publisher of much of Shaw's short fiction, and was anthologized in* Sailor Off the *Bremen* and Other Stories. *Shaw's blockbuster novels were* The Young Lions, Two Weeks in Another Town, *and* Rich Man, Poor Man. Rich Man, Poor Man *was made into one of television's most popular miniseries. Shaw died in 1984.*

Borough OF Cemeteries

*D*uring the cocktail hour, in Brownsville, the cab drivers gather in Lammanawitz's Bar and Grill and drink beer and talk about the world and watch the sun set slowly over the elevated tracks in the direction of Prospect Park.

"Mungo?" they say. "Mungo? He got a fish for a arm. A mackerel. He will pitch Brooklyn right into the first division of the International League."

"I saw the Mayor today. His Honor, himself. The Little Flower. What this country needs . . ."

"Pinky, I want that you should trust me for a glass of beer."

Pinky wiped the wet dull expanse of the bar. "Look, Elias. It is against the law of the State of New York," he said nervously, "to sell intoxicating liquors on credit."

"One glass of beer. Intoxicatin'!" Elias' lips curled. "Who yuh think I am, Snow White?"

"Do you want me to lose my license?" Pinky asked plaintively.

"I stay up nights worryin' Pinky might lose his license. My wife hears me cryin' in my sleep," Elias said. "One beer, J. P. Morgan."

Regretfully, Pinky drew the beer, with a big head, and sighed as he marked it down in the book. "The last one," he said, "positively the last one. As God is my witness."

"Yeah," Elias said. "Keep yer mouth closed." He drank the beer in one gulp, with his eyes shut. "My God," he said quietly, his eyes still shut, as he put the glass down. "Fer a lousy dime," he said to the room in general, "yuh get somethin' like that! Fer a lousy dime! Brooklyn is a wonderful place."

"Brooklyn stinks," said another driver, down the bar. "The borough of cemeteries. This is a first class place for graveyards."

"My friend Palangio," Elias said. "Il Doochay Palangio. Yuh don't like Brooklyn, go back to Italy. They give yuh a gun, yuh get shot in the behind in Africa." The rest of the drivers laughed and Elias grinned at his own wit. "I seen in the movies. Go back t' Italy, wit' the fat girls. Who'll buy me a beer?"

Complete silence fell over the bar, like taps over an army camp.

"My friends," Elias said bitterly.

"Brooklyn is a wonderful place," Palangio said.

"All day long," Elias said, reflectively rubbing his broken nose, "I push a hack. Eleven hours on the street. I now have the sum of three dollars and fifty cents in my pocket."

Pinky came right over. "Now, Elias," he said, "there is the small matter of one beer. If I knew you had the money . . ."

Elias impatiently brushed Pinky's hand off the bar. "There is somebody callin' for a beer down there, Pinky," he said. "Attend yer business."

"I think," Pinky grumbled, retreating, "that a man oughta pay his rightful debts."

"He thinks. Pinky thinks," Elias announced. But his heart was not with Pinky. He turned his back to the bar and leaned on his frayed elbows and looked sadly up at the tin ceiling. "Three dollars and fifty cents," he said softly. "An' I can't buy a beer."

"Whatsamatta?" Palangio asked. "Yuh got a lock on yuh pocket?"

"Two dollars an' seventy-fi' cents to the Company," Elias said. "An' seventy-fi' cents to my lousy wife so she don't make me sleep in the park. The lousy Company. Every day for a year I give 'em two dollars an' seventy-fi' cents an' then I own the hack. After a year yuh might as well sell that crate to Japan to put in bombs. Th' only way yuh can get it to move is t' drop it. I signed a contract. I need a nurse. Who wants t' buy me a beer?"

"I signed th' same contract," Palangio said. A look of pain came over his dark face. "It got seven months more to go. Nobody shoulda learned me how to write my name."

"If you slobs would only join th' union," said a little Irishman across from the beer spigots.

"Geary," Elias said. "The Irish hero. Tell us how you fought th' English in th' battle of Belfast."

"O.K., O.K.," Geary said, pushing his cap back excitably from his red hair. "You guys wanna push a hack sixteen hours a day for beans, don' let me stop yuh."

"Join a union, get yer hair parted down the middle by the cops," Elias said. "That is my experience."

"O.K., boys." Geary pushed his beer a little to make it foam. "Property-owners. Can't pay for a glass a beer at five o'clock in th' afternoon. What's the use a' talkin' t' yuh? Lemme have a beer, Pinky."

"Geary, you're a red," Elias said. "A red bastidd."

"A Communist," Palangio said.

"I want a beer," Geary said loudly.

"Times're bad," Elias said. "That's what's th' trouble."

"Sure." Geary drained half his new glass. "Sure."

"Back in 1928," Elias said, "I averaged sixty bucks a week."

"On New Year's Eve, 1927," Palangio murmured, "I made thirty-six dollars and forty cents."

"Money was flowin'," Elias remembered.

Palangio sighed, rubbed his beard bristles with the back of his hand. "I wore silk shirts. With stripes. They cost five bucks apiece. I had four girls in 1928. My God!"

"This ain't 1928," Geary said.

"Th' smart guy," Elias said. "He's tellin' us somethin'. This ain't 1928, he says. Join th' union, we get 1928 back."

"Why the hell should I waste my time?" Geary asked himself in disgust. He drank in silence.

"Pinky!" Palangio called. "Pinky! Two beers for me and my friend Elias."

Elias moved, with a wide smile, up the bar, next to Palangio. "We are brothers in misery, Angelo," he said. "Me and th' Wop. We both signed th' contract."

They drank together and sighed together.

"I had th' biggest pigeon flight in Brownsville," Elias said softly. "One hundred and twelve pairs of pedigreed pigeons. I'd send 'em up like fireworks, every afternoon. You oughta've seen 'em wheelin' aroun' an' aroun' over th' roofs. I'm a pigeon fancier." He finished his glass. "I got fifteen pigeons left. Every time I bring home less than seventy-five cents, my wife cooks one for supper. A pedigreed pigeon. My lousy wife."

"Two beers," Palangio said. He and Elias drank with grave satisfaction.

"Now," Elias said, "if only I didn't have to go home to my lousy wife. I married her in 1929. A lot of things've changed since 1929." He sighed. "What's a woman?" he asked. "A woman is a trap."

"You shoulda seen what I seen today," Palangio said. "My third fare. On Eastern Parkway. I watched her walk all th' way acrost Nostrand Avenue, while I was waitin' on the light. A hundred-and-thirty-pound girl. Blonde. Swingin' her hips like orchester music. With one of those little straw hats on top of her head, with the vegetables on it. You never saw nothin' like it. I held on to the wheel like I was drownin'. Talkin' about traps! She went to the St. George Hotel."

Elias shook his head. "The tragedy of my life," he said, "is I married young."

"Two beers," Palangio said.

"Angelo Palangio," Elias said, "yer name reminds me of music."

"A guy met her in front of the St. George. A big fat guy. Smilin' like he just seen Santa Claus. A big fat guy. Some guys . . ."

199

"Some guys . . ." Elias mourned. "I gotta go home to Annie. She yells at me from six to twelve, regular. Who's goin' to pay the grocer? Who's goin' to pay the gas company?" He looked steadily at his beer for a moment and downed it. "I'm a man who married at the age a' eighteen."

"We need somethin' to drink," Palangio said.

"Buy us two whiskys," Elias said. "What the hell good is beer?"

"Two Calverts," Palangio called. "The best for me and my friend Elias Pinsker."

"Two gentlemen," Elias said, "who both signed th' contract."

"Two dumb slobs," said Geary.

"Th' union man." Elias lifted his glass. "To th' union!" He downed the whisky straight. "Th' hero of th' Irish Army."

"Pinky," Palangio shouted. "Fill 'em up to the top."

"Angelo Palangio," Elias murmured gratefully.

Palangio soberly counted the money out for the drinks. "Now," he said, "the Company can jump in Flushing Bay. I am down to two bucks even."

"Nice," Geary said sarcastically. "Smart. You don't pay 'em one day, they take yer cab. After payin' them regular for five months. Buy another drink."

Palangio slowly picked up his glass and let the whisky slide down his throat in a smooth amber stream. "Don't talk like that, Geary," he said. "I don't want to hear nothin' about taxicabs. I am busy drinkin' with friends."

"You dumb Wop," Geary said.

"That is no way to talk," Elias said, going over to Geary purposefully. He cocked his right hand and squinted at Geary. Geary backed off, his hands up. "I don't like to hear people call my friend a dumb Wop," Elias said.

"Get back," Geary shouted, "before I brain yuh."

Pinky ran up excitably. "Lissen, boys," he screamed, "do you want I should lose my license?"

"We are all friends," Palangio said. "Shake hands. Everybody shake hands. Everybody have a drink. I hereby treat everybody to a drink."

200

Elias lumbered back to Palangio's side. "I am sorry if I made a commotion. Some people can't talk like gentlemen."

"Everybody have a drink," Palangio insisted.

Elias took out three dollar bills and laid them deliberately on the bar. "Pass the bottle around. This is on Elias Pinsker."

"Put yer money away, Elias." Geary pushed his cap around on his head with anger. "Who yuh think yuh are? Walter Chrysler?"

"The entertainment this afternoon is on me," Elias said inexorably. "There was a time I would stand drinks for twenty-five men. With a laugh, an' pass cigars out after it. Pass the bottle around, Pinky!"

The whisky flowed.

"Elias and me," Palangio said. "We are high class spenders."

"You guys oughta be fed by hand," Geary said. "Wards of the guvment."

"A man is entitled to some relaxation," Elias said. "Where's that bottle?"

"This is nice," Palangio said. "This is very nice."

"This is like the good old days," Elias said.

"I hate to go home," Palangio sighed. "I ain't even got a radio home."

"Pinky!" Elias called. "Turn on the radio for Angelo Palangio."

"One room," Palangio said. "As big as a toilet. That is where I live."

The radio played. It was soft and sweet and a rich male voice sang, "I married an angel."

"When I get home," Elias remembered, "Annie will kill a pedi-greed pigeon for supper, my lousy wife. An' after supper I push the hack five more hours and I go home and Annie yells some more and I get up tomorrow and push the hack some more." He poured himself another drink. "That is a life for a dog," he said. "For a Airedale."

"In Italy," Palangio said, "they got donkeys don't work as hard as us."

"If the donkeys were as bad off as you," Geary yelled, "they'd have sense enough to organize."

"I want to be a executive at a desk." Elias leaned both elbows on the bar and held his chin in his huge gnarled hands. "A long distance away from Brownsville. Wit' two thousand pigeons. In California, An' I should be a bachelor. Geary, can yuh organize that? Hey, Geary?"

"You're a workin' man," Geary said, "an' you're goin' to be a workin' man all yer life."

"Geary," Elias said. "You red bastidd, Geary."

"All my life," Palangio wept, "I am goin' to push a hack up an' down Brooklyn, fifteen, sixteen hours a day an' pay th' Company forever an' go home and sleep in a room no bigger'n a toilet. Without a radio. Jesus!"

"We are victims of circumstance," Elias said.

"All my life," Palangio cried, "tied to that crate!"

Elias pounded the bar once with his fist. "Th' hell with it! Palangio!" he said. "Get into that goddam wagon of yours."

"What do yuh want me to do?" Palangio asked in wonder.

"We'll fix 'em," Elias shouted. "We'll fix those hacks. We'll fix that Company! Get into yer cab, Angelo. I'll drive mine, we'll have a chicken fight."

"Yuh drunken slobs!" Geary yelled. "Yuh can't do that!"

"Yeah," Palangio said eagerly, thinking it over. "Yeah. We'll show 'em. Two dollars and seventy-fi' cents a day for life. Yeah. We'll fix 'em. Come on, Elias!"

Elias and Palangio walked gravely out to their cars. Everybody else followed them.

"Look what they're doin!" Geary screamed. "Not a brain between the both of them! What good'll it do to ruin the cabs?"

"Shut up," Elias said, getting into his cab. "We oughta done this five months ago. Hey, Angelo," he called, leaning out of his cab. "Are yuh ready? Hey Il Doochay!"

"Contact!" Angelo shouted, starting his motor. "Boom! Boom!"

The two cars spurted at each other, in second, head-on. As they hit, glass broke and a fender flew off and the cars skidded wildly and the metal noise echoed and re-echoed like artillery fire off the buildings.

Elias stuck his head out of his cab. "Are yuh hurt?" he called. "Hey, Il Doochay!"

"Contact!" Palangio called from behind his broken windshield. "The Dawn Patrol!"

"I can't watch this," Geary moaned. "Two workin' men." He went back into Lammanawitz's Bar and Grill.

The two cabs slammed together again and people came running from all directions.

"How're yuh?" Elias asked, wiping the blood off his face.

"Onward!" Palangio stuck his hand out in salute. "Sons of Italy!"

Again and again the cabs tore into each other.

"Knights of the Round Table," Palangio announced.

"Knights of Lammanawitz's Round Table," Elias agreed, pulling at the choke to get the wheezing motor to turn over once more.

Neil Simon

Neil Simon is undoubtedly the most successful commercial playwright on Broadway. His first play was Come Blow Your Horn, *produced in 1960 and written with his brother, Danny. In the next thirty years Broadway was rarely without a Simon play—* Barefoot in the Park, The Odd Couple, Plaza Suite, Last of the Red Hot Lovers, Chapter Two, *and many others. In the 1980s he wrote an autobiographical trilogy about Eugene Morris Jerome, Simon's alter ego:* Brighton Beach Memoirs, Biloxi Blues, *and* Broadway Bound. *This selection, from* Brighton Beach Memoirs, *is set in Brooklyn in 1937. Eugene, fifteen, lives with his parents and brother and his mother's widowed sister and her two daughters in a one-family house not far from the beach.*

FROM *Brighton Beach Memoirs*

*Brighton Beach, New York. Sep-
tember 1937. A wooden frame house, not too far from the beach. It is a
lower-middle-income area inhabited mostly by Jews, Irish and Germans.*

*The entrance to the house is to the right: a small porch and two steps up
that lead to the front door. Inside we see the dining room and living-room
area. Another door leads to the kitchen . . . A flight of stairs leads up to three
small bedrooms. Unseen are two other bedrooms. A hallway leads to other
rooms . . .*

It's around six-thirty and the late-September sun is sinking fast. KATE
JEROME, *about forty years old, is setting the table. Her sister,* BLANCHE MORTON,
thirty-eight, is working at a sewing machine. LAURIE MORTON, *aged thirteen, is
lying on the sofa reading a book.*

Outside on the grass stands EUGENE JEROME, *almost but not quite fifteen. He
is wearing knickers, a shirt and tie, a faded and torn sweater, Keds sneakers and
a blue baseball cap. He has a beaten and worn baseball glove on his left hand,*

and in his right hand he holds a softball that is so old and battered that it is ready to fall apart.

On an imaginary pitcher's mound, facing left, he looks back over his shoulder to an imaginary runner on second, then back over to the "batter." Then he winds up and pitches, hitting an offstage wall.

EUGENE   One out, a man on second, bottom of the seventh, two balls, no strikes . . . Ruffing checks the runner on second, gets the sign from Dickey, Ruffing stretches, Ruffing pitches—(*He throws the ball*) Caught the inside corner, steerike one! Atta baby! No hitter up there. (*He retrieves the ball*) One out, a man on second, bottom of the seventh, two balls, one strike . . . Ruffing checks the runner on second, gets the sign from Dickey, Ruffing stretches, Ruffing pitches—(*He throws the ball*) Low and outside, ball three. Come on, Red! Make him a hitter! No batter up there. In there all the time, Red.

BLANCHE   (*Stops sewing*) Kate, please. My head is splitting.

KATE   I told that boy a hundred and nine times. (*She yells out*) Eugene! Stop banging the wall!

EUGENE   (*Calls out*) In a minute, Ma! This is for the World Series! (*Back to his game*) One out, a man on second, bottom of the seventh, three balls, one strike . . . Ruffing stretches, Ruffing pitches—(*He throws the ball*) Oh, no! High and outside, JoJo Moore walks! First and second and Mel Ott lopes up to the plate . . .

BLANCHE   (*Stops again*) Can't he do that someplace else?

KATE   I'll break his arm, that's where he'll do it. (*She calls out*) Eugene, I'm not going to tell you again. Do you hear me?

EUGENE   It's the last batter, Mom. Mel Ott is up. It's a crucial moment in World Series history.

KATE Your aunt Blanche has a splitting headache.

BLANCHE I don't want him to stop playing. It's just the banging.

LAURIE (*Looks up from her book*) He always does it when I'm studying. I have a big test in history tomorrow.

EUGENE One pitch, Mom? I think I can get him to pop up. I have my stuff today.

KATE Your father will give you plenty of stuff when he comes home! You hear?

EUGENE All right! All right!

KATE I want you inside *now!* Put out the water glasses.

BLANCHE I can do that.

KATE Why? Is his arm broken? (*She yells out again*) And I don't want any back talk, you hear?
(*She goes back to the kitchen*)

EUGENE (*Slams the ball into his glove angrily. Then he cups his hand, making a megaphone out of it and announces to the grandstands*) "Attention, ladeees and gentlemen! Today's game will be delayed because of my aunt Blanche's headache . . ."

KATE Blanche, that's enough sewing today. That's all I need is for you to go blind.

BLANCHE I just have this one edge to finish . . . Laurie, darling, help your aunt Kate with the dishes.

LAURIE Two more pages, all right, Ma? I have to finish the Macedonian Wars.

KATE   Always studying, that one. She's gonna have some head on her shoulders. (*She calls out from the kitchen*) Eugene!!

EUGENE   I'm coming.

KATE   And wash your hands.

EUGENE   They're clean. I'm wearing a glove. (*He throws the ball into his glove again . . . then he looks out front and addresses the audience*) I hate my name! Eugene Morris Jerome . . . It is the second worst name ever given to a male child. The first worst is Haskell Fleischmann . . . How am I ever going to play for the Yankees with a name like Eugene Morris Jerome? You have to be a Joe . . . or a Tony . . . or Frankie . . . If only I was born Italian . . . All the best Yankees are Italian . . . My mother makes spaghetti with ketchup, what chance do I have?
(*He slams the ball into his glove again*)

LAURIE   I'm almost through, Ma.

BLANCHE   All right, darling. Don't get up too quickly.

KATE   (*To* LAURIE) You have better color today, sweetheart. Did you get a little sun this morning?

LAURIE   I walked down to the beach.

BLANCHE   Very slowly, I hope?

LAURIE   Yes, Ma.

BLANCHE   That's good.

EUGENE   (*Turns to the audience again*) She gets all this special treatment because the doctors say she has kind of a flutter in her heart . . . I got hit with a baseball right in the back of the skull, I saw two of everything for a week and I still had to carry a block of ice home every afternoon . . . Girls are treated like queens. Maybe that's what I should have been born—an Italian girl . . .

KATE   (*Picks up a sweat sock from the floor*) EUGENE!!

EUGENE   *What??*

KATE   How many times have I told you not to leave your things around the house?

EUGENE   A hundred and nine.

KATE   What?

EUGENE   You said yesterday, "I told you a hundred and nine times not to leave your things around the house."

BLANCHE   Don't be fresh to your mother, Gene!

EUGENE   (*To the audience*) Was I fresh? I swear to God, that's what she said to me yesterday . . . One day I'm going to put all this in a book or a play. I'm going to be a writer like Ring Lardner or somebody—that's if things don't work out first with the Yankees, or the Cubs, or the Red Sox, or maybe possibly the Tigers . . . If I get down to the St. Louis Browns, then I'll definitely be a writer.

LAURIE   Mom, can I have a glass of lemonade?

BLANCHE   It'll spoil your dinner, darling.

KATE   A small glass, it couldn't hurt her.

BLANCHE   All right. In a minute, angel.

KATE   I'll get it. I'm in the kitchen anyway.

EUGENE   (*To the audience*) Can you believe that? She'd better have a bad heart or I'm going to kill her one day . . . (*He gets up to walk into the house, then stops on the porch steps and turns to the audience again . . . confidentially*) Listen, I hope you don't repeat this to anybody . . . What I'm telling you are my secret memoirs. It's called, "The Unbelievable, Fantastic and Completely Private Thoughts of I, Eugene Morris Jerome, in this, the fifteenth year of his life, in the year nineteen hundred and thirty-seven, in the community of Brighton Beach, Borough of Brooklyn, Kings County, City of New York, Empire State of the American Nation—"

KATE   (*Comes out of the kitchen with a glass of lemonade and one roller skate*) A roller skate? On my kitchen floor? Do you want me dead, is that what you want?

EUGENE   (*Rushes into the house*) I didn't leave it there.

KATE   No? Then who? Laurie? Aunt Blanche? Did you ever see them on skates? (*She holds out the skate*) Take this upstairs . . . Come here!

EUGENE   (*Approaches, holding the back of his head*) Don't hit my skull, I have a concussion.

KATE   (*Handing the glass to* LAURIE) What would you tell your father if he came home and I was dead on the kitchen floor?

EUGENE   I'd say, "Don't go in the kitchen, Pa!"

KATE   (*Swings at him, he ducks and she misses*) Get upstairs! And don't come down with dirty hands.

EUGENE (*Goes up the stairs. He turns to the audience*) You see why I want to write all this down? In case I grow up all twisted and warped, the world will know why.

BLANCHE (*Still sewing*) He's a boy. He's young. You should be glad he's healthy and active. Before the doctors found out what Laurie had, she was the same way.

KATE Never. Girls are different. When you and I were girls, we kept the house spotless. It was Ben and Ezra who drove Momma crazy. (*We see* EUGENE, *upstairs, enter his room and take out a notebook and pencil and lie down on his bed, making a new entry in his "memoirs"*) . . . I've always been like that. I have to have things clean. Just like Momma. The day they packed up and left the house in Russia, she cleaned the place from top to bottom. She said, "No matter what the Cossacks did to us, when they broke into our house, they would have respect for the Jews."

LAURIE Who were the Cossacks?

KATE The same filthy bunch as live across the street.

LAURIE Across the street? You mean the Murphys?

KATE *All* of them.

LAURIE The Murphys are Russian?

BLANCHE The mother is nice. She's been very sweet to me.

KATE Her windows are so filthy, I thought she had black curtains hanging inside.

BLANCHE I was in their house. It was very neat. *Nobody* could be as clean as you.

KATE   What business did you have in their house?

BLANCHE   She invited me for tea.

KATE   To meet that drunken son of hers?

BLANCHE   No. Just the two of us.

KATE   I'm living here seven years, she never invited *me* for tea. Because she knows your situation. I know their kind. Remember what Momma used to tell us. "Stay on your own side of the street. That's what they have gutters for."

(*She goes back into the kitchen*)

Isaac
Bashevis
Singer

Born in Poland in 1904, Isaac Bashevis Singer studied to be a rabbi, but chose a writer's life instead. He emigrated to the United States in 1935 and wrote for the Jewish Daily Forward, *a Yiddish newspaper. Singer is best known for his short stories, which have been collected in* Gimpel the Fool, The Spinoza of Market Street, A Friend of Kafka, *and other volumes. "A Wedding in Brownsville" is anthologized in* Short Friday. *Singer won the Nobel Prize for literature in 1978. He died in 1991.*

$\mathcal{A}$ $\mathcal{W}edding$ IN $\mathcal{B}rownsville$

$\mathcal{T}$he wedding had been a burden to Dr. Solomon Margolin from the very beginning. True, it was to take place on a Sunday, but Gretl had been right when she said that was the only evening in the week they could spend together. It always turned out that way. His responsibilities to the community made him give away the evenings that belonged to her. The Zionists had appointed him to a committee; he was a board member of a Jewish scholastic society; he had become coeditor of an academic Jewish quarterly. And though he often referred to himself as an agnostic and even an atheist, nevertheless for years he had been dragging Gretl to Seders at Abraham Mekheles', a *Landsman* from Sencimin. Dr. Margolin treated rabbis, refugees, and Jewish writers without charge, supplying them with medicines and, if necessary, a hospital bed. There had been a time when he had gone regularly to the meetings of the Senciminer Society, had accepted positions in their ranks, and had attended all the parties. Now

214

Abraham Mekheles was marrying off his youngest daughter, Sylvia. The minute the invitation arrived, Gretl had announced her decision: she was not going to let herself be carted off to a wedding somewhere out in the wilds of Brownsville. If he, Solomon, wanted to go and gorge himself on all kinds of greasy food, coming home at three o'clock in the morning, that was his prerogative.

Dr. Margolin admitted to himself that his wife was right. When would he get a chance to sleep? He had to be at the hospital early Monday morning. Moreover he was on a strict fat-free diet. A wedding like this one would be a feast of poisons. Everything about such celebrations irritated him now: the Anglicized Yiddish, the Yiddishized English, the earsplitting music and unruly dances. Jewish laws and customs were completely distorted; men who had no regard for Jewishness wore skullcaps; and the reverend rabbis and cantors aped the Christian ministers. Whenever he took Gretl to a wedding or Bar Mitzvah, he was ashamed. Even she, born a Christian, could see that American Judaism was a mess. At least this time he would be spared the trouble of making apologies to her.

Usually after breakfast on Sunday, he and his wife took a walk in Central Park, or, when the weather was mild, went to the Palisades. But today Solomon Margolin lingered in bed. During the years, he had stopped attending the functions of the Senciminer Society; meanwhile the town of Sencimin had been destroyed. His family there had been tortured, burned, gassed. Many Senciminers had survived, and, later, come to America from the camps, but most of them were younger people whom he, Solomon, had not known in the old country. Tonight everyone would be there: the Senciminers belonging to the bride's family and the Tereshpolers belonging to the groom's. He knew how they would pester him, reproach him for growing aloof, drop hints that he was a snob. They would address him familiarly, slap him on the back, drag him off to dance. Well, even so, he had to go to Sylvia's wedding. He had already sent out the present.

The day had dawned, gray and dreary as dusk. Overnight, a heavy snow had fallen. Solomon Margolin had hoped to make up for the sleep he was going to lose, but unfortunately he had waked even earlier than usual. Finally he got up. He shaved himself meticulously at the bathroom mirror and also trimmed the gray hair at his temples. Today of all days he looked his age: there were bags under his eyes, and his face was lined. Exhaustion showed in his features. His nose appeared longer and sharper than usual; there were deep folds at the sides of his mouth. After breakfast he stretched out on the living-room sofa. From there he could see Gretl, who was standing in the kitchen, ironing—blonde, faded, middle-aged. She had on a skimpy petticoat, and her calves were as muscular as a dancer's. Gretl had been a nurse in the Berlin hospital where he had been a member of the staff. Of her family, one brother, a Nazi, had died of typhus in a Russian prison camp. A second, who was a Communist, had been shot by the Nazis. Her aged father vegetated at the home of his other daughter in Hamburg, and Gretl sent him money regularly. She herself had become almost Jewish in New York. She had made friends with Jewish women, joined Hadassah, learned to cook Jewish dishes. Even her sigh was Jewish. And she lamented continually over the Nazi catastrophe. She had her plot waiting for her beside his in that part of the cemetery that the Senciminers had reserved for themselves.

Dr. Margolin yawned, reached for the cigarette that lay in an ashtray on the coffee table beside him, and began to think about himself. His career had gone well. Ostensibly he was a success. He had an office on West End Avenue and wealthy patients. His colleagues respected him, and he was an important figure in Jewish circles in New York. What more could a boy from Sencimin expect? A self-taught man, the son of a poor teacher of Talmud? In person he was tall, quite handsome, and he had always had a way with women. He still pursued them—more than was good for him at his age and with his high blood pressure. But secretly Solomon Margolin had always felt that he was a failure. As a child he had been acclaimed a prodigy, reciting long passages of the Bible and studying the Talmud and Commentaries on his own. When he was a boy of eleven, he had sent for a responsum to the rabbi of Tarnow, who had referred to him in his reply as "great and illustrious." In his teens he had become a master in the *Guide for the Perplexed* and the

Kuzari. He had taught himself algebra and geometry. At seventeen he had attempted a translation of Spinoza's *Ethics* from Latin into Hebrew, unaware that it had been done before. Everyone predicted he would turn out to be a genius. But he had squandered his talents, continually changing his field of study; and he had wasted years in learning languages, in wandering from country to country. Nor had he had any luck with his one great love, Raizel, the daughter of Melekh the watchmaker. Raizel had married someone else and later had been shot by the Nazis. All his life Solomon Margolin had been plagued by the eternal questions. He still lay awake at night trying to solve the mysteries of the universe. He suffered from hypochondria and the fear of death haunted even his dreams. Hitler's carnage and the extinction of his family had rooted out his last hope for better days, had destroyed all his faith in humanity. He had begun to despise the matrons who came to him with their petty ills while millions were devising horrible deaths for one another.

Gretl came in from the kitchen.

"What shirt are you going to put on?"

Solomon Margolin regarded her quietly. She had had her own share of troubles. She had suffered in silence for her two brothers, even for Hans, the Nazi. She had gone through a prolonged change of life. She was tortured by guilt feelings toward him, Solomon. She had become sexually frigid. Now her face was flushed and covered with beads of sweat. He earned more than enough to pay for a maid, yet Gretl insisted on doing all the housework herself, even the laundry. It had become a mania with her. Every day she scoured the oven. She was forever polishing the windows of their apartment on the sixteenth floor and without using a safety belt. All the other housewives in the building ordered their groceries delivered, but Gretl lugged the heavy bags from the supermarket herself. At night she sometimes said things that sounded slightly insane to him. She still suspected him of carrying on with every female patient he treated.

Now husband and wife sized each other up wryly, feeling the strangeness that comes of great familiarity. He was always amazed at how she had lost her looks. No one feature had altered, but something in her aspect had given way: her pride, her hopefulness, her curiosity. He blurted out:

"What shirt? It doesn't matter. A white shirt."

"You're not going to wear the tuxedo? Wait, I'll bring you a vitamin."

"I don't want a vitamin."

"But you yourself say they're good for you."

"Leave me alone."

"Well, it's your health, not mine."

And slowly she walked out of the room, hesitating as if she expected him to remember something and call her back.

2

Dr. Solomon Margolin took a last look in the mirror and left the house. He felt refreshed by the half-hour nap he had had after dinner. Despite his age, he still wanted to impress people with his appearance—even the Senciminers. He had his illusions. In Germany he had taken pride in the fact that he looked like a *Junker,* and in New York he was often aware that he could pass for an Anglo-Saxon. He was tall, slim, blond, blue-eyed. His hair was thinning, had turned somewhat gray, but he managed to disguise these signs of age. He stooped a little, but in company was quick to straighten up. Years ago in Germany he had worn a monocle and though in New York that would have been too pretentious, his glance still retained a European severity. He had his principles. He had never broken the Hippocratic oath. With his patients he was honorable to an extreme, avoiding every kind of cant; and he had refused a number of dubious associations that smacked of careerism. Gretl claimed his sense of honor amounted to a mania. Dr. Margolin's car was in the garage—not a Cadillac like that of most of his colleagues—but he decided to go by taxi. He was unfamiliar with Brooklyn and the heavy snow made driving hazardous. He waved his hand and at once a taxi pulled over to the curb. He was afraid the driver might refuse to go as far as Brownsville, but he flicked the meter on without a word. Dr. Margolin peered through the frosted window into the wintry Sunday night but there was nothing to be seen. The New York streets sprawled out, wet, dirty, impenetrably dark. After a while, Dr. Margolin leaned back, shut his eyes, and retreated into his own warmth. His destination was a wedding. Wasn't the world, like this taxi, plunging away somewhere into the unknown toward a cosmic destination? Maybe a cosmic Brownsville, a cosmic wedding? Yes. But why did God—or whatever anyone wanted to call Him—create a Hitler, a Stalin? Why did He need world wars? Why heart attacks, cancers? Dr. Margolin took out a cigarette and lit it hesitantly. What had they been thinking of, those pious uncles of his, when they were digging their own graves? Was immortality possible? Was there such a thing as the soul? All the arguments for and against weren't worth a pinch of dust.

The taxi turned onto the bridge across the East River and for the first time Dr. Margolin was able to see the sky. It sagged low, heavy, red as glowing metal. Higher up, a violet glare suffused the vault of the heavens. Snow was sifting down gently, bringing a winter peace to the world, just as it had in the past—forty years ago, a thousand years ago, and perhaps a million years ago. Fiery pillars appeared to glow beneath the East River; on its surface, through black waves jagged as rocks, a tugboat was hauling a string of barges loaded with cars. A front window in the cab was open and icy gusts of wind blew in, smelling of gasoline and the sea. Suppose the weather never changed again? Who then would ever be able to imagine a summer day, a moonlit night, spring? But how much imagination—for what it's worth—does a man actually have? On Eastern Parkway the taxi was jolted and screeched suddenly to a stop. Some traffic accident, apparently. The siren on a police car shrieked. A wailing ambulance drew nearer. Dr. Margolin grimaced. Another victim. Someone makes a false turn of the wheel and all a man's plans in this world are reduced to nothing. A wounded man was carried to the ambulance on a stretcher. Above a dark suit and blood-spattered shirt and bow tie the face had a chalky pallor; one eye was closed, the other partly open and glazed. Perhaps he, too, had been going to a wedding, Dr. Margolin thought. He might even have been going to the same wedding as I. . . .

Some time later the taxi started moving again. Solomon Margolin was now driving through streets he had never seen before. It was New York, but it might just as well have been Chicago or Cleveland. They passed through an industrial district with factory buildings, warehouses of coal, lumber, scrap iron. Negroes, strangely black, stood about on the sidewalks, staring ahead, their great dark eyes full of a gloomy hopelessness. Occasionally the car would pass a tavern. The people at the bar seemed to have something unearthly about them, as if they were being punished here for sins committed in another incarnation. Just when Solomon Margolin was beginning to suspect that the driver, who had remained stubbornly silent the whole time, had gotten lost or else was deliberately taking him out of his way, the taxi entered a thickly populated neighborhood. They passed a synagogue, a funeral parlor, and there, ahead, was the wedding hall, all lit up, with its neon Jewish sign and Star of David. Dr. Margolin gave the driver a dollar tip and the man took it without uttering a word.

Dr. Margolin entered the outer lobby and immediately the comfortable intimacy of the Senciminers engulfed him. All the faces he saw were familiar, though he didn't recognize individuals. Leaving his hat and coat at the checkroom, he put on a skullcap and entered the hall. It was filled with people and music, with tables heaped with food, a bar stacked with bottles. The musicians were playing an Israeli march that was a hodgepodge of American jazz with Oriental flourishes. Men were dancing with men, women with women, men with women. He saw black skullcaps, white skullcaps, bare heads. Guests kept arriving, pushing their way through the crowd, some still in their hats and coats, munching hors d'oeuvres, drinking schnapps. The hall resounded with stamping, screaming, laughing, clapping. Flashbulbs went off blindingly as the photographers made their rounds. Seeming to come from nowhere, the bride appeared, briskly sweeping up her train, followed by a retinue of bridesmaids. Dr. Margolin knew everybody, and yet knew nobody. People spoke to him, laughed, winked, and waved, and he answered each one with a smile, a nod, a bow. Gradually he threw off all his worries, all his depression. He became half-drunk on the amalgam of odors: flowers, sauerkraut, garlic, perfume, mustard, and that nameless odor that only Senciminers emit. "Hello, Doctor!" "Hello, Schloime-Dovid, you don't recognize me, eh? Look, he forgot!" There were the encounters, the regrets, the reminiscences of long ago. "But after all, weren't we neighbors? You used to come to our house to borrow the Yiddish newspaper!" Someone had already kissed him: a badly shaven snout, a mouth reeking of whiskey and rotten teeth. One woman was so convulsed with laughter that she lost an earring. Margolin tried to pick it up, but it had already been trampled underfoot. "You don't recognize me, eh? Take a good look! It's Zissl, the son of Chaye Beyle!" "Why don't you eat something?" "Why don't you have something to drink? Come over here. Take a glass. What do you want? Whiskey? Brandy? Cognac? Scotch? With soda? With Coca-Cola? Take some, it's good. Don't let it stand. So long as you're here, you might as well enjoy yourself." "My father? He was killed. They were all killed. I'm the only one left of the entire family." "Berish the son of Feivish? Starved to death in Russia—they sent him to Kazakhstan. His wife? In Israel. She married a Lithuanian." "Sorele? Shot. Together with her children." "Yentl? Here at the wedding. She was standing here just a moment ago. There she is, dancing with that tall fellow." "Abraham Zilberstein? They burned him in the synagogue with twenty others. A mound of charcoal was all that was left, coal and ash." "Yosele Budnik? He passed away years ago. You must mean Yekele Budnik. He has a delicatessen store right here in Brownsville—married a widow whose husband made a fortune in real estate."

"*Lechayim,* Doctor! *Lechayim,* Schloime-Dovid! It doesn't offend you that I call you Schloime-Dovid? To me you're still the same Schloime-Dovid, the little boy with the blond side-curls who recited a whole tractate of the Talmud by heart. You remember, don't you? It seems like only yesterday. Your father, may he rest in peace, was beaming with pride. . . ." "Your brother Chayim? Your Uncle Oyzer? They killed everyone, everyone. They took a whole people and wiped them out with German efficiency: *gleichgeschaltet!*" "Have you seen the bride yet? Pretty as a picture, but too much makeup. Imagine, a grandchild of Reb

Todros of Radzin! And her grandfather used to wear two skullcaps, one in front and one in back." "Do you see that young woman dancing in the yellow dress? It's Riva's sister—their father was Moishe the candlemaker. Riva herself? Where all the others ended up: Auschwitz. How close we came ourselves! All of us are really dead, if you want to call it that. We were exterminated, wiped out. Even the survivors carry death in their hearts. But it's a wedding, we should be cheerful." "*Lechayim,* Schloime-Dovid! I would like to congratulate you. Have you a son or daughter to marry off? No? Well, it's better that way. What's the sense of having children if people are such murderers?"

3

It was already time for the ceremony, but someone still had not come. Whether it was the rabbi, the cantor, or one of the in-laws who was missing, nobody seemed able to find out. Abraham Mekheles, the bride's father, rushed around, scowled, waved his hand, whispered in people's ears. He looked strange in his rented tuxedo. The Tereshpol mother-in-law was wrangling with one of the photographers. The musicians never stopped playing for an instant. The drum banged, the bass fiddle growled, the saxophone blared. The dances became faster, more abandoned, and more and more people were drawn in. The young men stamped with such force that it seemed the dance floor would break under them. Small boys romped around like goats, and little girls whirled about wildly together. Many of the men were already drunk. They shouted boasts, howled with laughter, kissed strange women. There was so much commotion that Solomon Margolin could no longer grasp what was being said to him and simply nodded yes to everything. Some of the guests had attached themselves to him, wouldn't move, and kept pulling him in all directions, introducing him to more and more people from Sencimin and Tereshpol. A matron with a nose covered with warts pointed a finger at him, wiped her eyes, called him Schloimele. Solomon Margolin inquired who she was and somebody told him. Names were swallowed up in the tumult. He heard the same words over and over again: died, shot, burned. A man from Tereshpol tried to draw him aside and was shouted down by several Senciminers calling him an intruder who had no business there. A latecomer arrived, a horse and buggy driver from Sencimin who had become a millionaire in New York. His wife and children had perished, but, already, he had a new wife. The woman, weighted with diamonds, paraded about in a low-cut gown that bared a back, covered with blotches, to the waist. Her voice was husky. "Where did she come from? Who was she?" "Certainly no saint. Her first husband was a swindler who amassed a fortune and then dropped dead. Of what? Cancer. Where? In the stomach. First you don't have anything to eat, then you don't have anything to eat with. A man is always working for the second husband." "What is life anyway? A dance on the grave." "Yes, but as long as you're playing the game, you have to abide by the rules." "Dr. Margolin, why aren't you dancing? You're not among strangers. We're all from the same dust. Over there you weren't a doctor. You were only Schloime-Dovid, the son of the Talmud teacher. Before you know it, we'll all be lying side by side."

Margolin didn't recall drinking anything but he felt intoxicated all the same. The foggy hall was spinning like a carousel; the floor was rocking. Standing in a corner, he contemplated the dance. What different expressions the dancers wore. How many combinations and permutations of being, the Creator had brought together here. Every face told its own story. They were dancing together, these people, but each one had his own philosophy, his own approach. A man grabbed Margolin and for a while he danced in the frantic whirl. Then, tearing himself loose, he stood apart. Who was that woman? He found his eye caught by her familiar form. He knew her! She beckoned to him. He stood baffled. She looked neither young nor old. Where had he known her—that narrow face, those dark eyes, that girlish smile? Her hair was arranged in the old manner, with long braids wound like a wreath around her head. The grace of Sencimin adorned her—something he, Margolin, had long since forgotten. And those eyes, he was in love with those eyes and had been all his life. He half smiled at her and the woman

have accepted the world without her? And what will happen now with Gretl?—I'll give her everything, my last cent." He looked round toward the stairway to see if any of the guests had started to come up. The thought came to him that by Jewish law he was not married, for he and Gretl had had only a civil ceremony. He looked at Raizel.

"According to Jewish law, I'm a single man."

"Is that so?"

"According to Jewish law, I could lead you up there and marry you."

She seemed to be considering the import of his words.

"Yes, I realize . . ."

"According to Jewish law, I don't even need a ring. One can get married with a penny."

"Do you have a penny?"

He put his hand to his breast pocket, but his wallet was gone. He started searching in his other pockets. Have I been robbed? he wondered. But how? I was sitting in the taxi the whole time. Could someone have robbed me here at the wedding? He was not so much disturbed as surprised. He said falteringly:

"Strange, but I don't have any money."

"We'll get along without it."

"But how am I going to get home?"

"Why go home?" she said, countering with a question. She smiled with that homely smile of hers that was so full of mystery. He took her by the wrist and gazed at her. Suddenly it occurred to him that this could not be his Raizel. She was too young. Probably it was her daughter, who was playing along with him, mocking him. For God's sake, I'm completely confused! he thought. He stood bewildered, trying to untangle the years. He couldn't tell her age from her features. Her eyes were deep, dark, and melancholy. She also appeared confused, as if she, too, sensed some discrepancy. The whole thing is a mistake, Margolin told himself. But where exactly was the mistake? And what had happened to the wallet? Could he have left it in the taxi after paying the driver? He tried to remember how much cash he had had in it, but was unable to. "I must have had too much to drink. These people have made me drunk—dead drunk!" For a long time he stood silent, lost in some dreamless state, more profound than a narcotic trance. Suddenly he remembered the traffic collision he had witnessed on Eastern Parkway. An eerie suspicion came over him: Perhaps he had been more than a witness? Perhaps he himself had been the victim of that accident! That man on the stretcher looked strangely familiar. Dr. Margolin began to examine himself as though he were one of his own patients. He could find no trace of pulse or breathing. And he felt oddly deflated as if some physical dimension were missing. The sensation of weight, the muscular tension of his limbs, the hidden aches in his bones, all seemed to be gone. It can't be, it can't be, he murmured. Can one die without knowing it? And what will Gretl do? He blurted out:

"You're not the same Raizel."

"No? Then who am I?"

"They shot Raizel."

"Shot her? Who told you that?"

She seemed both frightened and perplexed. Silently she lowered her head like someone receiving the shock of bad news. Dr. Margolin continued to ponder. Apparently Raizel didn't realize her own condition. He had heard of such a state—what was it called? Hovering in the World of Twilight. The Astral Body wandering in semiconsciousness, detached from the flesh, without being able to reach its destination, clinging to the illusions and vanities of the past. But could there be any truth to all this superstition? No, as far as he was concerned, it was nothing but wishful thinking. Besides, this kind of survival would be less than oblivion. "I am most probably in a drunken stupor," Dr. Margolin decided. "All this may be one long hallucination, perhaps a result of food poisoning. . . ."

He looked up, and she was still there. He leaned over and whispered in her ear:

"What's the difference? As long as we're together."

"I've been waiting for that all these years."

"Where have you been?"

She didn't answer, and he didn't ask again. He looked around. The empty hall was full, all the seats taken. A ceremonious hush fell over the audience. The music played softly. The cantor intoned the benedictions. With measured steps, Abraham Mekheles led his daughter down the aisle.

Translated by CHANA FAERSTEIN *and* ELIZABETH POLLET

Betty Smith

Betty Smith wrote what was probably the most popular work ever set in Brooklyn. Published in 1943, A Tree Grows in Brooklyn *was an overnight success and sold over five million copies in sixteen languages. Smith was much like her heroine, Francie Nolan. Born and raised in Brooklyn, she was forced to leave school at fourteen to go to work. Although she had no secondary schooling she eventually studied at both the University of Michigan and Yale under special status. Smith moved to Chapel Hill, North Carolina, as a member of the faculty and lived there until her death in 1957. Although she wrote two other novels and many plays, nothing else approached the success of* A Tree Grows in Brooklyn.

FROM *A Tree Grows in Brooklyn*

Serene was a word you could put to Brooklyn, New York. Especially in the summer of 1912. Somber, as a word, was better. But it did not apply to Williamsburg, Brooklyn. Prairie was lovely and Shenandoah had a beautiful sound, but you couldn't fit those words into Brooklyn. Serene was the only word for it; especially on a Saturday afternoon in summer.

Late in the afternoon the sun slanted down into the mossy yard belonging to Francie Nolan's house, and warmed the worn wooden fence. Looking at the shafted sun, Francie had that same fine feeling that came when she recalled the poem they recited in school.

> This is the forest primeval. The murmuring
> pines and the hemlocks,
> Bearded with moss, and in garments green,
> indistinct in the twilight,
> Stand like Druids of eld.

The one tree in Francie's yard was neither a pine nor a hemlock. It had pointed leaves which grew along green switches which radiated from the bough and made a tree which looked like a lot of opened green umbrellas. Some people called it the Tree of Heaven. No matter where its seed fell, it made a tree which struggled to reach the sky. It grew in boarded-up lots and out of neglected rubbish heaps and it was the only tree that grew out of cement. It grew lushly, but only in the tenement districts.

You took a walk on a Sunday afternoon and came to a nice neighborhood, very refined. You saw a small one of these trees through the iron gate leading to someone's yard and you knew that soon that section of Brooklyn would get to be a tenement district. The tree knew. It came there first. Afterwards, poor foreigners seeped in and the quiet old brownstone houses were hacked up into flats, feather beds were pushed out on the windowsills to air and the Tree of Heaven flourished. That was the kind of tree it was. It liked poor people.

That was the kind of tree in Francie's yard. Its umbrellas curled over, around and under her third-floor fire escape. An eleven-year-old girl sitting on this fire escape could imagine that she was living in a tree. That's what Francie imagined every Saturday afternoon in summer.

Oh, what a wonderful day was Saturday in Brooklyn. Oh, how wonderful anywhere! People were paid on Saturday and it was a holiday without the rigidness of a Sunday. People had money to go out and buy things. They ate well for once, got drunk, had dates, made love and stayed up until all hours; singing, playing music, fighting and dancing because the morrow was their own free day. They could sleep late—until late mass anyhow.

On Sunday, most people crowded into the eleven o'clock mass. Well, some people, a few, went to early six o'clock mass. They were given credit for this but they deserved none for they were the ones who had stayed out so late that it was morning when they got home. So they went to this early mass, got it over with and went home and slept all day absolved from sin.

For Francie, Saturday started with the trip to the junkie. She and her brother, Neeley, like other Brooklyn kids, collected rags, paper, metal, rubber, and other junk and hoarded it in locked cellar bins or in boxes hidden under the bed. All week Francie walked home slowly from school with her eyes in the gutter looking for tin foil from cigarette packages or chewing gum wrappers. This was melted in the lid of a jar. The junkie wouldn't take an unmelted ball of foil because too many kids put iron washers in the middle to make it weigh heavier. Sometimes Neeley found a seltzer bottle. Francie helped him break the top off and melt it down for lead. The junkie wouldn't buy a complete top because he'd get into trouble with the soda water people. A seltzer bottle top was fine. Melted, it was worth a nickel.

Francie and Neeley went down into the cellar each evening and emptied the dumbwaiter shelves of the day's accumulated trash. They owned this privilege because Francie's mother was the janitress. They looted the shelves of paper, rags and deposit bottles. Paper wasn't worth much. They got only a penny for ten pounds. Rags brought two cents a pound and iron, four. Copper was good—ten cents a pound. Sometimes Francie came across a bonanza: the bottom of a discarded wash boiler. She got it off with a can opener, folded it, pounded it, folded it and pounded it again.

Soon after nine o'clock of a Saturday morning, kids began spraying out of all the side streets onto Manhattan Avenue, the main thoroughfare. They made their slow way up the Avenue to Scholes Street. Some carried their junk in their arms. Others had wagons made of a wooden soap box with solid wooden wheels. A few pushed loaded baby buggies.

Francie and Neeley put all their junk into a burlap bag and each grabbed an end and dragged it along the street; up Manhattan Avenue, past Maujer, Ten Eyck, Stagg to Scholes Street. Beautiful names for ugly streets. From each side street hordes of little ragamuffins emerged to swell the main tide. On the way to Carney's, they met other kids coming back empty-handed. They had sold their junk and already squandered the pennies. Now, swaggering back, they jeered at the other kids.

"Rag picker! Rag picker!"

Francie's face burned at the name. No comfort knowing that the taunters were rag pickers too. No matter that her brother would straggle back, empty-handed with his gang and taunt later comers the same way. Francie felt ashamed.

Carney plied his junk business in a tumbledown stable. Turning the corner, Francie saw that both doors were hooked back hospitably and she imagined that the large, bland dial of the swinging scale blinked a welcome. She saw Carney, with his rusty hair, rusty mustache and rusty eyes presiding at the scale. Carney liked girls better than boys. He would give a girl an extra penny if she did not shrink when he pinched her cheek.

Because of the possibility of this bonus, Neeley stepped aside and let Francie drag the bag into the stable. Carney jumped forward, dumped the contents of the bag on the floor and took a preliminary pinch out of her cheek. While he piled the stuff onto the scale, Francie blinked, adjusting her eyes to the darkness, and was aware of the mossy air and the odor of wetted rags. Carney slewed his eyes at the dial and spoke two words: his offer. Francie knew that no dickering was permitted. She nodded yes, and Carney flipped the junk off and made her wait while he piled the paper in one corner, threw the rags in another and sorted out the metals. Only then did he reach down in his pants pocket, haul up an old leather pouch tied with a wax string and count out old green pennies that looked like junk too. As she whispered, "Thank you," Carney fixed a rusty junked look on her and pinched her cheek hard. She stood her ground. He smiled and added an extra penny. Then his manner changed and he became loud and brisk.

"Come on," he hollered to the next one in line, a boy. "Get the lead out!" He timed the laugh. "And I don't mean junk." The children laughed dutifully. The laughter sounded like the bleating of lost little lambs but Carney seemed satisfied.

Francie went outside to report to her brother. "He gave me sixteen cents and a pinching penny."

"That's your penny," he said, according to an old agreement.

She put the penny in her dress pocket and turned the rest of the money over to him. Neeley was ten, a year younger than Francie. But he was the boy; he handled the money. He divided the pennies carefully.

"Eight cents for the bank." That was the rule; half of any money they got from anywhere went into the tin-can bank that was nailed to the floor in the darkest corner of the closet. "And four cents for you and four cents for me."

Francie knotted the bank money in her handkerchief. She looked at her own five pennies realizing happily that they could be changed into a whole nickel.

Neeley rolled up the burlap bag, tucked it under his arm and pushed his way in Cheap Charlie's with Francie right behind him. Cheap Charlie's was the penny candy store next to Carney's which catered to the junk trade. At the end of a Saturday, its cash box was filled with greenish pennies. By an unwritten law, it was a boys' store. So Francie did not go all the way in. She stood by the doorway.

The boys, from eight to fourteen years of age, looked alike in straggling knickerbockers and broken-peaked caps. They stood around, hands in pockets and thin shoulders hunched forward tensely. They would grow up looking like that; standing the same way in other hangouts. The only difference would be the cigarette seemingly permanently fastened between their lips, rising and falling in accent as they spoke.

Now the boys churned about nervously, their thin faces turning from Charlie to each other and back to Charlie again. Francie noticed that some already had their summer hair-cut: hair cropped so short that there were nicks in the scalp where the clippers had bitten too deeply. These fortunates had their caps crammed into their pockets or pushed back on the head. The unshorn ones whose hair curled gently and still babyishly at the nape of the neck, were ashamed and wore their caps pulled so far down over their ears that there was something girlish about them in spite of their jerky profanity.

Cheap Charlie was not cheap and his name wasn't Charlie. He had taken that name and it said so on the store awning and Francie believed it. Charlie gave you a pick for your penny. A board with fifty numbered hooks and a prize hanging from each hook, hung behind the counter. There were a few fine prizes; roller skates, a catcher's mitt, a doll with real hair and so on. The other hooks held blotters, pencils and other penny articles. Francie watched as Neeley bought a pick. He removed the dirty card from the ragged envelope. Twenty-six! Hopefully Francie looked at the board. He had drawn a penny penwiper.

"Prize or candy?" Charlie asked him.

"Candy. What do you think?"

It was always the same. Francie had never heard of anyone winning above a penny prize. Indeed the skate wheels were rusted and the doll's hair was dust-filmed as though these things had waited there a long time like Little Boy Blue's toy dog and tin soldier. Someday, Francie resolved, when she had fifty cents, she would take all the picks and win everything on the board. She figured that would be a good business deal: skates, mitt, doll and all the other things for fifty cents. Why the skates alone were worth four times that much! Neeley would have to come along that great day because girls seldom patronized Charlie's. True, there were a few girls there that Saturday . . . bold, brash ones, too developed for their age; girls who talked loud and horseplayed around with the boys—girls whom the neighbors prophesied would come to no good.

Francie went across the street to Gimpy's candy store. Gimpy was lame. He was a gentle man, kind to little children . . . or so everyone thought until that sunny afternoon when he inveigled a little girl into his dismal back room.

Francie debated whether she should sacrifice one of her pennies for a Gimpy Special: the prize bag. Maudie Donavan, her once-in-a-while girl friend, was about to make a purchase. Francie pushed her way in until she was standing behind Maudie. She pretended that she was spending the penny. She held her breath as Maudie, after much speculation, pointed dramatically at a bulging bag in the showcase. Francie would have picked a smaller bag. She looked over her friend's shoulder; saw her take out a few pieces of stale candy and examine her prize—a coarse cambric handkerchief. Once Francie had gotten a small bottle of strong scent. She debated again whether to spend a penny on a prize bag. It was nice to be surprised even if you couldn't eat the candy. But she reasoned she had been surprised by being with Maudie when she made her purchase and that was almost as good.

Francie walked up Manhattan Avenue reading aloud the fine-sounding names of the streets she passed: Scholes, Meserole, Montrose and then Johnson Avenue. These last two avenues were where the

Italians had settled. The district called Jew Town started at Siegel Street, took in Moore and McKibbon and went past Broadway. Francie headed for Broadway.

And what was on Broadway in Williamsburg, Brooklyn? Nothing—only the finest nickel and dime store in all the world! It was big and glittering and had everything in the world in it . . . or so it seemed to an eleven-year-old girl. Francie had a nickel. Francie had power. She could buy practically anything in that store! It was the only place in the world where that could be.

Arriving at the store, she walked up and down the aisles handling any object her fancy favored. What a wonderful feeling to pick something up, hold it for a moment, feel its contour, run her hand over its surface and then replace it carefully. Her nickel gave her this privilege. If a floorwalker asked whether she intended buying anything, she could say yes, buy it and show him a thing or two. Money was a wonderful thing, she decided. After an orgy of touching things, she made her planned purchase—five cents' worth of pink-and-white peppermint wafers.

She walked back home down Graham Avenue, the Ghetto street. She was excited by the filled pushcarts—each a little store in itself—the bargaining, emotional Jews and the peculiar smells of the neighborhood; baked stuffed fish, sour rye bread fresh from the oven, and something that smelled like honey boiling. She stared at the bearded men in their alpaca skullcaps and silkolene coats and wondered what made their eyes so small and fierce. She looked into tiny hole-in-the-wall shops and smelled the dress fabrics arranged in disorder on the tables. She noticed the feather beds bellying out of windows, clothes of Oriental-bright colors drying on the fire escapes and the half-naked children playing in the gutters. A woman, big with child, sat patiently at the curb in a stiff wooden chair. She sat in the hot sunshine watching the life on the street and guarding within herself her own mystery of life.

Francie remembered her surprise that time when mama told her that Jesus was a Jew. Francie had thought that He was a Catholic. But mama knew. Mama said that the Jews had never looked on Jesus as anything but a troublesome Yiddish boy who would not work at the

236

carpentry trade, marry, settle down and raise a family. And the Jews believed that their Messiah was yet to come, mama said. Thinking of this, Francie stared at the pregnant Jewess.

"I guess that's why the Jews have so many babies," Francie thought. "And why they sit so quiet . . . waiting. And why they aren't ashamed the way they are fat. Each one thinks that she might be making the real little Jesus. That's why they walk so proud when they're that way. Now the Irish women always look so ashamed. They know that they can never make a Jesus. It will be just another Mick. When I grow up and know that I am going to have a baby, I will remember to walk proud and slow even though I am not a Jew."

It was twelve when Francie got home. Mama came in soon after with her broom and pail which she banged into a corner with that final bang which meant that they wouldn't be touched again until Monday.

Mama was twenty-nine. She had black hair and brown eyes and was quick with her hands. She had a nice shape, too. She worked as a janitress and kept three tenement houses clean. Who would ever believe that mama scrubbed floors to make a living for the four of them? She was so pretty and slight and vivid and always bubbling over with intensity and fun. Even though her hands were red and cracked from the sodaed water, they were beautifully shaped with lovely, curved, oval nails. Everyone said it was a pity that a slight pretty woman like Katie Nolan had to go out scrubbing floors. But what else could she do considering the husband she had, they said. They admitted that, no matter which way you looked at it, Johnny Nolan was a handsome lovable fellow far superior to any man on the block. But he *was* a drunk. That's what they said and it was true.

Francie made mama watch while she put the eight cents in the tin-can bank. They had a pleasant five minutes conjecturing about how much was in the bank. Francie thought there must be nearly a hundred dollars. Mama said eight dollars would be nearer right.

Mama gave Francie instructions about going out to buy something for lunch. "Take eight cents from the cracked cup and get a quarter loaf of Jew rye bread and see that it's fresh. Then take a nickel, go to Sauerwein's and ask for the end-of-the-tongue for a nickel."

"But you have to have a pull with him to get it."

"Tell him that your mother *said,*" insisted Katie firmly. She thought something over. "I wonder whether we ought to buy five cents' worth of sugar buns or put that money in the bank."

"Oh, Mama, it's *Saturday.* All week you said we could have dessert on Saturday."

"All right. Get the buns."

The little Jewish delicatessen was full of Christians buying Jew rye bread. She watched the man push her quarter loaf into a paper bag. With its wonderful crisp yet tender crust and floury bottom, it was easily the most wonderful bread in the world, she thought, when it was fresh. She entered Sauerwein's store reluctantly. Sometimes he was agreeable about the tongue and sometimes he wasn't. Sliced tongue at seventy-five cents a pound was only for rich people. But when it was nearly all sold, you could get the square end for a nickel if you had a pull with Mr. Sauerwein. Of course there wasn't much tongue to the end. It was mostly soft, small bones and gristle with only the memory of meat.

It happened to be one of Sauerwein's agreeable days. "The tongue came to an end, yesterday," he told Francie. "But I saved it for you because I know your mama likes tongue and I like your mama. You tell her that. Hear?"

"Yes sir," whispered Francie. She looked down on the floor as she felt her face getting warm. She hated Mr. Sauerwein and would *not* tell mama what he had said.

At the baker's, she picked out four buns, carefully choosing those with the most sugar. She met Neeley outside the store. He peeped into the bag and cut a caper of delight when he saw the buns. Although he had eaten four cents' worth of candy that morning, he was very hungry and made Francie run all the way home.

Papa did not come home for dinner. He was a free-lance singing waiter which meant that he didn't work very often. Usually he spent Saturday morning at Union Headquarters waiting for a job to come in for him.

Francie, Neeley, and mama had a very fine meal. Each had a thick slice of the "tongue," two pieces of sweet-smelling rye bread spread with unsalted butter, a sugar bun apiece and a mug of strong hot coffee with a teaspoon of sweetened condensed milk on the side.

There was a special Nolan idea about the coffee. It was their one great luxury. Mama made a big potful each morning and reheated it for dinner and supper and it got stronger as the day wore on. It was an awful lot of water and very little coffee but mama put a lump of chicory in it which made it taste strong and bitter. Each one was allowed three cups a day *with milk*. Other times you could help yourself to a cup of black coffee anytime you felt like it. Sometimes when you had nothing at all and it was raining and you were alone in the flat, it was wonderful to know that you could have *something* even though it was only a cup of black and bitter coffee.

Neeley and Francie loved coffee but seldom drank it. Today, as usual, Neeley let his coffee stand black and ate his condensed milk spread on bread. He sipped a little of the black coffee for the sake of formality. Mama poured out Francie's coffee and put the milk in it even though she knew that the child wouldn't drink it.

Francie loved the smell of coffee and the way it was hot. As she ate her bread and meat, she kept one hand curved about the cup enjoying its warmth. From time to time, she'd smell the bitter sweetness of it. That was better than drinking it. At the end of the meal, it went down the sink.

Mama had two sisters, Sissy and Evy, who came to the flat often. Every time they saw the coffee thrown away, they gave mama a lecture about wasting things.

Mama explained: "Francie is entitled to one cup each meal like the rest. If it makes her feel better to throw it away rather than to drink it, all right. *I* think it's good that people like us can waste something once in a while and get the feeling of how it would be to have lots of money and not have to worry about scrounging."

This queer point of view satisfied mama and pleased Francie. It was one of the links between the ground-down poor and the wasteful rich. The girl felt that even if she had less than anybody in Williamsburg, somehow she had more. She was richer because she had something to waste. She ate her sugar bun slowly, reluctant to have done with its sweet taste, while the coffee got ice-cold. Regally, she poured it down the sink drain feeling casually extravagant. After that, she was ready to go to Losher's for the family's semi-weekly supply of stale bread. Mama told her that she could take a nickel and buy a stale pie if she could get one that wasn't mashed too much.

Losher's bread factory supplied the neighborhood stores. The bread was not wrapped in wax paper and grew stale quickly. Losher's redeemed the stale bread from the dealers and sold it at half price to the poor. The outlet store adjoined the bakery. Its long narrow counter filled one side and long narrow benches ran along the other two sides. A huge double door opened behind the counter. The bakery wagons backed up to it and unloaded the bread right onto the counter. They sold two loaves for a nickel, and when it was dumped out, a pushing crowd fought for the privilege of buying it. There was never enough bread and some waited until three or four wagons had reported before they could buy bread. At that price, the customers had to supply their own wrappings. Most of the purchasers were children. Some kids tucked the bread under their arms and walked home brazenly letting all the world know that they were poor. The proud ones wrapped up the bread, some in old newspapers, others in clean or dirty flour sacks. Francie brought along a large paper bag.

She didn't try to get her bread right away. She sat on a bench and watched. A dozen kids pushed and shouted at the counter. Four old men dozed on the opposite bench. The old men, pensioners on their families, were made to run errands and mind babies, the only work left for old worn-out men in Williamsburg. They waited as long as they could before buying because Losher's smelled kindly of baking bread, and the sun coming in the windows felt good on their old backs. They sat and dozed while the hours passed and felt that they were filling up time. The waiting gave them a purpose in life for a little while and, almost, they felt necessary again.

Francie stared at the oldest man. She played her favorite game, figuring out about people. His thin tangled hair was the same dirty gray as the stubble standing on his sunken cheeks. Dried spittle caked the corners of his mouth. He yawned. He had no teeth. She watched, fascinated and revolted, as he closed his mouth, drew his lips inward until there was no mouth, and made his chin come up to almost meet his nose. She studied his old coat with the padding hanging out of the torn sleeve seam. His legs were sprawled wide in helpless relaxation and one of the buttons was missing from his grease-caked pants opening. She saw that his shoes were battered and broken open at the toes. One shoe was laced with a much-knotted shoe string, and the other with a bit of dirty twine. She saw two thick dirty toes with creased gray toenails. Her thoughts ran. . . .

"He is old. He must be past seventy. He was born about the time Abraham Lincoln was living and getting himself ready to be president. Williamsburg must have been a little country place then and maybe Indians were still living in Flatbush. That was so long ago." She kept staring at his feet. "He was a baby once. He must have been sweet and clean and his mother kissed his little pink toes. Maybe when it thundered at night she came to his crib and fixed his blanket better and whispered that he mustn't be afraid, that mother was there. Then she picked him up and put her cheek on his head and said that he was her own sweet baby. He might have been a boy like my brother, running in and out of the house and slamming the door. And while his mother scolded him she was thinking that maybe he'll be president someday. Then he was a young man, strong and happy. When he walked down the street, the girls smiled and turned to watch him. He smiled back and maybe he winked at the prettiest one. I guess he must have married and had children and they thought he was the most wonderful papa in the world the way he worked hard and bought them toys for Christmas. Now his children are getting old too, like him, and *they* have children and nobody wants the old man anymore and they are waiting for him to die. But he don't want to die. He wants to keep on living even though he's so old and there's nothing to be happy about anymore."

The place was quiet. The summer sun streamed in and made dusty, down-slanting roads from the window to the floor. A big green fly buzzed in and out of the sunny dust. Excepting for herself and the dozing old men, the place was empty. The children who waited for bread had gone to play outside. Their high screaming voices seemed to come from far away.

Suddenly Francie jumped up. Her heart was beating fast. She was frightened. For no reason at all, she thought of an accordion pulled out full for a rich note. Then she had an idea that the accordion was closing . . . closing . . . closing. . . . A terrible panic that had no name came over her as she realized that many of the sweet babies in the world were born to come to something like this old man someday. She had to get out of that place or it would happen to her. Suddenly she would be an old woman with toothless gums and feet that disgusted people.

At that moment, the double doors behind the counter were banged open as a bread truck backed up. A man came to stand behind the counter. The truck driver started throwing bread to him which he piled up on the counter. The kids in the street who had heard the doors thrown open piled in and milled around Francie who had already reached the counter.

"I want bread!" Francie called out. A big girl gave her a strong shove and wanted to know who she thought she was. "Never mind! Never mind!" Francie told her. "I want six loaves and a pie not too crushed," she screamed out.

Impressed by her intensity, the counter man shoved six loaves and the least battered of the rejected pies at her and took her two dimes. She pushed her way out of the crowd dropping a loaf which she had trouble picking up as there was no room to stoop over in.

Outside, she sat at the curb fitting the bread and the pie into the paper bag. A woman passed, wheeling a baby in a buggy. The baby was waving his feet in the air. Francie looked and saw, not the baby's foot, but a grotesque thing in a big, worn-out shoe. The panic came on her again and she ran all the way home.

The flat was empty. Mama had dressed and gone off with Aunt Sissy to see a matinee from a ten-cent gallery seat. Francie put the bread and pie away and folded the bag neatly to be used the next time. She went into the tiny, windowless bedroom that she shared with Neeley and sat on her own cot in the dark waiting for the waves of panic to stop passing over her.

After a while Neeley came in, crawled under his cot and pulled out a ragged catcher's mitt.

"Where you going?" she asked.

"Play ball in the lots."

"Can I come along?"

"No."

She followed him down to the street. Three of his gang were waiting for him. One had a bat, another a baseball and the third had nothing but wore a pair of baseball pants. They started out for an empty lot over towards Greenpoint. Neeley saw Francie following but said nothing. One of the boys nudged him and said,

"Hey! Your sister's followin' us."

"Yeah," agreed Neeley. The boy turned around and yelled at Francie:

"Go chase yourself!"

"It's a free country," Francie stated.

"It's a free country," Neeley repeated to the boy. They took no notice of Francie after that. She continued to follow them. She had nothing to do until two o'clock when the neighborhood library opened up again.

It was a slow, horseplaying walk. The boys stopped to look for tin foil in the gutter and to pick up cigarette butts which they would save and smoke in the cellar on the next rainy afternoon. They took time out to bedevil a little Jew boy on his way to the temple. They detained him while they debated what to do with him. The boy waited, smiling humbly. The Christians released him finally with detailed instructions as to his course of conduct for the coming week.

"Don't show your puss on Devoe Street," he was ordered.

"I won't," he promised. The boys were disappointed. They had expected more fight. One of them took out a bit of chalk from his pocket and drew a wavy line on the sidewalk. He commanded,

"Don't you even step over that line."

The little boy, knowing that he had offended them by giving in too easily, decided to play their way.

"Can't I even put one foot in the gutter, fellers?"

243

"You can't even *spit* in the gutter," he was told.

"All right." He sighed in pretended resignation.

One of the bigger boys had an inspiration. "And keep away from Christian girls. Get me?" They walked away leaving him staring after them.

"Gol-*lee!*" he whispered rolling his big brown Jewish eyes. The idea that those *Goyem* thought him man enough to be capable of thinking about *any* girl, Gentile or Jew, staggered him and he went his way saying gol-*lee* over and over.

The boys walked on slowly, looking slyly at the big boy who had made the remark about the girls, and wondering whether he would lead off into a dirty talk session. But before this could start, Francie heard her brother say,

"I know that kid. He's a white Jew." Neeley had heard papa speak so of a Jewish bartender that he liked.

"They ain't no such thing as a white Jew," said the big boy.

"Well, if there was such a thing as a white Jew," said Neeley with that combination of agreeing with others and still sticking to his own opinions, which made him so amiable, "he would be it."

"There never could be a white Jew," said the big boy, "even in supposing."

"Our Lord was a Jew." Neeley was quoting mama.

"And other Jews turned right around and killed him," clinched the big boy.

Before they could go deeper in theology, they saw another little boy turn onto Ainslee Street from Humboldt Avenue carrying a basket on his arm. The basket was covered with a clean ragged cloth. A stick stuck up from one corner of the basket, and, on it, like a sluggish flag stood six pretzels. The big boy of Neeley's gang gave a command and they made a tightly-packed run on the pretzel seller. He stood his ground, opened his mouth and bawled, "Mama!"

A second-story window flew open and a woman clutching a crepe-paperish kimona around her sprawling breasts, yelled out,

"Leave him alone and get off this block, you lousy bastards."

Francie's hands flew to cover her ears so that at confession she would not have to tell the priest that she had stood and listened to a bad word.

"We ain't doing nothing, Lady," said Neeley with that ingratiating smile which always won over his mother.

"You bet your life, you ain't. Not while I'm around." Then without changing her tone she called to her son, "And get upstairs here, you. I'll learn you to bother me when I'm taking a nap." The pretzel boy went upstairs and the gang ambled on.

"That lady's tough." The big boy jerked his head back at the window.

"Yeah," the others agreed.

"My old man's tough," offered a smaller boy.

"Who the hell cares?" inquired the big boy languidly.

"I was just saying," apologized the smaller boy.

"My old man ain't tough," said Neeley. The boys laughed.

They ambled along, stopping now and then to breathe deeply of the smell of Newtown Creek, which flowed its narrow tormented way a few blocks up Grand Street.

"God, she stinks," commented the big boy.

"Yeah!" Neeley sounded deeply satisfied.

"I bet that's the worst stink in the world," bragged another boy.

"Yeah."

And Francie whispered yeah in agreement. She was proud of that smell. It let her know that nearby was a waterway, which, dirty though it was, joined a river that flowed out to the sea. To her, the stupendous stench suggested far-sailing ships and adventure and she was pleased with the smell.

Just as the boys reached the lot in which there was a ragged diamond tramped out, a little yellow butterfly flew across the weeds. With man's instinct to capture anything running, flying, swimming or crawling, they gave chase, throwing their ragged caps at it in advance of their coming. Neeley caught it. The boys looked at it briefly, quickly lost interest in it and started up a four-man baseball game of their own devising.

They played furiously, cursing, sweating and punching each other. Every time a stumble bum passed and loitered for a moment, they

245

clowned and showed off. There was a rumor that the Brooklyn Dodgers had a hundred scouts roaming the streets of a Saturday afternoon watching lot games and spotting promising players. And there wasn't a Brooklyn boy who wouldn't rather play on the Bums' team than be president of the United States.

After a while, Francie got tired of watching them. She knew that they would play and fight and show off until it was time to drift home for supper. It was two o'clock. The librarian should be back from lunch by now. With pleasant anticipation, Francie walked back towards the library.

William
Styron

*William Styron was born in Newport News,
Virginia, in 1925. At twenty-six he won praise
for his first novel,* Lie Down in Darkness,
*about the disintegration of a wealthy Virginia
family. Two books followed,* The Long March
and Set This House on Fire, *before the contro-
versial success of* The Confessions of Nat
Turner *in 1967.* Turner *won a Pulitzer Prize.
It was thirteen years before the publication of his
next novel,* Sophie's Choice. *In this excerpt from*
Sophie's Choice, *Stingo, an aspiring writer
from Virginia, moves to Yetta Zimmerman's
"Pink House" and finds himself "in the unimaginable reaches of Brooklyn, an ineffective and
horny Calvinist among all these Jews."*

FROM *Sophie's Choice*

I stayed long enough at the University Residence Club to receive the check from my father. Given proper management, the money should last me through the summer, which was just beginning, and maybe even into the fall. But where to live? The University Residence Club was no longer for me a possibility, spiritual or physical. The place had reduced me to such a shambles of absolute impotence that I found that I could not even indulge myself in my occasional autoerotic diversions, and was reduced to performing furtive pocket jobs during midnight strolls through Washington Square. My sense of solitariness was verging, I knew, on the pathological, so intensely painful was the isolation I felt, and I suspected that I would be even more lost if I abandoned Manhattan, where at least there were familiar landmarks and amiable Village byways as points of reference to make me feel at home. But I simply could no longer afford either the Manhattan prices or the rent—even single rooms were becoming beyond my means—and so I had to search the classified ads for accommodations in Brooklyn. And that is how, one fine day in June, I got out of the Church Avenue station of the BMT with my Marine Corps seabag and suitcase, took several intoxicating breaths of the pickle-fragrant air of Flatbush, and walked down blocks of gently greening sycamores to the rooming house of Mrs. Yetta Zimmerman.

Yetta Zimmerman's house may have been the most openheartedly monochromatic structure in Brooklyn, if not in all of New York. A large rambling wood and stucco house of the nondescript variety erected, I should imagine, sometime before or just after the First World War, it would have faded into the homely homogeneity of other large nondescript dwellings that bordered on Prospect Park had it not been for its striking—its overwhelming—pinkness. From its second-floor dormers and cupolas to the frames of its basement-level windows, the house was unrelievedly pink. When I first saw the place I was instantly reminded of the façade of some back-lot castle left over from the MGM movie version of *The Wizard of Oz*. The interior also was pink. The floors, walls, ceilings and even most of the furniture of each hallway and room varied slightly in hue—due to an uneven paint job—from the tender *rosé* of fresh lox to a more aggressive bubble-gum coral, but everywhere there was pink, pink admitting rivalry from no other color, so that after only a few minutes contemplating my prospective room under the proud eye of Mrs. Zimmerman, I felt at first amused—it was a cupid's bower in which one could only barely restrain raucous laughter—and then really grimly trapped, as if I were in a Barricini candy store or the infants' department at Gimbels. "I know, you're thinking about the pink," Mrs. Zimmerman had said, "everybody does. But then it gets you. It wears on you—nice, really nice that is, I mean. Pretty soon, most people they don't want no other color." Without my questioning, she added that her husband, Sol—her late husband—had lucked into a fantastic bargain in the form of several hundred gallons of Navy surplus paint, used for that—*"you know"*—and halted, finger quizzically laid aside her porous spatulate nose. "Camouflage?" I ventured. To which she replied, "Yeah, that's it. I guess they didn't have much use for pink on those boats." She said that Sol had painted the house himself. Yetta was squat and expansive, sixty or thereabouts, with a slightly mongoloid cast to her cheerful features that gave her the look of a beaming Buddha.

That day I had been persuaded almost at once. First, it was cheap. Then, pink or not, the room she showed me on the ground floor was agreeably spacious, airy, sun-filled, and clean as a Dutch parlor. Furthermore, it possessed the luxury of a kitchenette and a small private bathroom in which the toilet and tub appeared almost jarringly white against the prevailing peppermint. I found the privacy itself seduction enough, but there was also a bidet, which lent a risqué note and, electrically, unconscionably stirred my expectations. I also was greatly taken by Mrs. Zimmerman's overview of her establishment, which she expounded as she led me around the premises. "I call this place Yetta's Liberty Hall," she said, every now and then giving me a nudge. "What I like to see is my tenants enjoy life. They're usually young people, my tenants, and I like to see them enjoy life. Not that I don't gotta have rules." She lifted the pudgy nub of a forefinger and began to tick them off. "Rule number one: no playing the radio after eleven o'clock. Rule number two: you gotta turn off all lights when you leave the room, I got no need to pay extra to Con Edison. Rule three: positively no smoking in bed, you get caught smoking in bed—*out.* My late husband, Sol, had a cousin burned himself up that way, plus a whole house. Rule number four: full week's payment due every Friday. End of the rules! Everything else is Yetta's Liberty Hall. Like what I mean is, this place is for grownups. Understand, I'm running no brothel, but you wanta have a girl in your room once in a while, have a girl in your room. You be a gentleman and quiet and have her out of there at a reasonable hour, you'll have no quarrel with Yetta about a girl in your room. And the same thing goes for the young ladies in my house, if they want to entertain a boyfriend now and then. What's good for the gander is good for the goose, I say, and if there's one thing I hate, it's hypocrisy."

This extraordinary broad-mindedness—deriving from what I could only assume was an Old World appreciation of *volupté*—put the final seal on my decision to move to Yetta Zimmerman's, despite the all too problematical nature of the free hand I had been given. Where would I get a girl? I wondered. Then I was suddenly furious at myself for my

250

lack of enterprise. Certainly the license that Yetta (we were soon on a first-name basis) had given me meant that this important problem would soon take care of itself. The salmon-hued walls seemed to acquire a wanton glow, and I vibrated with inward pleasure. And a few days later I took up residence there, warmly anticipating a summer of carnal fulfillment, philosophical ripening and steady achievement in the creative task I had cut out for myself.

My first morning—a Saturday—I rose late and strolled over to a stationery store on Flatbush Avenue and bought two dozen Number 2 Venus Velvet pencils, ten lined yellow legal pads and a "Boston" pencil sharpener, which I got permission from Yetta to screw to the frame of my bathroom door. Then I sat down in a pink straight-backed wicker chair at an oaken desk, also painted pink, whose coarse-grained and sturdy construction reminded me of the desks used by schoolmarms in the grammar-school classrooms of my childhood, and with a pencil between thumb and forefinger confronted the first page of the yellow legal pad, its barrenness baneful to my eye. How simultaneously enfeebling and insulting is an empty page! Devoid of inspiration, I found that nothing would come, and although I sat there for half an hour while my mind fiddled with half-jelled ideas and nebulous conceits, I refused to let myself panic at my stagnation; after all, I reasoned, I had barely settled into these strange surroundings. The previous February, during my first few days at the University Residence Club, before starting work at McGraw-Hill, I had written a dozen pages of what I planned to be the prologue of the novel—a description of a ride on a railroad train to the small Virginia city which was to provide the book's locale. Heavily indebted in tone to the opening passages of *All the King's Men,* using similar rhythms and even the same second-person singular to achieve the effect of the author grabbing the reader by the lapels, the passage was, I knew, to say the least, derivative, yet I also knew that there was much in it that was powerful and fresh. I was proud of it, it was a good beginning, and now I took it out of its manila folder and reread it for perhaps the ninetieth time. It still pleased me and I would not have wanted to change a line. Move over, Warren, this is Stingo arriving, I said to myself. I put it back in its folder.

251

The yellow page remained empty. I felt restless, a little goatish, and in order to keep the curtain drawn down over my brain's ever-handy peep show of lewd apparitions—harmless, but in relation to work distracting—I got up and paced the room, which the summer sun bathed in a lurid flamingo light. I heard voices, footsteps in the room above—the walls I realized were paper-thin—and I looked up and glared at the pink ceiling. I began to detest the omnipresent pink and doubted gravely that it would "wear" on me, as Yetta had said. Because of the problems of weight and volume involved, I had brought only what I considered essential books with me; few in number, they included *The American College Dictionary,* Roget's *Thesaurus,* my collection of John Donne, Oates and O'Neill's *Complete Greek Drama,* the *Merck Manual of Diagnosis and Therapy* (essential to my hypochondria), the *Oxford Book of English Verse* and the Holy Bible. I knew I could eventually build up my library piecemeal. Meanwhile, now to help summon my own muse, I tried to read Marlowe, but for some reason that lilting music failed to stir me as it usually did.

I put the book aside and moseyed into the tiny bathroom, where I began to take inventory of the articles I had placed in the medicine chest. (Years later I would be fascinated to discover a hero of J. D. Salinger duplicating my ceremony, but I claim priority.) This was a ritual, deeply rooted in the soil of inexplicable neurosis and materialistic urgency, which I have gone through many times since when vision and invention have flagged to the point of inertia, and both writing and reading have become burdensome to the spirit. It is a mysterious need to restore a tactile relationship with mere things. One by one with my fingertips I examined them where I had placed them the night before, there on the shelves of the wall cabinet, which like everything else had fallen prey to Sol Zimmerman's loony incarnadine paintbrush: a jar of Barbasol shaving cream, a bottle of Alka-Seltzer, a Schick injector razor, two tubes of Pepsodent toothpaste, a Dr. West's toothbrush with medium bristles, a bottle of Royall Lyme after-shave lotion, a Kent comb, an "injecto-pack" of Schick injector blades, an unopened cellophane-wrapped box of three dozen rolled and lubricated Trojan condoms with "receptacle tips," a jar of Breck's antidandruff shampoo, a tube of Rexall nylon dental floss, a jar of Squibb multivitamins, a bottle of Astring-o-sol mouthwash. I touched them all gently, examined the labels, and even unscrewed the cap of the Royall Lyme shaving lotion and inhaled the fruity citrus aroma, receiving considerable satisfaction from the total medicine-chest experience, which took about a minute and a half. Then I closed the door of the cabinet and returned to my writing table.

Sitting down, I lifted my gaze and looked out the window and was suddenly made aware of another element which must have worked on my subconscious and caused me to be drawn to this place. It was such a placid and agreeable view I had of the park, this corner known as the Parade Grounds. Old sycamore trees and maples shaded the sidewalks at the edge of the park, and the dappled sunlight aglow on the gently sloping meadow of the Parade Grounds gave the setting a serene, almost pastoral quality. It presented a striking contrast to remoter parts of the neighborhood. Only short blocks away traffic flowed turbulently on Flatbush Avenue, a place intensely urban, cacophonous, cluttered, swarming with jangled souls and nerves; but here the arboreal green and the pollen-hazy light, the infrequent trucks and cars, the casual pace of the few strollers at the park's border, all created the effect of an outlying area in a modest Southern city—Richmond perhaps, or Chattanooga or Columbia. I felt a sharp pang of homesickness, and abruptly wondered what in God's name was I doing here in the unimaginable reaches of Brooklyn, an ineffective and horny Calvinist among all these Jews?

John Tunis

Born in Boston in 1889 and a graduate of Harvard, John Tunis was best known for his sports writing, both for adults and children. He also had stints as a sportswriter for the New York Evening Post *and a sports broadcaster for NBC radio. Tunis was incredibly prolific, author of many books of nonfiction and fiction and over two thousand articles in magazines including* Collier's, Reader's Digest, The New Yorker, *and* The Saturday Evening Post. Keystone Kids *was published in 1943. Tunis died in 1975.*

Winter. Snow was falling that evening in mid-February when Spike got back after work to their room in Mrs. Hampton's boardinghouse on McGavock Street to find Bob triumphantly waving a telegram.

"It's from him, from Jack MacManus! Says he's passing through town next week and wants to see us about the contract. Gee, Spike, I sure hope we can fix things up. It looks like you were right after all."

As the business manager of the pair, Spike had confidence in his dealings with the Dodger management that was not entirely shared by his brother. Before leaving Brooklyn last fall he had consulted Fat Stuff at some length as to what kind of a contract they should ask for the next season. The veteran's opinion was that the Dodgers' Keystone Kids deserved a substantial raise.

"What'd you boys knock down this year?"

"I was paid on a basis of three thousand five, and Bobby three

---

charming; MacManus aroused and crazy mad; MacManus eager and attentive; MacManus keen and sober; MacManus keen and not so sober. He was truly a man of moods. He could be agreeable and friendly, as he had been when they'd first come up, and in two minutes he could be as cold as ice.

To Spike's relief, MacManus was in his genial mood. "I really oughtn't to do this, but I'm fond of you boys and, confidentially, I'm going to break one of our club rules. Those raises are back in your contracts."

Spike was pleased by this generosity but somehow managed to keep his self-control.

"Yessir. Thank you very much indeed, sir."

"Then it's settled?"

"Nosir."

"What d'you mean, no?"

"Insufficient moolah, Mr. MacManus. We got good jobs down here; we can live on what we earn. And I feel we're worth fifteen to the club, sir."

Would he get mad? Would he rant and roar? Would he bellow and call names over the phone? Not at all.

"O.K., Spike," he replied in his suavest tone. "I'm terribly sorry. I always liked you two boys, fine type of fellows, kind of lads we like to have on the club. But this is your last chance. Come now, don't you want to take a few days to think things over?"

"We have, sir."

"All right, all right. That's everything I've got to say then." Once again the telephone clicked decisively.

More unpleasant was the arrival of a letter which followed immediately. It was a nice letter, too nice in fact. The genial and charming MacManus wrote that they would both be missed next summer on the team. But after all business was business, so he wished them good luck in their new venture.

"What new venture?" snorted Bob. "Now then, see what you've done! You sure pulled a boner this time. He's through with us; he's washed us up. Because why? Just on account you're so doggoned stub-

straight," answered Spike, talking baseball figures to the old pitcher.

He thought awhile. "Well, let's see. The team finished up in third place, and you boys both had more than a little to do with our standing. Judging by your play out there, I'd say you were worth considerable more next year. Guess you oughta double it, say fifteen. Split it anyway you like—or they do."

But the contracts that arrived unsigned in Nashville shortly after Christmas called for a five-thousand-dollar salary to Spike and four to Bob. Somewhat to Bob's distress, Spike insisted on returning them immediately, unsigned, with a polite letter. "There's some guys think it's fine to holler and curse the management, but I think we'd be smart to leave Ginger an out."

"Yeah, an' suppose they don't take the out. Suppose they don't come back at us."

"They will," Spike assured him. "They got to. They don't expect you to sign the first contract; they just send it out in hopes, that's all."

He was correct. The contract was returned with a raise of a thousand dollars apiece, making eleven thousand in all. Once again Bob was worried. Not Spike.

"No, sir, we're in a strong position. They need us bad out there round second base, and they know it. Besides, we got a leverage on 'em; we can make a living outside of baseball and they realize it. You got a good electrical job, haven't you? O.K., and I can always work in the L. and N. freight house. We got something to bargain with, boy."

"But we don't want to do that; we don't want to work here in Nashville. We wanna play baseball."

"Sure we do. But we can if we hafta, see? Point is, they need us bad. Now just sit tight and wait and see."

The contract went back unsigned.

Three days later a telephone call came for Spike in the Louisville and Nashville freight house where he was working. It caught him when the boss and three helpers were able to listen with interest. They only heard Spike's answers but they got enough to understand the meaning of the conversation.

"Spike?" It was the taut, aggressive voice of Ginger Crane. "Spike,

let's get down to brass tacks. How much do you boys want any

"We want fifteen, Ginger, split any way you folks like up t

"Wow! Boy, have you got a nerve! For a couple of rookies in t leagues, you got your gall. When I broke in with the Senat '35 . . .'"

Spike knew that record. "Yeah? This boy Wakefield, the ki signed with the Tigers, got forty-two five," he answered in ba terminology, hoping the railway men around wouldn't get it.

"What say? I don't believe it. Those are newspaper figures. A rate, you boys haven't proved a thing so far, not a thing . . .'"

"Nothing except we made eighteen doubleplays that last mo

"What's that mean? Now that Ed Davis's arm is mended, I pro shan't use your brother except as a utility infielder next season."

"Well, Ginger, that's what we feel we're worth—fifteen."

"O.K., Spike, you know your own business best. I'd be mighty to see you go, but that's how things are. So long, and good luck to both."

He hung up. The click of the telephone had an impressively de tone that was unpleasant to hear, and Spike turned back to the mouthed freight-hands feeling unusually foolish.

Three or four days later a telegram arrived informing them tha raises were revoked. This really bothered both boys. What did mean? They decided that it meant that if they signed now they'd to do so at the figures of their original contracts—five and four thou respectively. With difficulty Spike withstood his brother's pleas to for a contract and sign immediately. A week later he was glad he ha weakened. A letter came from the manager saying he had no auth to treat further with them, and that from now on negotiations wer the hands of Jack MacManus, the fiery-tempered owner of the Dodg The letter didn't describe him that way, however.

No word came from that worthy, either, for almost ten days, then late in January, when they were both worried and having trou getting to sleep at night, a telephone call caught them one evening the boardinghouse. Spike took the call, wondering just which M Manus he would find at the other end. There was MacManus genial a

born. You held out for a few thousand and where are we? We're out, that's where we are!"

Spike, too, was upset this time. He simply wouldn't have believed it, and somehow even yet it didn't make sense. He knew enough baseball to realize that Ed Davis with his arm at its best was not as good a man as Bob around second, not from any angle. And they needed a fast pair at that keystone sack if they hoped to overhaul the Pirates or the Cards, who were also improved. The fans liked them, too, the fans were for them, the fans and the writers as well.

"Shucks, I b'lieve he's stalling. If he isn't, he isn't. We must sit tight, Bob. We aren't through, not by any means. Nine thousand is just fish-cakes; so is eleven. Maybe Grouchy will take us on. I hear they're talking of Grouchy as manager for the Cards next season."

But both boys spent some bad nights for a week until suddenly a wire arrived from Buffalo, New York. "HAVE A CHANCE TO BUY YOUR CONTRACTS STOP WOULD YOU PLAY WITH US PLEASE REPLY BY WESTERN UNION COLLECT IMMEDIATELY REGARDS STEVE O'HARE MANAGER."

Bob agreed at once to Spike's reply. "IF WE WOULDNT PLAY WITH THE DODGERS WE CERTAINLY WOULDNT PLAY WITH BUFFALO SPIKE AND BOB RUSSELL."

Then followed another week of uncertainty and suspense until the telegram came from MacManus, who was on his way South, saying that he would stop off en route. Now Bob began to feel that possibly Spike's tactics had been correct. But he was extremely nervous as they both went upstairs in the elevator of the Andrew Jackson that evening to the boss's room, Spike in his working overalls, Bob in the clothes he wore on his electrical job. This was the older brother's idea. He wanted the owner of the club to see they weren't fooling.

That evening it was the genial MacManus, agreeable, affable, putting them at their ease, remembering they didn't smoke, pouring out double Cokes for them; in short, Mac at his most charming. Two contracts were spread out on a table in one corner of the room. Evidently this time he meant business.

He lighted a cigarette. "Now, boys, I'm going to be frank with you; I'm going to put my cards on the table and take you both behind the scenes so you'll understand why we cannot under any consideration pay you more than eleven thousand dollars. Let me explain. These figures I'm telling you are seen by no one except the owner and stockholders of the club. They concern things you maybe never thought about, you probably didn't even know.

"Boys, we get, as the visiting team, twenty-three cents for every customer when we're away from home. We pay out twenty-three cents for every customer to all visiting clubs at Ebbets Field. Those are National League rules. We have nothing to say about them. Now where does all the money we take in go? Last year we played to a million here at home and over a million on the road. Well, we spent $180,000 on salaries, yours and Fat Stuff's and Razzle's and the Slugger's and the rest. That doesn't count what we pay our manager, the Doc, the rubbers, the clubhouse boy, and so forth and so on. Then we spent $19,856 for railroad fares. You travel well, don't you, boys? Yep, and that costs us money. Your uniforms were worth exactly $4,626. We spent $8,111 for baseballs. Your bats alone cost the club $632."

He spoke the words slowly, rolling over the figures on his tongue.

"I made out a check the other day to the Brooklyn Laundry for $6,789 for cleaning your uniforms, your underwear, and the towels. Away from home your hotel bills amounted to $17,146."

He was certainly a wonderful man. Figures rippled from his lips as he continued.

"And so on. You like a nice, good bounding ball, don't you, Spike, when you get set out there at short? You, too, Bob? So do the other boys. O.K. Our sprinkler system to keep the grass fresh and the turf solid so you'll get good bounds meant $10,000 last summer. Know what the lights cost? About $1,000 a month. I spent two-fifty grand repairing the stands and having the posts sunk in concrete last year. Then there's the amortization, depreciation, ushers' wages, groundkeepers, loss due to rain . . ."

Bob was dazed by this Niagara of figures. So, too, was Spike. But not completely. He interrupted the owner. "Yessir, yessir, I can see you have to spend a lot of money."

He suddenly produced a bill from his pocket and extended it toward the businessman.

"Mr. MacManus, sir, here's a five spot if it'll help you any."

MacManus started in his chair. He would either lose his temper or laugh heartily at himself. There was a moment of tension in the room, broken by his explosion of merriment.

He roared with laughter. "Spike, you're a card! Well now, boys, what do you say? This'll give you an inside, a really inside picture of the situation. You both started well for us but, of course, we have to recognize that you slumped a bit there toward the end."

"Yessir. And we made forty-eight doubleplays while we were up with the club, Mr. MacManus. That's . . . that's . . ."

By the expression on his face, Spike saw the owner had been talking with Ginger Crane.

"Doubleplays! Doubleplays! Do doubleplays get a man on first? Hits win ballgames. Now, boys, I'm sure we understand each other. I've got just so much money, and even if you made a doubleplay in every chance you handled I couldn't pay you five cents more. I've put back those ups in your contract; that means eleven between the two of you. But I want to be generous, I want to do the right thing by you. I appreciate you did a good job jumping in there the way you both did the end of the season. So suppose we say twelve. That gives you six apiece. Six for both of you, how's that, hey?"

He looked at them closely, seeing Bob's tense, eager expression. What the older boy was thinking and how he would respond to this offer Jack MacManus had no idea nor could his brother, searching that face for a hint, guess either.

"Yes, sir. Yes, Mr. MacManus," said Spike at last. "I'd like to be able to sign up but it just wouldn't be fair to you, sir. We wouldn't be able to do our best for you."

Now MacManus was annoyed. He had made concessions, too many concessions. They'd sign now, by ginger, or else . . .

"Boys, this is your last chance. I really mean business." He looked it, too. His grimness frightened Bob, who turned to his brother.

"Spike, I think we oughta sign for twelve, don't you?"

Then Jack MacManus, a rare judge of human nature, made one of his rare mistakes.

261

"O.K. If he won't sign, how 'bout you putting your John Hancock on that contract, Bob? I promise you won't be sorry."

No one spoke. The silence lasted and lasted.

"You mean . . . I should leave Spike, Mr. MacManus?" What was the man saying? Leave Spike and go back up there alone? Not a chance!

MacManus, shrewd, intelligent, realized instantly he had made a bad mistake. But before he could correct himself the boy replied.

"Thank you very much indeed, sir, but I reckon I better stick with my brother."

"What? Why, you young fatheads! You fresh young bushers . . . throwing away your last chance . . . you two chowderheads! This *is* your last chance . . . don't you appreciate . . ."

Now he was angry. MacManus liked to jockey with other people, but he enjoyed winning these battles and he usually did win. When losing he didn't enjoy himself at all. And he was losing, he knew he was losing, although the two scared boys did not. For almost the first time in the long weeks of indecision, Spike was thoroughly frightened as the Dodger owner, red in the face, rose from his chair, strode across the room, took the two contracts off the table and hurled them over.

"Take 'em, take 'em, you young bushers, you fresh young rookies . . . you . . ."

They reached over and each picked up a contract from the floor. Both contracts were made out in typewritten figures for the same sum— seven thousand five hundred dollars!

Derek Walcott

Derek Walcott was born in St. Lucia in 1930. He published three volumes of verse between 1948 and 1953, but did not gain fame until his book In a Green Light *in 1962. He has also published* Selected Poems, The Castaway, The Gulf, *and other volumes of poetry. Walcott is a forceful voice for Caribbean culture, and most of his work deals with sorting out its often conflicting origins. Walcott is also a playwright and his work includes* Henri Christophe, Drums and Colours, Remembrance, *and* Pantomime. *His autobiographical poem "Another Life" was published in 1973. His most recent work is* Omeros, *a narrative epic. Walcott was awarded the Nobel Prize for literature in 1992.*

A Letter FROM Brooklyn

An old lady writes me in a spidery style,
Each character trembling, and I see a veined hand
Pellucid as paper, travelling on a skein
Of such frail thoughts its thread is often broken;
Or else the filament from which a phrase is hung
Dims to my sense, but caught, it shines like steel,
As touch a line, and the whole web will feel.
She describes my father, yet I forget her face
More easily than my father's yearly dying;
Of her I remember small, buttoned boots and the place
She kept in our wooden church on those Sundays
Whenever her strength allowed;
Grey haired, thin voiced, perpetually bowed.

"I am Mable Rawlins," she writes, "and know both your parents";
He is dead, Miss Rawlins, but God bless your tense:

264

"Your father was a dutiful, honest,
Faithful and useful person."
For such plain praise what fame is recompense?
"A horn-painter, he painted delicately on horn,
He used to sit around the table and paint pictures."
The peace of God needs nothing to adorn
It, nor glory nor ambition.
"He is twenty-eight years buried," she writes, "he was called home,
And is, I am sure, doing greater work."

The strength of one frail hand in a dim room
Somewhere in Brooklyn, patient and assured,
Restores my sacred duty to the Word.
"Home, home," she can write, with such short time to live,
Alone as she spins the blessings of her years;
Not withered of beauty if she can bring such tears,
Nor withdrawn from the world that breaks its lovers so;
Heaven is to her the place where painters go,
All who bring beauty on frail shell or horn,
There was all made, thence their lux-mundi drawn,
Drawn, drawn, till the thread is resilient steel,
Lost though it seems in the darkening periods,
And there they return to do work that is God's.

So this old lady writes, and again I believe.
I believe it all, and for no man's death I grieve.

Walt Whitman

Walt Whitman is Brooklyn's most famous writer. Born on Long Island, the son of a carpenter, Whitman and his family moved to Brooklyn in 1823 when he was four years old. As his family's fortunes rose and fell, Whitman moved in and out of the borough until he found regular work as a newspaperman on the Long Island Star, The Brooklyn Daily Eagle, *and* The Brooklyn Freeman. *Forced to leave the newspaper business because of his radical editorials, Whitman embarked on an itinerant life that included carpentry, journalism, and poetry. "Crossing Brooklyn Ferry" appeared in the second edition of* Leaves of Grass. *Whitman's work, with its unorthodox form and sensual content, was revolutionary to his contemporaries. He was reviled by the establishment and championed by other writers, including Emerson, William Rosetti, and Horace Traubel. The Bard of Brooklyn died in 1892.*

Crossing Brooklyn Ferry

Flood-tide below me! I see you face to face!
Clouds of the west—sun there half an hour high—I see you also face to
  face.

Crowds of men and women attired in the usual costumes, how curious
  you are to me!
On the ferry-boats the hundreds and hundreds that cross, returning
  home, are more curious to me than you suppose,
And you that shall cross from shore to shore years hence are more to me,
  and more in my meditations, than you might suppose.

2

The impalpable sustenance of me from all things at all hours of the day,
The simple, compact, well-join'd scheme, myself disintegrated, every
    one disintegrated yet part of the scheme,
The similitudes of the past and those of the future,
The glories strung like beads on my smallest sights and hearings, on the
    walk in the street and the passage over the river,
The current rushing so swiftly and swimming with me far away,
The others that are to follow me, the ties between me and them,
The certainty of others, the life, love, sight, hearing of others.

Others will enter the gates of the ferry and cross from shore to shore,
Others will watch the run of the flood-tide,
Others will see the shipping of Manhattan north and west, and the
    heights of Brooklyn to the south and east,
Others will see the islands large and small;
Fifty years hence, others will see them as they cross, the sun half an hour
    high,
A hundred years hence, or ever so many hundred years hence, others will
    see them,
Will enjoy the sunset, the pouring-in of the flood-tide, the falling-back
    to the sea of the ebb-tide.

3

It avails not, time nor place—distance avails not,
I am with you, you men and women of a generation, or ever so many
    generations hence,
Just as you feel when you look on the river and sky, so I felt,
Just as any of you is one of a living crowd, I was one of a crowd,

Just as you are refresh'd by the gladness of the river and the bright flow,
  I was refresh'd,
Just as you stand and lean on the rail, yet hurry with the swift current,
  I stood yet was hurried,
Just as you look on the numberless masts of ships and thick-stemm'd
  pipes of steamboats, I look'd.

I too many and many a time cross'd the river of old,
Watched the Twelfth-month sea-gulls, saw them high in the air float-
  ing with motionless wings, oscillating their bodies,
Saw how the glistening yellow lit up parts of their bodies and left the
  rest in strong shadow,
Saw the slow-wheeling circles and the gradual edging toward the south,
Saw the reflection of the summer sky in the water,
Had my eyes dazzled by the shimmering track of beams,
Look'd at the fine centrifugal spokes of light round the shape of my head
  in the sunlit water,
Look'd on the haze on the hills southward and south-westward,
Look'd on the vapor as it flew in fleeces tinged with violet,
Look'd toward the lower bay to notice the vessels arriving,
Saw their approach, saw aboard those that were near me,
Saw the white sails of schooners and sloops, saw the ships at anchor,
The sailors at work in the rigging or out astride the spars,
The round masts, the swinging motion of the hulls, the slender ser-
  pentine pennants,
The large and small steamers in motion, the pilots in their pilothouses,
The white wake left by the passage, the quick tremulous whirl of the
  wheels,
The flags of all nations, the falling of them at sunset,
The scallop-edged waves in the twilight, the ladled cups, the frolicsome
  crests and glistening,
The stretch afar growing dimmer and dimmer, the gray walls of the
  granite storehouses by the docks,
On the river the shadowy group, the big steam-tug closely flank'd on
  each side by the barges, the hay-boat, the belated lighter,

On the neighboring shore the fires from the foundry chimneys burning
    high and glaringly into the night,
Casting their flicker of black contrasted with wild red and yellow light
    over the tops of houses, and down into the clefts of streets.

4

These and all else were to me the same as they are to you,
I loved well those cities, loved well the stately and rapid river,
The men and women I saw were all near to me,
Others the same—others who look back on me because I look'd forward
    to them,
(The time will come, though I stop here to-day and to-night.)

5

What is it then between us?
What is the count of the scores or hundreds of years between us?

Whatever it is, it avails not—distance avails not, and place avails not,
I too lived, Brooklyn of ample hills was mine,
I too walk'd the street of Manhattan island, and bathed in the waters
    around it,
I too felt the curious abrupt questionings stir within me,
In the day among crowds of people sometimes they came upon me,
In my walks home late at night or as I lay in my bed they came upon
    me,

I too had been struck from the float forever held in solution,
I too had receiv'd identity by my body,
That I was I knew was of my body, and what I should be I knew I should
be of my body.

6

It is not upon you alone the dark patches fall,
The dark threw its patches down upon me also,
The best I had done seem'd to me blank and suspicious,
My great thoughts as I supposed them, were they not in reality meagre?
Nor is it you alone who know what it is to be evil,
I am he who knew what it was to be evil,
I too knitted the old knot of contrariety,
Blabb'd, blush'd, resented, lied, stole, grudg'd,
Had guile, anger, lust, hot wishes I dared not speak,
Was wayward, vain, greedy, shallow, sly, cowardly, malignant,
The wolf, the snake, the hog, not wanting in me,
The cheating look, the frivolous word, the adulterous wish, not want-
ing,
Refusals, hates, postponements, meanness, laziness, none of these want-
ing,
Was one with the rest, the days and haps of the rest,
Was call'd by my nighest name by clear loud voices of young men as
they saw me approaching or passing,
Felt their arms on my neck as I stood, or the negligent leaning of their
flesh against me as I sat,
Saw many I loved in the street or ferry-boat or public assembly, yet
never told them a word,
Lived the same life with the rest, the same old laughing, gnawing,
sleeping.

Play'd the part that still looks back on the actor or actress,
The same old role, the role that is what we make it, as great as we like,
Or as small as we like, or both great and small.

7

Closer yet I approach you,
What thought you have of me now, I had as much of you—I laid in my
   stores in advance,
I consider'd long and seriously of you before you were born.

Who was to know what should come home to me?
Who knows but I am enjoying this?
Who knows, for all the distance, but I am as good as looking at you
   now, for all you cannot see me?

8

Ah, what can ever be more stately and admirable to me than mast-
   hemm'd Manhattan?
River and sunset and scallop-edg'd waves of flood-tide?
The sea-gulls oscillating their bodies, the hay-boat in the twilight, and
   the belated lighter?

What gods can exceed these that clasp me by the hand, and with voices
   I love call me promptly and loudly by my nighest name as I approach?

What is more subtle than this which ties me to the woman or man that
    looks in my face?
Which fuses me into you now, and pours my meaning into you?

We understand then do we not?
What I promis'd without mentioning it, have you not accepted?
What the study could not teach—what the preaching could not accom-
    plish is accomplish'd, is it not?

9

Flow on, river! flow with the flood-tide, and ebb with the ebb-tide!
Frolic on, crested and scallop-edg'd waves!
Gorgeous clouds of the sunset! drench with your splendor me, or the
    men and women generation after me!
Cross from shore to shore, countless crowds of passengers!
Stand up, tall masts of Mannahatta! stand up, beautiful hills of Brook-
    lyn!
Throb, baffled and curious brain! throw out questions and answers!
Suspend here and everywhere, eternal float of solution!
Gaze, loving and thirsting eyes, in the house or street or public assem-
    bly!
Sound out, voices of young men! loudly and musically call me by my
    nighest name!
Live, old life! play the part that looks back on the actor or actress!
Play the old role, the role that is great or small according as one makes
    it!
Consider, you who peruse me, whether I may not in unknown ways be
    looking upon you;
Be firm, rail over the river, to support those who lean idly, yet haste
    with the hasting current;

Fly on, sea-birds! fly sideways, or wheel in large circles high in the air;

Receive the summer sky, you water, and faithfully hold it till all down-
cast eyes have time to take it from you!

Diverge, fine spokes of light, from the shape of my head, or any one's
head, in the sunlit water!

Come on, ships from the lower bay! pass up or down, white-sail'd
schooners, sloops, lighters!

Flaunt away, flags of all nations! be duly lower'd at sunset!

Burn high your fires, foundry chimneys! cast black shadows at nightfall!
cast red and yellow light over the tops of the houses!

Appearances, now or henceforth, indicate what you are,

You necessary film, continue to envelop the soul,

About my body for me, and your body for you, be hung our divinest
aromas,

Thrive, cities—bring your freight, bring your shows, ample and sufficient rivers,

Expand, being than which none else is perhaps more spiritual,

Keep your places, objects than which none else is more lasting.

You have waited, you always wait, you dumb, beautiful ministers,

We receive you with free sense at last, and are insatiate henceforward,

Not you any more shall be able to foil us, or withhold yourselves from
us,

We use you, and do not cast you aside—we plant you permanently
within us,

We fathom you not—we love you—there is perfection in you also,

You furnish your parts toward eternity,

Great or small, you furnish your parts toward the soul.

Thomas Wolfe

Another transplanted Southerner, Thomas Wolfe was born in Asheville, North Carolina. His most famous novel, Look Homeward, Angel, *and much of his other work are based on his Southern family. The short story "Only the Dead Know Brooklyn" is unusual for its setting and use of dialect. Wolfe moved to Brooklyn in the 1930s, occupying several apartments in and around Brooklyn Heights. In 1934, Wolfe made the mistake of mentioning his address in an interview. After the article appeared, his fans swarmed his brownstone and Wolfe was forced to move to a hotel. After a short illness, Thomas Wolfe died in 1938.*

$Only$ THE $Dead\ Know$ $Brooklyn$

Dere's no guy livin' dat knows Brooklyn t'roo an' t'roo, because it'd take a guy a lifetime just to find his way aroun' duh f—— town.

So like I say, I'm waitin' for my train t' come when I sees dis big guy standin' deh—dis is duh foist I eveh see of him. Well, he's lookin' wild, y'know, an' I can see dat he's had plenty, but still he's holdin' it; he talks good an' is walkin' straight enough. So den, dis big guy steps up to a little guy dat's standin' deh, an' says, "How d'yuh get t' Eighteent' Avenoo an' Sixty-sevent' Street?" he says.

"Jesus! Yuh got me, chief," duh little guy says to him. "I ain't been heah long myself. Where is duh place?" he says. "Out in duh Flatbush section somewhere?"

"Nah," duh big guy says. "It's out in Bensonhoist. But I was neveh deh befoeh. How d'yuh get deh?"

"Jesus," duh little guy says, scratchin' his head, y'know—yuh could see duh little guy didn't know his way about—"yuh got me, chief. I neveh hoid of it. Do any of youse guys know where it is?" he says to me.

"Sure," I says. "It's out in Bensonhoist. Yuh take duh Fourt' Avenoo express, get off at Fifty-nint' Street, change to a Sea Beach local deh, get off at Eighteent' Avenoo an' Sixty-toid, an' den walk down foeh blocks. Dat's all yuh got to do," I says.

"G'wan!" some wise guy dat I neveh seen befoeh pipes up. "Whatcha talkin' about?" he says—oh, he was wise, y'know. "Duh guy is crazy! I tell yuh what yuh do," he says to duh big guy. "Yuh change to duh West End line at Toity-sixt'," he tells him. "Get off at Noo Utrecht an' Sixteent' Avenoo," he says. "Walk two blocks oveh, foeh blocks up," he says, "an' you'll be right deh." Oh, a *wise* guy, y'know.

"Oh, yeah?" I says. "Who told *you* so much?" He got me sore because he was so wise about it. "How long you been livin' heah?" I says.

"All my life," he says. "I was bawn in Williamsboig," he says. "An' I can tell you t'ings about dis town you neveh hoid of," he says.

"Yeah?" I says.

"Yeah," he says.

"Well, den, you can tell me t'ings about dis town dat nobody else has eveh hoid of, either. Maybe you make it all up yoehself at night," I says, "befoeh you go to sleep—like cuttin' out papeh dolls, or somp'n."

"Oh, yeah?" he says. "You're pretty wise, ain't yuh?"

"Oh, I don't know," I says. "Duh boids ain't usin' my head for Lincoln's statue yet," I says. "But I'm wise enough to know a phony when I see one."

"Yeah?" he says. "A wise guy, huh? Well, you're so wise dat someone's goin' t'bust yuh one right on duh snoot some day," he says. "Dat's how wise *you* are."

Well, my train was comin', or I'da smacked him den and dere, but when I seen duh train was comin', all I said was, "All right, mugg! I'm sorry I can't stay to take keh of you, but I'll be seein' yuh sometime, I hope, out in duh cemetery." So den I says to duh big guy, who'd been standin' deh all duh time, "You come wit me," I says. So when we gets

277

onto duh train I says to him, "Where yuh goin' out in Bensonhoist?" I says. "What numbeh are yuh lookin' for?" I says. *You* know—I t'ought if he told me duh address I might be able to help him out.

"Oh," he says. "I'm not lookin' for no one. I don't know no one out deh."

"Then whatcha goin' out deh for?" I says.

"Oh," duh guy says, "I'm just goin' out to see duh place," he says. "I like duh sound of duh name—Bensonhoist, y'know—so I t'ought I'd go out an' have a look at it."

"Whatcha tryin t'hand me?" I says. "Whatcha tryin t'do—kid me?" *You* know, I t'ought duh guy was bein' wise wit me.

"No," he says, "I'm tellin' yuh duh troot. I like to go out an' take a look at places wit nice names like dat. I like to go out an' look at all kinds of places," he says.

"How'd yuh know deh was such a place," I says, "if yuh neveh been deh befoeh?"

"Oh," he says, "I got a map."

"A *map?*" I says.

"Sure," he says, "I got a map dat tells me about all dese places. I take it wit me every time I come out heah," he says.

And Jesus! Wit dat, he pulls it out of his pocket, an' so help me, but he's *got* it—he's tellin' duh troot—a big map of duh whole f—— place with all duh different pahts mahked out. You know—Canarsie an' East Noo Yawk an' Flatbush, Bensonhoist, Sout' Brooklyn, duh Heights, Bay Ridge, Greenpernt—duh whole goddam layout, he's got it right deh on duh map.

"You been to any of dose places?" I says.

"Sure," he says, "I been to most of 'em. I was down in Red Hook just last night," he says.

"Jesus! Red Hook!" I says. "Whatcha do down deh?"

"Oh," he says, "nuttin' much. I just walked aroun'. I went into a coupla places an' had a drink," he says, "but most of the time I just walked aroun'."

"Just walked aroun'?" I says.

"Sure," he says, "just lookin' at t'ings, y'know."

"Where'd yuh go?" I asts him.

"Oh," he says, "I don't know duh name of duh place, but I could find it on my map," he says. "One time I was walkin' across some big fields where deh ain't no houses," he says, "but I could see ships oveh deh all lighted up. Dey was loadin'. So I walks across duh fields," he says, "to where duh ships are."

"Sure," I says, "I know where you was. You was down to duh Erie Basin."

"Yeah," he says, "I guess dat was it. Dey had some of dose big elevators an' cranes an' dey was loadin' ships, an' I could see some ships in drydock all lighted up, so I walks across duh fields to where dey are," he says.

"Den what did yuh do?" I says.

"Oh," he says, "nuttin' much. I came on back across duh fields after a while an' went into a coupla places an' had a drink."

"Didn't nuttin' happen while yuh was in dere?" I says.

"No," he says. "Nuttin' much. A coupla guys was drunk in one of duh places an' started a fight, but dey bounced 'em out," he says, "an' den one of duh guys stahted to come back again, but duh bartender gets his baseball bat out from under duh counteh, so duh guy goes on."

"Jesus!" I said. "Red Hook!"

"Sure," he says. "Dat's where it was, all right."

"Well, you keep outa deh," I says. "You stay away from deh."

"Why?" he says. "What's wrong wit it?"

"Oh," I says, "it's a good place to stay away from, dat's all. It's a good place to keep out of."

"Why?" he says. "Why is it?"

Jesus! Whatcha gonna do wit a guy as dumb as dat? I saw it wasn't no use to try to tell him nuttin', he wouldn't know what I was talkin' about, so I just says to him, "Oh, nuttin'. Yuh might get lost down deh, dat's all."

"Lost?" he says. "No, I wouldn't get lost. I got a map," he says. A map! Red Hook! Jesus.

* * *

So den duh guy begins to ast me all kinds of nutty questions: how big was Brooklyn an' could I find my way aroun' in it, an' how long would it take a guy to know duh place.

"Listen!" I says. "You get dat idea outa yoeh head right now," I says. "You ain't neveh gonna get to know Brooklyn," I says. "Not in a hunderd yeahs. I been livin' heah all my life," I says, "an' I don't even know all deh is to know about it, so how do you expect to know duh town," I says, "when you don't even live heah?"

"Yes," he says, "but I got a map to help me find my way about."

"Map or no map," I says, "yuh ain't gonna get to know Brooklyn wit no map," I says.

"Can you swim?" he says, just like dat. Jesus! By dat time, y'know, I begun to see dat duh guy was some kind of nut. He'd had plenty to drink, of course, but he had dat crazy look in his eye I didn't like. "Can you swim?" he says.

"Sure," I says. "Can't you?"

"No," he says. "Not more'n a stroke or two. I neveh loined good."

"Well, it's easy," I says. "All yuh need is a little confidence. Duh way I loined, me older bruddeh pitched me off duh dock one day when I was eight yeahs old, cloes an' all. 'You'll swim,' he says. 'You'll swim all right—or drown.' An' believe me, I *swam!* When yuh know yuh got to, you'll do it. Duh only t'ing yuh need is confidence. An' once you've loined," I says, "you've got nuttin' else to worry about. You'll neveh forget it. It's somp'n dat stays wit yuh as long as yuh live."

"Can yuh swim good?" he says.

"Like a fish," I tells him. "I'm a regulah fish in duh wateh," I says. "I loined to swim right off duh docks wit all duh oddeh kids," I says.

"What would you do if yuh saw a man drownin'?" duh guy says.

"Do? Why, I'd jump in an' pull him out," I says. "Dat's what I'd do."

"Did yuh eveh see a man drown?" he says.

"Sure," I says. "I see two guys—bot' times at Coney Island. Dey got out too far, an' neider one could swim. Dey drowned befoeh anyone could get to 'em."

"What becomes of people after dey've drowned out heah?" he says.

280

"Drowned out where?" I says.

"Out heah in Brooklyn."

"I don't know whatcha mean," I says. "Neveh hoid of no one drownin' heah in Brooklyn, unless you mean a swimmin' pool. Yuh can't drown in Brooklyn," I says. "Yuh gotta drown somewhere else—in duh ocean, where dere's wateh."

"Drownin'," duh guy says, lookin' at his map. "Drownin'." Jesus! I could see by den he was some kind of nut, he had dat crazy expression in his eyes when he looked at you, an' I didn't know what he might do. So we was comin' to a station, an' it wasn't my stop, but I got off anyway, an' waited for duh next train.

"Well, so long, chief," I says. "Take it easy, now."

"Drownin'," duh guy says, lookin' at his map. "Drownin'."

Jesus! I've t'ought about dat guy a t'ousand times since den an' wondered what eveh happened to 'm goin' out to look at Bensonhoist because he liked duh name! Walkin' aroun' t'roo Red Hook by himself at night an' lookin' at his map! How many people did I see get drowned out heah in Brooklyn! How long would it take a guy wit a good map to know all deh was to know about Brooklyn!

Jesus! What a nut *he* was! I wondeh what eveh happened to 'im, anyway! I wondeh if someone knocked him on duh head, or if he's still wanderin' aroun' in duh subway in duh middle of duh night wit his little map! Duh poor guy! Say, I've got to laugh, at dat, when I t'ink about him! Maybe he's found out by now dat he'll neveh live long enough to know duh whole of Brooklyn. It'd take a guy a lifetime to know Brooklyn t'roo an' t'roo. An' even den, yuh wouldn't know it all.

$\mathcal{P}ermissions$

$\mathcal{A}bout$ THE $\mathcal{E}ditors$

ANDREA WYATT SEXTON was born in Brooklyn, and grew up there and in Washington, D.C. Her first book, *Three Rooms,* was published in 1970 by Oyez Press. She now resides with her husband and daughter in Washington, where she works for the Democratic National Committee. She is currently at work on other anthologies as well as her seventh book of poems, *13 Ways of Looking at the Sea.*

ALICE LECCESE POWERS was raised on Long Island, but she often visited her extended Italian-American family in Brooklyn. A free-lance writer and editor, she has been published in *The Washington Post, The Baltimore Sun, Newsday,* and many other newspapers and magazines. Ms. Powers now lives in Washington, D.C., with her husband and three daughters.